T5-BQA-139

Library of
Davidson College

The South Pacific Foreign Affairs Handbook

The South Pacific Foreign Affairs Handbook

Steve Hoadley

ALLEN & UNWIN
in association with the New Zealand Institute of
International Affairs

320.99
H678s

©Steve Hoadley, 1992
This book is copyright under the Berne Convention.
All rights reserved. No reproduction without permission.

First published in 1992
Allen & Unwin Pty Ltd
8 Napier Street, North Sydney, NSW 2059 Australia

National Library of Australia
Cataloguing-in-Publication entry:

Hoadley, Steve.
   The South Pacific foreign affairs handbook.

   Bibliography.
   Includes index.
   ISBN 1 86373 176 8.

   1. Oceania—Politics and government. 2. Oceania—
   Economic conditions. 3. Oceania—Foreign relations.
   I. Title.

320.995

Set in 10/11pt Times by DOCUPRO, Ryde

Printed by Chong Moh Offset Printing Pte Ltd, Singapore

94-913
ACW-2411

Contents

Figures

Tables

Preface

This is a book of facts, figures and observations on the foreign affairs of South Pacific states. It aims to be a sympathetic introduction for those approaching the Pacific island region for the first time. It hopes also to be a useful synthesis for those with previous experience looking at island affairs from a new angle.

The method has been to arrange and present essential information on the international relations of South Pacific countries without becoming enmeshed in political, parochial, or intellectual disputes. The theme is that South Pacific foreign affairs are best understood in terms of how island leaders strike balances between their insular political and economic heritage on the one hand and the opportunities and risks facing their countries in the global arena on the other.

In gathering material and writing it up for this book I have enjoyed the stimulation, generosity and assistance of the following institutions and the individuals associated with them: the University of Auckland, especially the Political Studies Department, the New Zealand and Pacific Collection, and the Research Committee; the New Zealand Institute of International Affairs, particularly the Research Committee; the New Zealand Ministry of External Relations and Trade, notably officers devoted to South Pacific affairs, and their Australian, American, British, French and Japanese counterparts; numerous island governments and various international agencies located in or concentrating on the Pacific islands; academic specialists on the South Pacific, especially those from Australia, but also those based in Hawaii, New Zealand, Japan and France; and all who have commented constructively on early drafts of this book, particularly the editorial staff of Allen & Unwin.

I wish to thank all those persons who have contributed directly and indirectly to the writing and publishing of this handbook. Each has helped me in my endeavour to make the South Pacific region more visible, understandable and accessible.

Note: in December 1991 the Soviet Union ceased to exist. Its international role was assumed by the Russian Republic. Passages in this book referring to Soviet interests, diplomacy, and other activities in the South Pacific should be interpreted in light of this and subsequent developments.

1   Studying the South Pacific

Much has been written about outside interests in the South Pacific, particularly on colonial and post-colonial involvement, political and strategic rivalry, nuclear testing and deployment, and natural resource exploitation (Alley 1984; Hayes 1986; Walker 1988; Ravenhill 1989; Dorrance 1990a; Mediansky 1991). Many outside analysts have treated the Pacific island region as a strategic, political or economic resource to be cultivated by friends and denied to rivals. The island countries have been perceived as units to be managed in pursuit of larger goals held by outside governments or enterprises. The foreign policies of island governments have been assumed to be derivatives of those of their Western patrons, and their domestic politics were viewed as parochial, even obstructive, from a global perspective.

Orientation

This book takes the South Pacific as centre stage and casts the island governments as the leading players. It views the region's geography, resource-base, and historical experiences as authentic influences on current interests and aspirations and on the policies adopted to pursue them. Island governments' foreign policy institutions, goals, initiatives, and achievements are seen as legitimate outcomes of local and regional political processes.

This South Pacific viewpoint is adopted to provide a perspective that is lacking in much Western official and academic analysis so that islanders and outsiders can approach each other with a clear awareness of their varying interests, objectives and capabilities. A century of colonialism and ensuing decades of post-independence economic and cultural penetration have made islanders well aware of outsiders' activities. Now the obligation rests on outsiders to take islanders with equal seriousness. Also, a book about island foreign affairs can possibly make island leaders more aware of their assets and accomplishments—and their weaknesses—and therefore better equipped to negotiate mutually beneficial accommodations with the outside powers whose interests impinge on the South Pacific.

The language of this book is the language of a political scientist. Consequently it may distort or omit the nuances of islanders' traditional interactions. However, in the 1990s island governments deal intensively with outside governments and agencies, and with each other in formal institutions such as the South Pacific Forum, in which English is the common tongue, where the terms of international diplomacy, economics, law and science are widely employed. Thus this book describes island institutions and their regional activities in formal terms, as elements of the modern international system.

Definitions

The key terms used in this book are defined as follows. The term *South Pacific* is used throughout in its geo-political sense to denote the small island countries and waters of the southern and central Pacific Ocean region, including those which lie just north of the equator, such as the Micronesian groups. The following islands lying in Pacific waters, but close to and governed by the Pacific rim powers, are excluded: the Ryukyu, Ogasawara (Bonin) and Kurile islands of Japan; the islands of the Aleutian chain and the American state of Hawaii; New Zealand's Kermadec and Chatham islands; the offshore islands of Australia such as Lord Howe, Norfolk and Torres Strait islands; small Pacific outliers of Taiwan, the Philippines and Indonesia; the South American Galapagos and Easter islands; and the islands of the Southern Ocean near Antarctica.

The most widely accepted delineation of the region is provided by the South Pacific Commission. The commission deals with 22 island countries, which are included in the outlined area of the map in Figure 1.1 and listed in Table 2.2. This definition of the South Pacific is adopted in this book, and 'South Pacific', which is widely used by Pacific island leaders themselves, for example in naming the South Pacific Forum, is adopted as the preferred term.

Readers should be aware that there are complementary and over-

Figure 1.1 Map of the South Pacific Commission area

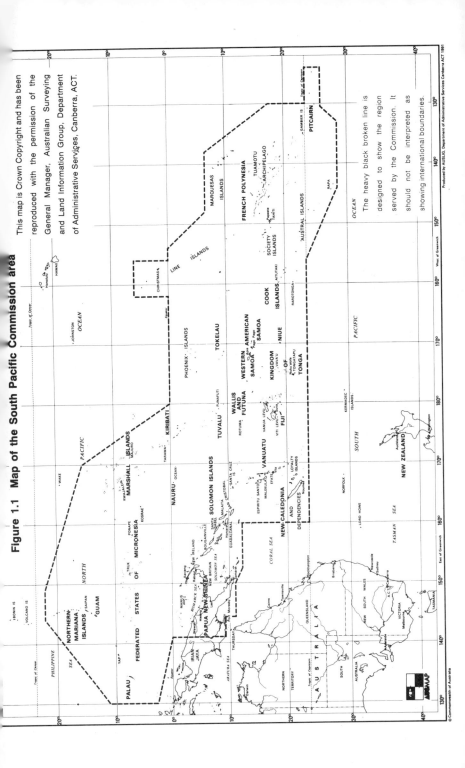

This map is Crown Copyright and has been reproduced with the permission of the General Manager, Australian Surveying and Land Information Group, Department of Administrative Services, Canberra, ACT.

The heavy black broken line is designed to show the region served by the Commission. It should not be interpreted as showing international boundaries.

© Commonwealth of Australia

Produced by AUSLIG, Department of Administrative Services Canberra ACT 1991 lapping terms in general use elsewhere. US officials and scholars tend to use the term *Pacific islands*. This reflects their post-World War II preoccupation with the administration and decolonisation of the United Nations Strategic Trust Territory of the Pacific Islands lying just north of the equator, and their continuing strategic interests in that part of the Pacific. Nevertheless Americans, and this author, recognise 'Pacific islands' as virtually synonymous with 'South Pacific', and it is so employed in this book as a variation. New Zealanders tend to favour 'South Pacific', by which they often mean mainly the Polynesian countries to their north. Australians too use 'South Pacific', but sometimes employ the term *Southwest Pacific* to stress their predominant interests in the Melanesian island groups nearest their continent.

Japanese and French analysts and several international agencies tend to use the term *Oceania*. Because this term sometimes includes and sometimes excludes Australia, New Zealand and parts of Indonesia, it has to be defined before it can be used without ambiguity. Another term requiring definition is *Australasia*, which centres on Australia but sometimes includes parts of Asia and the Pacific islands and sometimes not. The term *South Seas*, popular among fiction and travel writers, is more useful to evoke nostalgia and romance than to analyse modern political and economic relations. Neither 'Oceania' nor 'Australasia' nor 'South Seas' is used in this book except under specifically defined circumstances, and readers are warned of their variable and imprecise connotations.

Political terms also are notoriously slippery, and an attempt to clarify a few key terms in their South Pacific context is offered below:

- A *country* is an island group populated predominantly by an historically rooted and relatively homogeneous population and now administered as a geographical unit within a recognised boundary. The term *nation* is often used as a synonym, particularly when the emphasis is on the common ethnic origins and current consensual beliefs of the inhabitants. The term can also connote state or government, as in the term 'inter*nation*al relations', defined below; so caution is recommended when using this term.
- A *state* is a nation in a country with an independent and sovereign government. In the South Pacific there are ten sovereign ex-colonial states and four states in free association with a former colonial power. They are listed in Table 2.2. The eight remaining island countries may be described as *territories* or *dependencies* of outside powers (France, Britain, New Zealand and the United States), enjoying varying degrees of local self-government.
- *Governments* are authoritative decision-making bodies with capacity

to administer and power to enforce decisions throughout their countries. In the South Pacific the majority of governments are indigenous but some, in the dependencies, are still extraregional to a greater or lesser extent.

- Governments make *foreign policies*, which are stable goals, and plans and initiatives for achieving them applied to relationships between their own country and countries and agencies external to it. Foreign policies vary over time as new leaders emerge and as parties, groups and enterprises attempt to influence the government of the day in their favour.

- Governments conduct *diplomatic relations*, that is, formal government-to-government contact through ministers, ambassadors or officials. *Foreign relations* is a related but looser term including relations encouraged but not actually conducted by governments such as trade and cultural exchange conducted by entrepreneurs or voluntary associations.

- *Foreign affairs* is a collective term for the total array of external relationships of a country, many of which are conducted by non-governmental agencies and individuals, for example trade, migration and tourism, and also smuggling, poaching and pollution.

- A stable network of foreign affairs may be called *regional affairs*, as in 'South Pacific affairs'. An alternative term used in Chapter 4 is *regional system*. Likewise, a stable network of foreign relations, particularly if it is extensive, as is the case in the present era of global diplomacy and institutions, is called *international relations*—a term particularly favoured by political scientists.

This book on South Pacific foreign affairs is thus about activities that cross the legal boundaries into or out of one or more of the 22 South Pacific countries. The emphasis falls on foreign relations, that is, the policies and activities of the governments of island countries and of outside countries with interests in the Pacific islands that have consequences for South Pacific regional affairs. This includes the governments' roles in stimulating and regulating private sector activities. Inasmuch as foreign affairs are influenced by domestic affairs and vice versa, these internal–external linkages are taken into account in this book.

Sources

The text and tables are based mainly on Western and South Pacific official sources. This is an inevitable consequence of the limited nature of information accumulation and publication in the Pacific island region. Official sources are thus appropriate for this book on foreign affairs managed by governments. The narrowness and shallowness of education during the colonial period, the recency of independence, leaders' initial preoccupation with domestic affairs, the youth and diminutive size of foreign affairs bureaucracies, and the paucity of resources available for policy research, analysis and reporting in government and academia alike—all these have combined to retard the publication and circulation of indigenous accounts, leaving the field to outsiders by default. Notwithstanding the extensive writing done by missionaries in fields related to evangelical and social work, the Rockefeller Foundation in health improvements and anthropologists on culture, most publications on policy-related activity have tended to be generated by government agencies. Records were produced by the colonial governments (the United States, Britain, France, Germany, Australia, New Zealand and Japan), and the archives of these countries are the richest source of materials on the 1800s and first half of the 1900s. Western scholars have exploited these materials, and a number of reliable histories are now available in academic libraries.

World War II and its aftermath of restoration of order, then of decolonisation, stimulated a burst of research and reporting on contemporary policy by officials concerned with strategy and the administration of dependent and developing territories. This tradition continues, with informative publications and unpublished reports emerging from the departments of State, Defense and the Interior in Washington and from ministries of Foreign Affairs and related agencies in London, Paris and Tokyo. In recent years official publications by the Department of Foreign Affairs and Trade and the Parliament of the Commonwealth of Australia in Canberra, and the Ministry of External Relations and Trade in Wellington, have become recognised as informative and balanced accounts and are widely used by both island and outside governments, and by scholars, as accessible sources of reliable information.

Recently the island governments have begun to compile and issue periodic reports, statistics, development plans, investment and tourist prospectuses, speeches and press releases, and other publications. When available and appropriate, these are excerpted or summarised in this book. The objection that an official publication may be biased in favour of the issuing government may be valid, but it is not relevant if the objective of a passage is to portray a particular government's point of view, as is frequently the case in the country chapters that follow.

A persistent problem with official statistics is tardiness and inaccessibility, not because of secrecy but because of overburdened and inexperienced island bureaucracies' incapacity to collate, print and distribute detailed information in a timely manner. Thus much reliance is placed on international agencies with access, analytical capacity, and publishing and dissemination facilities. A number of intergovernmental organisations issue useful publications, comprising reports of activities, compilations of statistics and research-based

Table 1.1   International agencies providing information on the South Pacific

- **Asian Development Bank (ADB).** Contact: Publicity Department, ADB, PO Box 789, 2300 Roxas Boulevard, Manila, Republic of the Philippines. See especially *Key Indicators of Developing Member Countries of the ADB* (annual) and *Asian Development Outlook* (annual) for statistics and analysis, and the quarterly *Asian Development Review* for occasional interpretive articles.

- **Economic and Social Commission for Asia and the Pacific (ESCAP).** Contact: Publications Officer, ESCAP Pacific Operations Centre (EPOC), Port Vila, Vanuatu; or Publications Officer, ESCAP, United Nations Building, Rajadamnern Avenue, Bangkok, Thailand. See especially the *Economic and Social Survey of Asia and the Pacific* (annual) and *Statistical Yearbook for Asia and the Pacific*. Also useful is the *United Nations International Trade Statistics Yearbook*.

- **International Monetary Fund (IMF).** Contact: Publications Services, IMF, 700 19th Street, NW, Washington, DC, 20431, USA. See especially the *International Financial Statistics Yearbook* and its monthly counterpart, and *World Economic Outlook*.

- **Organization for Economic Cooperation and Development (OECD): Development Assistance Committee (DAC).** Contact: OECD Publications, 2 rue André-Pascal, 75775 Paris Cedex 16, France. See especially the DAC annual review, *Development Cooperation*, for aid statistics.

- **South Pacific Commission (SPC).** Contact: SPC Publications Section, BP D5, Noumea Cedex, New Caledonia. See especially the *South Pacific Economies: Statistical Summary* (most recent edition 1989), *Statistical Bulletin of the South Pacific* (occasional), *Pacific Impact: Quarterly Review of the SPC* and *South Pacific Conference Report* (annual).

- **South Pacific Forum Secretariat.** Contact: Information and Publications Officer, Forum Secretariat, GPO Box 856, Suva, Fiji. See especially the secretariat's annual report and brochures on its sectoral programmes, the communiqués of the annual South Pacific Forum meetings, the *SPARTECA Guide for Pacific Island Exporters* and the country-by-country *Trade and Investment Guide* (1982).

- **United Nations Development Programme (UNDP).** Contact: UNDP, Victoria Parade and Gorrie Street, Suva, Fiji; or UNDP, Credit House, Musgrave Street, Port Moresby, Papua New Guinea; or UNDP, Lauofo Meti's Building, Four Corners, Matautu-uta, Apia, Western Samoa. See the *Annual Report* and periodical *World Development*.

- **World Bank.** Contact: Publications Office, World Bank, 1818 H Street, NW, Washington, DC, 20433, USA. See especially the *World Development Report* (annual).

analyses, either annually or occasionally. Among these organisations are the Asian Development Bank (ADB), the International Monetary Fund (IMF) the United Nations Development Programme (UNDP) and the World Bank, each of which issues an annual report, with statistics, touching on South Pacific countries, and most of which sponsor special topic studies on an occasional basis. The United Nations Trusteeship Council and Special Committee on Decolonisation produce reports by their visiting missions to dependent territories. More focused on the South Pacific are two regional organisations: the South Pacific Forum Secretariat and the South Pacific Commission. The secretariat's publications are mainly news releases and occasional reports. The commission, in contrast, publishes a widely used compendium of comparative statistics entitled *South Pacific Economies*. Intergovernmental organisations publishing material relevant to the South Pacific, and their contact addresses, are listed in Table 1.1.

In recent decades a number of university-based and independent institutions have emerged to support research and sponsor publications on current South Pacific affairs. The leading institutions are:

- the Center for Pacific Island Studies at the University of Hawaii;
- the Pacific Islands Development Program and related agencies of the East–West Center, in Hawaii; and
- the National Centre for Development Studies, the Centre for Strategic and Defence Studies, the Peace Research Centre, and the Research School of Pacific Studies, all at the Australian National University, in Canberra.

Also active but less accessible because they rarely publish in English are institutes in Japan, France, Germany and the Soviet Union. These and other institutions, varying greatly in focus and level of activity, issue publications of relevance to the South Pacific. The most active and accessible South Pacific study institutions are listed in Table 1.2, the more obscure ones in the Crocombe article in the source note.

Table 1.2 South Pacific studies institutions and publications

AUSTRALIA

- **Centre for Melanesian Studies**, Department of Geography, James Cook University, Townsville, Queensland 4811, Australia. Publishes occasional papers.

- **Centre for Pacific Studies**, University of New South Wales, Kensington, NSW 2033, Australia. Publishes an informative newsletter of activities and events around the Pacific.

- **National Centre for Development Studies**, Australian National University, GPO Box 4, Canberra, ACT, 2601, Australia. Publishes books, reports, a newsletter and the semiannual *Pacific Economic Bulletin* and maintains the South Pacific Economic and Social Data Base.

- **Peace Research Centre**, Australian National University, GPO Box 4, Canberra, ACT 2601, Australia. Publishes the quarterly *Pacific Research*, books, monographs and working papers.

- **Research Institute for Asia and the Pacific**, University of Sydney, Sydney, NSW 2006, Australia. Encourages research and publishes occasional papers.

- **Research School of Pacific Studies**, Australian National University, GPO Box 4, Canberra, ACT 2601, Australia. Teaching, seminars, research and publishing undertaken by approximately 100 staff members is reported in the occasional bulletin *Pacific Islands Research*. Also note the respected *Journal of Pacific History*.

- **Strategic and Defence Studies Centre**, Australian National University, GPO Box 4, Canberra, ACT 2601, Australia. Publishes books, working papers and a newsletter.

NEW ZEALAND

- **Centre for Pacific Studies**, University of Auckland, Private Bag, Auckland 1, New Zealand. Occasional books and monographs.

- **Macmillan Brown Centre for Pacific Studies**, University of Canterbury, Christchurch, New Zealand. Offers fellowships for research.

- **New Zealand Institute of International Affairs**, Victoria University, Box 600, Wellington, New Zealand. Publishes occasional monographs and the bimonthly journal *New Zealand International Review*.

- **Polynesian Society**, Anthropology Department, University of Auckland, Private Bag, Auckland 1, New Zealand. Publishes the periodical *Journal of the Polynesian Society*.

UNITED STATES

- **Center for Pacific Island Studies**, University of Hawaii, Honolulu, Hawaii, 96822, USA. Publishes the scholarly quarterly *The Contemporary Pacific: A Journal of Island Affairs* and *Pacific News from Manoa* (newsletter).

- **Center for Pacific Rim Studies**, Pacific Alaska University, Anchorage, Alaska, USA. Publishes the semiannual journal *Pacifica*.

- **Institute for Polynesian Studies**, Brigham Young University, Laie, Hawaii, 96762, USA.

- **Pacific Islands Development Program**, East–West Center, Honolulu, Hawaii, 96848, USA. Publishes reports, monographs and books.

- **The Micronesian Institute**, 1275 K Street NSW, Suite 360, Washington, DC 20005–4006, USA. Conducts training courses and issues an occasional newsletter.

- **Pacific Basin Development Council**, 567 South King Street, Suite 325, Honolulu, Hawaii, 96813, USA. Conducts studies and issues publications, mainly on US flag territories and Hawaii.

- **Pacific Islands Development Program**, East–West Center, 1777 East-West Road, Honolulu, Hawaii 96848, USA. Publishes occasional papers and research reports.

JAPAN

- **Committee for Oceania and Pacific Island Countries**, Foundation for Advanced Information and Research, Toranomon Central Building, 1-7-1 Nishi-Shimbashi, Minato-ku, Tokyo 105, Japan. Undertaking studies to be published in English and Japanese.

- **Faculty of General Social Science** (from 1 April 1992), Gunma University, 1375 Aramaki-cho, Maebashi City, Gunma Prefecture, Japan. Encourages academic research and publication by faculty and associates.

- **Japan–Micronesian Association and the Institute of Pacific Studies**, Asia Center of Japan, 8-10-32 Akasaka, Minato-ku, Tokyo, Japan. Publishes a newsletter in Japanese.

- **The Pacific Society**, 4-1-6 Akasaka, Minato-ku, Tokyo, Japan. Publishes the quarterly *Journal of the Pacific Society* in English and Japanese.

- **Research Center for the South Pacific**, Kagoshima University, 21 Korimoto, 1-chome, Kagoshima 890, Japan. Issues a semiannual newsletter *South Pacific Study* in English and occasional papers in Japanese. Sponsors seminars and exchanges with South Pacific universities.

SOUTH PACIFIC COUNTRIES

- **French University of the South Pacific**, Noumea (New Caledonia) and Papeete (Tahiti). New tertiary institutions with research, publishing and regional education exchange potential. Establishment pending

- **Institute of Pacific Studies**, University of the South Pacific, Box 1168, Suva, Fiji. Publishes books, monographs and the periodical *Pacific Perspective*. Extensive publications list available on request.

- **Micronesian Area Research Center**, University of Guam, Mangilao 96913, Guam. Extensive publications.

- **ORSTOM**, BPAS, Cedex Noumea, New Caledonia. Publishes research in French. Emphasis on physical and natural sciences; undertakes cooperative projects.

- **Pacific Studies Institute**, PO Box 20820, Marianas PO 96921, Commonwealth of Northern Marianas, USA.

Source: Crocombe, 1989b, pp. 115–38; Centre for South Pacific Studies, 1990.

Special mention must be made of the Institute of Pacific Studies at the University of the South Pacific, in Suva, Fiji. This institute, supported by subsidies and grants by island and outsider governments, international organisations and private foundations, is unique inasmuch as it is directed and staffed by, and publishes predominantly works by, Pacific island scholars. It claims to have published works by 800 Pacific island authors. Its publications list is extensive, ranging over history, culture, development and politics. Its books and journals are establishing themselves as an indigenous baseline against which to measure the reliability of outsiders' writings on the region. However, the institute has done relatively little on current international affairs and foreign policies in the region—a gap that this book is intended to fill until an island author produces a work on the subject from an indigenous perspective.

Finally there are commercial publications, of which the most reliable is the *Pacific Islands Yearbook*, issued most recently in its sixteenth edition in 1989. A number of other handbooks shading off into tourist guides, covering one or more island countries, are published from year to year. The two leading commercial periodicals are *Pacific Islands Monthly* and *Islands Business Pacific*. Others dealing mainly or in part with the South Pacific are listed in Table 1.3. Newspapers reporting on events in the South Pacific are too numerous to list separately but are found in most island capitals and most major cities of the Pacific rim and should be recognised as useful, although sometimes superficial, records of day-to-day developments. The leading indigenous papers are Papua New Guinea's *Post–Courier* and Fiji's *Fiji Times*. The *Sydney Morning Herald*, the *New Zealand Herald* and the *Los Angeles Times* also carry island news, emphasising Melanesia, Polynesia and Micronesia respectively.

Table 1.3 Commercial periodicals on the South Pacific

- *American Pacific Business Directory*. A regional directory of business, governments and organisations published periodically by Pacific Information Bank, PO Box 1310, Saipan, MP 96950, Commonwealth of Northern Marianas, USA.

- *The Asia–Pacific Business and Trade Directory*. Published annually by Universal Business Directories, 360 Dominion Road, Auckland 3, New Zealand. Incorporated the *Pacific Islands Business and Trade Directory* after 1986.

- *Asia Year Book*. Published annually by Review Publishing Company, 181 Gloucester Road, Hong Kong, with chapters and statistics on Fiji, Papua New Guinea, and Asia–Pacific regional institutions and affairs.

- *Country Report: Analysis of Economic and Political Trends* (quarterly) and *Country Profile: Annual Survey of Political and Economic Background* (annual) cover the principal island states. Published by The Economist Intelligence Unit, 40 Duke Street, London W1A 1DW, United Kingdom.

- *The Far East and Australasia*. Published annually by Europa Publications, 18 Bedford Square, London WC1 3JN, United Kingdom.

- *Far Eastern Economic Review*. A weekly news magazine published by Review Publishing Company, 181 Gloucester Road, Hong Kong, with occasional coverage of Pacific island events.

- *Islands Business Pacific*. Published monthly by Islands Business Ltd, 24 Des Voeux Road, Suva, Fiji.

- *Oceania: A Regional Study* (1985). Edited by Frederica M. Bunge and Melinda W. Cooke. Published by the Department of the Army and distributed by the US Government Printing Office, Washington, DC, USA. Updated irregularly.

- *Oceania Economic Handbook* (1990). Published by Euromonitor, 87 Turnmill St., London EC1M 50U, United Kingdom.

- *Pacific Business Guide* (1986). Published occasionally by World of Information, 21 Gold Street, Saffron Walden, Essex, United Kingdom.

- *Pacific Islands Monthly*. Published monthly by Fiji Times Ltd, 20 Gordon Street, GPO Box 1167, Suva, Fiji.

- *Pacific Islands Yearbook* (16th edn 1989). Edited by Norman and Ngaire Douglas. Published by Angus and Robertson Publishers, 31 Waterloo Road, North Ryde, NSW 2113, Australia.

- *Pacific Report*. Newsletter published fortnightly by Pacific Report Ltd, Box 25, Monaro Crescent PO, ACT 2603, Australia.

- *The Pacific Review*. Published quarterly by Oxford University Press, Walton Street, Oxford OX2 6DP, United Kingdom. Scholarly, mostly on the Pacific rim.

- *The Political Handbook of the World* (1990). Published annually by CSA Publications, State University of New York, Binghamton, New York 13901, USA.

- *The South Sea Digest*. Published fortnightly. GPO Box 4245, Sydney, NSW 2001, Australia.

- *The Statesman's Year-Book*. Published annually by Macmillan Publishers, Basingstoke, Hampshire, RG21 2XS, United Kingdom.

- *The Washington Pacific Report*. Published twice a month. P O Box 2918, Washington, DC, 20013, USA.

2   Political and economic heritage

The present governments of the South Pacific are recent in origin, but the resources they command have been shaped by long-term political and economic forces. Their external goals are influenced by the cultures, experiences and resources of the peoples they represent. This chapter sketches the origins of island governments with particular attention to milestone events of the pre-colonial, colonial and independence periods, and assesses the natural, human, institutional and economic resources on which governments must base their participation in international affairs.

Origins and identity

The forebears of the South Pacific peoples are thought to have migrated from southern China and eastern Southeast Asia, probably over a long period in small groups. First came negroid peoples, presumed to be the ancestors of the Melanesians. Later migrations and developments brought forth the Micronesian and Polynesian cultures (Beaglehole 1934; Day 1966; Delpar 1980; Dodge 1976; Friis 1967; Oliver 1951, all *passim*). It is customary to divide the Pacific islands into these three ethnic and cultural sub-regions, as shown in Figure 2.1.

Migratory experiences and environmental challenges, and perhaps vestiges of their civilisations of origin, gave rise among Polynesians and Micronesians to hierarchically stratified socio-political institutions led by chiefs and nobles supported by a priestly caste and

Figure 2.1 Map of Melanesia, Micronesia and Polynesia

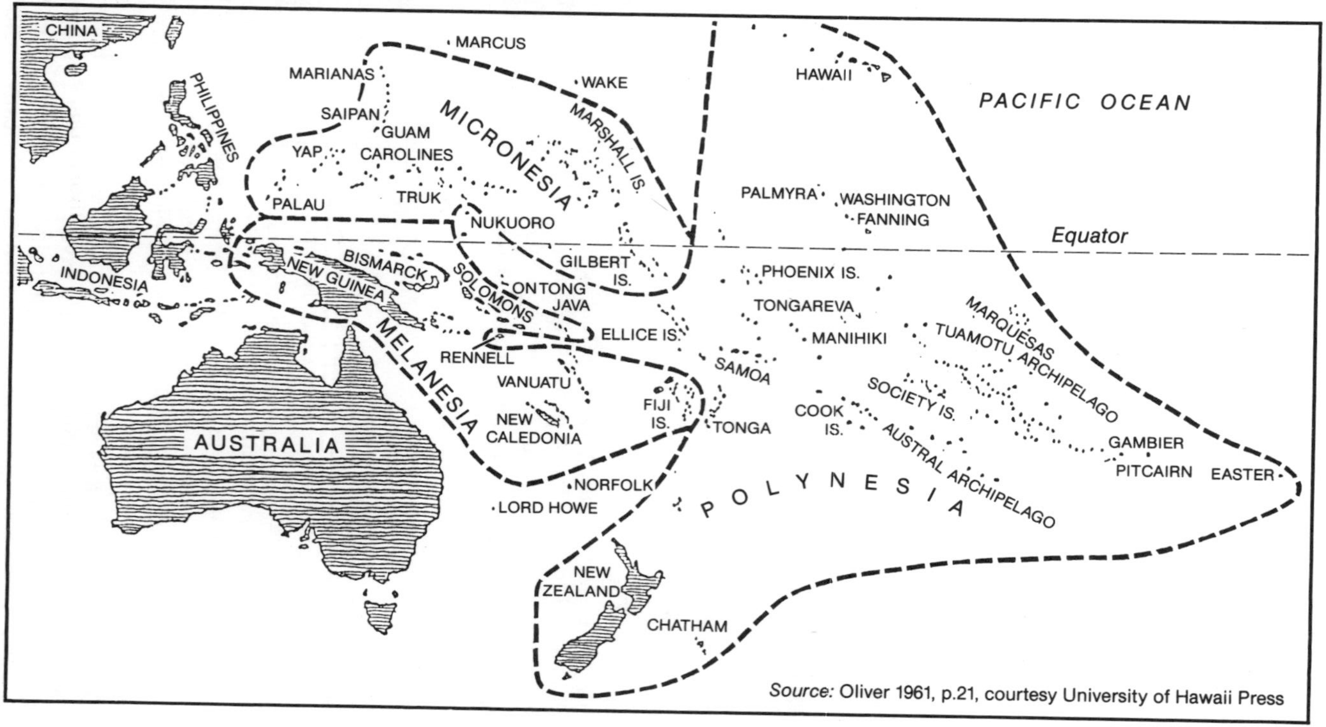

Source: Oliver 1961, p.21, courtesy University of Hawaii Press

elaborate mythologies and artforms. In Melanesia more diverse, dispersed and individualistic patterns of tribal and family organisations prevailed, defying generalisation. It is plausible that the relative scarcity of land resources in the small Pacific islands, and the collective effort required to reach and settle them, necessitated a greater degree of social coordination for survival among the Polynesians and Micronesians than among the geographically better endowed Melanesians. Distant migrations, the evolution of complex socio-political forms and an epic mythology have endowed present-day Polynesian political leaders with a cosmopolitan outlook, manifested by their adaptability in incorporating religious, educational and governmental institutions from the West.

Although the political nationalism that stirred in Europe after the 1500s had no counterpart in the South Pacific, there was among the islands a vague awareness of the special nature of the island world, hinted at by myths, art forms and proto-religious ceremonies. Trade was conducted by tribes specialising in barter and long distance travel by outrigger, and there was some contact with Chinese traders, leading one historian to observe that well before the arrival of the Europeans 'most Oceanians were trade conscious and eager for new goods' (Oliver 1951, p. 104).

Early outside influences

Significant contacts and influences from outside the Pacific began only after island societies had long been established. Only in 1520–21 did the first European, Ferdinand Magellan, transit the Pacific. A century of contacts by Spanish explorers was followed by a Dutch century, roughly from 1615 to 1722. Then followed the British and French century, from the mid 1700s to the beginnings of colonialism in the mid 1800s. These early explorations and contacts are noted in the chronology in Table 2.1.

By the early 1800s James Cook and others had charted most of the Pacific islands, but no permanent European settlements beyond scattered encampments by sealers, pedlars, and beachcombers had been established. Religious and political rivalries between Britain and France during the Napoleonic Wars, the rise of the United States as an economic rival to both and the rise of German imperialism were three influences propelling Europeans and their governments into the region as the 1800s progressed. As in the prior century, European motives had little to do with the intrinsic value of the Pacific islands or with their people or institutions, but much to do with European ambitions and rivalries, including the search for new lands or routes and for trade or plunder. This historical tendency

Table 2.1 Chronology of exploration and early contacts

1513 Spanish explorer Vasco Nuñez de Balboa crossed the Panama isthmus and became the first European to sight the Pacific Ocean.

1520–21 Ferdinand Magellan, a Portuguese in the service of Spain, rounded South America in search of the Indies and crossed the Pacific to Guam and eventually the Philippines.

1542–45 Spaniard Inigo Ortiz de Retes, after a failed attempt to establish a colony in the Philippines, sailed along the northern coast of the island of New Guinea and gave it its name.

1565 Spain initiated the regular galleon route from Mexico to the Philippines; Guam was a waystation and the Mariana Islands subsequently became a Spanish colony.

1567–68 Alvaro de Mendana set out from Peru to find the legendary southern continent, establish a settlement and convert the natives to Christianity, but got only to Santa Isabel in the Solomons and, in a second expedition in 1595 to Santa Cruz Island.

1577–80 Francis Drake became the first Englishman to enter the Pacific during his circumnavigation of the globe.

1605 Pedro Fernandes de Quiros, believing that he had found the southern continent, gave his landfall in the Solomons the name Australia del Espiritu Santo. His lieutenant Luis Vaez de Torres skirted the southern shore of New Guinea, proving it was an island, and gave his name to the Torres Strait.

1616 In search of new routes and trade opportunities, Willem Schouten and Jacob Le Maire touched on northern Tonga, Futuna and Alofi on their way from Holland to the Dutch East Indies.

1642–43 Sent by the Dutch East India Company to learn more about Terra Australis Incognita, particularly trade prospects, Abel Tasman discovered numerous islands now part of Tonga, Fiji and Papua New Guinea as well as Tasmania and New Zealand.

1700 William Dampier, an Englishman, traversed the strait between New Britain and New Ireland.

1722 Jacob Roggeveen, challenging the Dutch East India Company's monopoly, discovered eastern Samoa and Easter Island.

1764–65 The British Admiralty sent Commodore John Byron to locate a northwest passage to the Orient; he failed but discovered islands in the Tuamotu, Cook and Tokelau groups.

1765–66 The Admiralty sent Samuel Wallis and Philip Carteret on voyages of discovery and scientific investigation; they discovered Tahiti, Wallis and Pitcairn, and islands in the Melanesian region.

1767 France, competing with Britain for prestige and opportunities, sent Louis Antoine de Bougainville to the Pacific where he touched on Tahiti, Samoa, the New Hebrides and the islands off New Guinea, discovering and giving his name to Bougainville Island.

1768–71 The Admiralty and the Royal Society sent Captain James Cook on an expedition whose objects included astronomical and natural science observations and also search for the southern continent and other new lands. Cook mapped and commented on findings in Tahiti, Leeward and Rurutu islands, and New Zealand and Australia.

1772–75 Cook on his second voyage discovered and mapped islands in the Tuamotu, Cook, Tonga and Marquesas groups and also Palmerston, Niue, New Caledonia and Norfolk islands.

1776–79 Cook, ostensibly searching for the northwest passage, discovered and mapped Atiu, Tubuai and Christmas islands and made landfall in Hawaii, where he was killed.

1785–88 Comte de Jean-François de Galaup La Perouse, French, explored the northern and southern Pacific before perishing in Vanikoro, Solomon Islands.

1789 The HMS *Bounty* mutiny took place, leading to British settlement of Pitcairn Island.

1791 Captain John Ingraham, American, discovered islands in the northern Marquesas.

1791–92 British captains George Vancouver and John Broughton discovered the Chatham Islands and Rapa and visited many Hawaiian islands.

1792–93 Frenchman Antoine de Bruni D'Entrecasteaux visited numerous islands in his search for the missing La Perouse expedition.

1815–26 Otto von Kotzebue and F.G.B. von Bellingshausen were the first to explore the islands flying the Russian flag; they surveyed parts of the Tuamotus, Society, Marshall and Fiji islands.

Source: Oliver 1968; Beaglehole 1934; Craig and King 1981; Douglas and Douglas 1989; *Concise World Atlas* 1987; all *passim.*

of outsiders to see Pacific islands as objects rather than subjects persists to the present.

In the 1800s the islanders were visited by whalers, traders, planters, blackbirders (indentured labour recruiters), and company merchants in growing numbers. Collectively they led to:

- depletion of coastal sea life;
- stimulation of demand for European trade goods, guns and alcohol;
- exacerbation of local feuds and consequent disorder;
- depopulation of islands by disease and forced labour; and
- alienation of communal lands.

The age of exploration gave way to the age of colonialism in 1797 when the London Missionary Society set up stations in Tahiti and Tongatapu, from which Protestantism, mainly Anglicanism, Methodism and Presbyterianism, spread rapidly to the Cook Islands, Samoa, Fiji and the Melanesian archipelago in the succeeding four decades. The American Boston Mission, set up in Hawaii in 1820, stimulated the spread of Protestantism westwards to the Marshalls,

Carolines and Gilberts. Catholicism was introduced by the Spanish in the Marianas in the 1600s and by the French in Tahiti in 1836 but did not prosper until buttressed by French colonial initiatives in French Polynesia and New Caledonia.

The War of 1812 and the British blockade of Atlantic ports induced American whalers, sealers and traders to move into the Pacific. They were followed by planters, sandalwood buyers, black-birders and large merchant companies from several European countries, including Germany. Fraud, plunder and cruelty turned island hospitality to bitterness and led to flare-ups of violence by rivals and by islanders exacting vengeance. Missionaries and settlers pressed their home governments for protection. European tensions intensified Anglo-French rivalry, and the establishment of British colonies in Australia in 1788 and New Zealand in 1840 increased the pressure on the Colonial Office to take a more active role to keep order in the South Pacific and to limit the influence of the French, and later the Germans. But the British government, well aware of the risks and costs of direct rule and preoccupied with imperial affairs in eastern Africa and southern Asia, was reluctant to act, and the initiative passed to the French.

Colonialism

The first South Pacific colony, not counting the Spanish Marianas, New South Wales and New Zealand, was established when the French government annexed the Marquesas and declared a protectorate over Tahiti in 1842 (Aldrich 1990, *passim*). In 1853 France annexed New Caledonia, and Wallis and Futuna islands became French soon after. Britain hesitated another two decades before arranging with local chiefs to administer Fiji in 1874, and another decade after that before offering protection, in irregular succession, to Papua, Solomon Islands, Cook Islands, Gilbert and Ellice Islands, Niue, Ocean Island, Tonga and, in condominium with France, the New Hebrides, between 1884 and 1906. Newly unified Germany entered the South Pacific first as a commercial power; then between 1884 and 1899 it annexed New Guinea and its offshore islands, Nauru and Western Samoa and acquired the Marianas, Caroline and Marshall islands from Spain. In 1899 the United States acquired Guam as a result of the Spanish–American war and got American Samoa with its deepwater harbour at Pago Pago, through a trilateral agreement with Britain and Germany.

Colonial governments followed, often reluctantly except for the French, at the insistence of the British and Americans who demanded order and protection for their commercial pursuits, Protestant missionary societies which desired to curb the growth of

Catholicism and of social abuses such as blackbirding, and the governments of Australia and New Zealand which wished to deny nearby islands to French, German and US colonialism. The process was piecemeal and apparently without design by Britain and the United States; it was motivated by strong ambitions in France and Germany, and later Japan, but proceeded pragmatically. Colonialism was not unwelcome to many islanders to the extent that it curbed local feuds, controlled the depredations of blackbirders, unscrupulous merchants and swindlers, and brought religious, educational and material benefits, including modern medicine and public works.

World War I spelled the end of Germany in the South Pacific, displaced by Japan in Micronesia, Australia in Melanesia and New Zealand in Western Samoa. Phosphate-rich Nauru was taken over and exploited by a commission set up by Britain, Australia and New Zealand. The tiny isolated islands of Midway, Wake, Howland, Baker, Jarvis, and Johnston were subsequently claimed by the United States, and Canton and Enderbury by Britain, as stepping stones for new trans-Pacific air routes. The Kingdom of Tonga remained self-governing and nominally independent, but was obliged to seek the protection of Britain. The colonisation of the South Pacific was virtually complete.

Self-government

World War I brought a surge of idealism, expressed by President Woodrow Wilson's Fourteen Points advocating the self-determination of nations. Good intentions led the colonial powers first to devote resources to public works, health, education and economic development in their colonies, and then, prodded by nativist and proto-nationalist agitation in Fiji, Western Samoa, New Guinea and Solomon Islands, to consider steps towards self-government. The disruptive impact of World War II weakened colonial authority and hastened the devolution of power to formerly subject peoples. The gratitude felt by colonial governments for islanders' support in the war against Japan, the formation of the United Nations Trusteeship Council, whose terms of reference implied decolonisation, and the rush to independence by scores of Asian and African countries, all converged to create a climate of decolonisation in the South Pacific. These forces, and requests by island elites for a larger voice in their own affairs, notably in Western Samoa, led Britain, Australia and New Zealand to set up and empower institutions for self-government and eventually grant independence to the majority of their possessions.

Decolonisation was neither as precipitous nor as violent as it had been in other parts of the world. Nationalism and ideological extremism were moderated by Christianity and genuine respect for the colonial powers by local leaders, who were inducted and prepared by education and training schemes well in advance of scheduled transfers of power. The widespread use of English and the establishment of British-inspired educational systems promoted consensus. Only in Vanuatu, divided between anglophone and francophone parties and stirred by French planter intrigue, did discord erupt into violence and a secessionist movement, and then only on the island of Espiritu Santo.

The process of achieving self-government is still unfolding. At the time of writing the Trust Territory of Palau is awaiting removal by referendum of an antinuclear constitutional blockage to attain self-governing status in free association with the United States. The territories of New Caledonia and French Polynesia are constitutionally still parts of France, whose government in Paris decides on foreign affairs, defence and finance, but they are increasingly self-governing in domestic and trade policy. Elsewhere, such as in Guam—an unincorporated territory of the United States whose economy is buoyed by the presence of military bases—demands for the further devolution of powers are being heard with increasing frequency, but continued association with the US seems to be the wish of the majority in the absence of a practical alternative. The same is broadly true in the Commonwealth of Northern Marianas and the territory of American Samoa, in Tokelau (administered by New Zealand) and in Pitcairn (administered by Britain). The political status of the 22 countries of the South Pacific Commission is summarised in Table 2.2.

Most of the current governments of the South Pacific are parliamentary systems, reflecting their British origins and continued Commonwealth ties, but a few have presidential features, reflecting US and French influences. They are, with several exceptions, liberal democracies in broad outline, but many have unique archaic elements that give prominence to traditional leaders, either overtly as in the case of the king and nobles of Tonga and the Council of Chiefs of Fiji, or implicitly through customary leadership styles in weak political-party systems as in the Melanesian states. There is a general acceptance of the Anglo-American and French ideals of respect for human rights and civil liberties and their protection by constitutions, laws and institutions of justice, and gross abuses are few in comparison with other parts of the developing world. However, in practice South Pacific governments operate in personalistic and idiosyncratic ways not predictable by examination of their formal Western-modelled institutions. This gives the foreign policies of island states a unique character (Fairbairn 1991, p. 25).

Table 2.2 Political status of 22 South Pacific countries

Country	Status of Sovereignty	Self-government
American Samoa	Territory of USA	Substantial
Cook Islands	Free association, NZ (1965)[b]	Total
Federated States of Micronesia	Free association, US (1986)	Total
Fiji	Independent (1970)	Total
French Polynesia	Territory of France	Substantial
Guam	Territory of USA	Substantial
Kiribati	Independent(1979)[a]	Total
Marshall Islands	Free association, USA (1986)	Total
Nauru	Independent (1968)[a]	Total
New Caledonia	Territory of France	Substantial
Niue	Free association, NZ (1974)[b]	Total
Northern Mariana Islands	Commonwealth of USA	Total
Palau (Belau)	Trust territory, USA	Substantial
Papua New Guinea	Independent (1975)[a]	Total
Pitcairn	Dependency of UK	Limited
Solomon Islands	Independent (1978)[a]	Total
Tokelau	Dependency of NZ	Limited
Tonga	Independent (1970)[a]	Total
Tuvalu	Independent (1978)[a]	Total
Vanuatu	Independent (1980)[a]	Total
Wallis and Futuna	Territory of France	Substantial
Western Samoa	Independent (1962)[a]	Total

[a] Member of Commonwealth [b] Recognises Queen Elizabeth II as sovereign.

Source: Crocombe 1989a; New Zealand Government 1990b; Douglas and Douglas 1989; all *passim*.

Regional security

Since the Japanese thrust into the South Pacific, the region has known no military threat from an external power bent on territorial acquisition. There has been uneasiness about Indonesian military operations on the border with Papua New Guinea and about Soviet naval patrolling and penetration via fishing agreements. Communist Chinese and Libyan diplomatic initiatives have been viewed with suspicion. There has been criticism of US, French and even Australian and New Zealand military activities and potential for interference in island affairs. There has been concern that outside rivalries might intrude into the South Pacific and recommendations of security consultations to prevent, or deal with, this possibility. Military or subversion threat scenarios have been projected by outside officials, journalists, and scholars (Dorrance 1990a; Mediansky 1991).

In practice, the South Pacific has remained a benign region in which the overt use, threat, or stationing—with a few US and French exceptions—of military forces has been unnecessary. Island leaders are well aware that their countries are distant from the cockpits of world power politics and that invasion or attack are highly unlikely. They are content pragmatically to rely on friendly outside powers, particularly the United States, Australia and New Zealand, confident that they are committed by their own self-interests (see Chapter 3) to protect the Pacific islands. Island governments—with the exceptions of Papua New Guinea, Fiji and Tonga—have opted not to set up military forces or to participate in alliances. Rather, they rely on police establishments to deal with internal disturbances and small-scale external threats such as smuggling and poaching.

'Security' to island leaders means primarily political and economic security (Hegarty and Polomka 1989; Henningham and Ball 1991). This connotes raising standards of living to dissolve social and ethnic tensions and enhance political stability. It entails gaining trade and immigration access to, and aid and investment from, wealthy outsiders while avoiding political interference by them. Thus the region benefits because outside powers have preferred diplomacy and economic cooperation over military rivalry. Also, the new international law of recognition of post-colonial 'quasi-states' as nominal equals in the international community shelters the region from overt intervention and induces compensatory assistance (Jackson 1990). Island governments and their regional organisations are respected and supported by virtually all outside governments and international agencies with interests in the region. Island states can base their political, economic, and regional policies on this secure and supportive international environment.

Economic heritage

The predominant physical characteristic of the South Pacific region is maritime space punctuated irregularly by small island groups. The basic resources are people, land and sea. The total population of the South Pacific region was 5 660 500 in 1987. Populations were unevenly distributed, numbering less than 100 in Pitcairn, 1600 in Tokelau, 2500 in Niue and 8500 in Tuvalu, but exceeding 3 463 300 in Papua New Guinea—greater than New Zealand (see Table 2.3). Population densities also varied greatly, from Papua New Guinea with 7 inhabitants per square kilometre, New Caledonia with 8 and Vanuatu with 12, to serious pressures on land resources (more than 100 inhabitants per square kilometre) in American Samoa, Federated States of Micronesia, Guam, Marshall Islands, Nauru, Tokelau, Tonga and Tuvalu.

The United Nations Convention on the Law of the Sea legitimised

Table 2.3 Population, land area, density and sea area

Country	Population	Land area (km²)	Density (per km²)	Sea area (000 km²)
American Samoa	36 700	197	186	390
Cook Islands	17 100	240	71	1 839
Federated States of Micronesia	97 700	701	139	2 978
Fiji	725 500	18 272	40	1 290
French Polynesia	176 800	3 265	54	5 030
Guam	119 800	541	221	218
Kiribati	67 700	690	98	3 550
Marshall Islands	37 800	181	209	2 131
Nauru	8 800	21	419	320
New Caledonia	153 500	19 103	8	1 740
Niue	2 500	259	10	390
Northern Mariana Islands	20 600	471	44	777
Palau (Belau)	14 000	494	28	629
Papua New Guinea	3 463 300	462 243	7	3 120
Pitcairn	100	5	20	800
Solomon Islands	292 000	27 556	11	1 340
Tokelau	1 600	10	160	290
Tonga	94 800	699	136	700
Tuvalu	8 500	26	327	900
Vanuatu	145 000	11 880	12	680
Wallis and Futuna	14 700	255	58	300
Western Samoa	162 000	2 935	55	120
Total	5 660 500	550 044	10	29 523

Source: South Pacific Commission 1989a, p. 4.

island states' claims to Exclusive Economic Zones (EEZs) within 200 miles (about 322 kilometres) of their shores (United Nations 1983; Buchholz 1987; Slatyer 1987; Prescott 1988). The area encompassed by the maritime boundaries of island states is 29 523 000 square kilometres, of which 550 044 square kilometres are land, or a sea/land ratio of 54 to 1. If the giant bulk of Papua New Guinea is excluded, the ratio of sea to land is about 336 to 1. The explorer Magellan, the first European to traverse the region, in 1520–21 sailed from the southern tip of South America past hundreds of islands without sighting any until he encountered the Mariana Islands (Oliver 1951, p. 87). Modern Pacific travellers spend hours in the air with few land sightings to break the seascape. Nine island countries command over 1 million square kilometres of sea, and six more command over 500 000 square kilometres, but Western Samoa, constricted by its neighbours' EEZs, commands only 120 000 square kilometres.

Fish and seabed resources

The ocean may be vast, but it is far from uniform or empty. The sea varies in depth from reefs, shallows and continental shelves to the Mariana Trench—the deepest spot on earth, 11 022 metres below sea level. Marine life varies from sea vegetation, shellfish and coastal fish, which provide islanders with food, tools and artefacts, to the large offshore and migratory species that are in global demand and offer commercial opportunities. The most valuable of these is the tuna.

In the 1980s approximately 650 000 tonnes of tuna were taken each year from Pacific waters by local and outside boats; the annual catch was valued at over US$500 million (Doulman 1987a, p. x; Doulman 1991, p.81). In 1986 fish and seafood exports comprised 15.8 per cent of total exports from South Pacific countries, being second only to minerals in value and the leading export earner of Solomon Islands, Kiribati and American Samoa (South Pacific Commission 1989a, p. 15). Licensing of EEZ fishing rights to outsiders, principally Japan, Korea, Taiwan and the Soviet Union, and revenues from the 1987 United States–South Pacific Regional Fisheries Treaty, are significant sources of revenue also for Tuvalu, Federated States of Micronesia, Marshall Islands and Vanuatu (Hamnett and Kiste 1988, pp. 18–19). Exploitation of fish resources is thus a major objective of island governments, particularly in small countries where there are few economic alternatives. To this end the island governments in 1979 established the Forum Fisheries Agency and continue to support and benefit from its activities.

Offshore seabed and subsoil resources have great potential, although their exploitation and thus their contribution to particular South Pacific economies vary greatly and lie in the distant future for most. Oil, gas and coal are now extracted from northern Pacific offshore areas and off the island of New Guinea and it is anticipated that a rise of world prices will intensify exploration and exploitation in the South Pacific in the coming century. Already discovered on the seabed are nodules of minerals precipitated from seawater. The nodules range from 1 to 20 centimetres in diameter, are concentrated in some places at 100 000 tons per square mile (39 230 tonnes per square kilometre), and contain not only manganese, which gives the nodules their customary name, but also nickel, copper, cobalt, molybdenum, aluminium, titanium, magnesium, iron and lead (Luard 1974, p. 14). A 1959 study estimated the total at 1700 billion tons (1727 billion tonnes) for the Pacific as a whole (Mero 1959, *passim*). One extrapolation estimated that at the 1960 rate of world consumption the Pacific seabed reserves of manganese would last

400 000 years, aluminium would last 20 000 years, nickel would last 150 000 years, copper would last 6000 years, and cobalt would last 200 000 years (Luard 1974, pp. 15–16). Also of importance and more accessible are phosphates, sand and gravel, and precious corals (Howorth 1990, p. 69). The United Nations in the 1970s sponsored an agency to help states in the region to evaluate and manage these potential seabed resources; that agency is now known as the South Pacific Applied Geoscience Commission (SOPAC).

Minerals, agriculture and forestry

Generally speaking, the Pacific islands taper off from substantial continental landforms in the southwest to peaks of submerged volcanic ranges in the central South Pacific area to tiny coral atolls north of the equator. The larger Melanesian islands are endowed with minerals, including copper and oil in Papua New Guinea, gold in Solomon Islands and Fiji, nickel in New Caledonia, and phosphates in Nauru. In 1986 these resources comprised 46.8 per cent of the total value of South Pacific exports (South Pacific Commission 1989a, p. 17).

Also in Melanesia is the bulk of the land. Papua New Guinea alone accounts for 88 per cent of the region's land area, and the Solomons, Vanuatu and Fiji account for another 11 per cent. The larger islands support plantations whose sugar, coffee, tea and cocoa generated 23.0 per cent and whose forestry products generated 5.4 per cent of total South Pacific exports in 1986 (South Pacific Commission 1989a, pp. 15–16).

In the small island countries of the central and north Pacific, land areas are small relative to the population, arable land is scarce and fresh groundwater is sometimes in short supply. Fish, foodstuffs, building material, clothing and artefacts are made for local consumption, but little is exported. The principal agricultural exports are copra, bananas, citrus fruit and foodcrops such as taro, the latter mainly to islanders living abroad. Philatelic sales to collectors around the world rival exports of copra in value for the microstates of Polynesia, and indeed stamps are the principal export of Tuvalu. The prospects of increasing earnings from exports are dim, not because of market barriers because there are none, but because of the lack of modern production technology, uncertain supply and quality, low demand abroad and high transportation costs (Robertson 1986, pp. 161–2).

Export earnings

The value of the principal products exported by South Pacific countries in 1986, and their proportion of the total, are summarised in Table 2.4. The figures show dependency on mineral ores (46.8 per cent) and basic foods and beverages (45.3 per cent). Manufacturing is not a major source of export income. It is found mainly in Papua New Guinea, based on mineral, food and timber processing, and in Fiji, based on processing sugar and on making garments for export. Fish canning is the major industry of Solomon Islands and American Samoa. Tonga and Western Samoa are making efforts to attract light labour intensive industry such as textiles and garments. Otherwise, exports comprise relatively unprocessed commodities whose prices are vulnerable to international market fluctuations beyond the control of island producers and whose production is vulnerable to local disturbances, such as interethnic disputes as in New Caledonia and Fiji or secessionist movements as in Bougainville. Natural disasters such as periodic hurricanes threaten production at source; strikes, bankruptcies and costs threaten transportation to market; and unforeseen events such as pest infestation and changing consumer tastes threaten market access.

Efforts to increase export earnings have been made by island governments with the encouragement of outside aid and technical assistance agencies, and to a limited degree these efforts have yielded a small but steady annual increase (see Table 2.5). However, the parallel growth of import costs has nullified export gains and left a net and growing deficit in the balance of merchandise trade.

Table 2.4 Exports of principal products, 1986

Product	Value A $000	%
Minerals, oil	1 275 353	46.8
Coffee, tea, cocoa	438 694	16.1
Fish, seafoods	431 222	15.8
Sugar, sugar products	186 845	6.9
Other foods, edible oils	176 456	6.5
Wood, wood products	152 779	5.6
Shells, corals, pearls	17 945	0.6
Clothing, footwear	9 510	0.4
Miscellaneous	35 399	1.3
Total	2 723 035	100.0

Source: Adapted from South Pacific Commission 1989, pp. 16–17.

Table 2.5 Value and balance of merchandise trade, 1970–87

Year	Exports (US$ million)	Imports (US$ million)	Balance (US$ million)
1970	480	926	−446
1975	1 149	1 860	−771
1980	2 139	3 477	−1 340
1985	1 937	3 359	−1 422
1986	2 036	3 649	−1 613
1987	2 312	4 009	−1 697

Source: United Nations 1988, pp. 990–1.

The pattern is not uniform, however. The broader land-resource base of the larger island countries is reflected in the favourable trade balances of Papua New Guinea and Solomon Islands, and of phosphate-rich Nauru, contrasted with the negative balances of merchandise trade incurred by all the other countries in 1986 (South Pacific Commission 1989a, p. 15).

Tourism, remittances and rubbish

Unorthodox resources of small Pacific islands are tapped to generate income, including their image as unspoiled and exotic retreats from the tensions of the West and Japan. The numbers of tourists and their relative impact are unevenly spread. The biggest impact is doubtless on Guam, whose nearly 500 000 visitors, predominantly from Japan, number ten times the population. Table 2.6 summarises visitor arrivals in 1987 and their impact expressed as a percentage of the indigenous population. The table also shows that the predominant source of visitors to each country is usually the former colonial power.

Tourism is a major earner also for French Polynesia, New Caledonia, Cook Islands, Fiji, Western Samoa, Tonga, Vanuatu and Solomon Islands (Hamnett and Kiste 1988, pp. 20–1). A study of gross tourist receipts by the latter five countries from the mid 1970s to the mid 1980s showed very substantial contributions to invisible export earnings, gross domestic product (GDP) and local paid employment, as reported in Table 2.7.

An unorthodox export resource is people. Tens of thousands of islanders have migrated to Australia, New Zealand and the United States in search of education and jobs. Significant portions of the populations of Tonga and Western Samoa, and a majority of Cook Islanders and Niueans, live abroad, mainly in New Zealand (Hamnett and Kiste 1988, p. 6). Emigrants typically send remittances

Table 2.6 Overseas visitors by origin and destination, 1987

Country	Visitors	% of indigenous population	Main Source
American Samoa	45 127	123.0	USA 17%
Fiji	189 866	26.2	Australia 34%
French Polynesia	142 820	80.8	USA 49%
Guam	483 954	404.0	Japan 85%
Kiribati	3 905	5.8	USA 32%
Marshall Islands	3 131	8.3	—
New Caledonia	58 034	37.8	France, Japan 25% each
Niue	2 040	81.6	NZ 78%
Northern Mariana Islands	194 242	942.9	USA 17%
Palau (Belau)	16 695	119.3	Japan 41%
Papua New Guinea	34 970	1.0	Australia 49%
Solomon Islands	12 555	4.3	Australia 39%
Tonga	20 591	21.7	USA, NZ 20% each
Vanuatu	14 642	10.1	Australia 45%
Western Samoa	47 675	29.4	NZ 28%

Source: South Pacific Commission 1989a, p 25.

Table 2.7 Tourism's contribution to five island economies

Country	Year	% of exports	% of GDP	% of jobs
Fiji	1987	35	16–22	31
Solomon Islands	1981	4–5	3–4	1
Tonga	1986	68	14	2
Vanuatu	1984	27	11	20
Western Samoa	1979	16–25	3–4	3

Source: Dwyer 1986, pp. 237, 240; Australia Government 1989b, p. 26; Cole 1991, p. 37.

back to their families, and often return home with savings and educational and occupational skills. The substantial contribution of remittances relative to other sources of foreign exchange earnings is shown in Table 2.8. Empty atolls for the disposal of US rubbish have attracted offers to six island governments; and although none has accepted, the temptation remains strong (*Islands Business Pacific* 1991c, p. 40).

Aid and borrowing

Besides tourism, remittances and other invisible (that is, non-merchandise) receipts, the most prominent corrective for most island

Table 2.8 Relative contributions of remittances, aid, and exports and tourism to foreign exchange earnings, mid 1980s

Country	Remittances (%)	Aid (%)	Exports and Tourism (%)	Total (%)
Kiribati	12	49	39	100
Tonga	42	32	26	100
Tuvalu	8	71	21	100
Vanuatu	8	28	64	100
Western Samoa	31	31	38	100

Source: Australia Government 1989b, p. 132.

states to the deficit on current account, or overall trade balance, is official development assistance or aid. Aid is a government-to-government transfer; it comes in a variety of forms including grants for projects, grants to subsidise the government's budget, grants to development banks or trust funds, and low interest loans for various purposes. The South Pacific enjoys the highest per capita aid receipts of any region in the developing world, and this aid helps to maintain a satisfactory standard of living despite meagre resources and export earnings.

Aid receipts vary from recipient to recipient, with the smaller Polynesian and Micronesian countries typically receiving more per capita aid than the larger Melanesian countries, partly compensating for their weaker resource bases. Table 2.9 summarises the relative impact of aid by expressing it in terms of per capita value and percentage of government expenditure of each recipient. In general, the principal donors are the former colonial countries, each favouring its former colonies or trust territories.

Creditworthiness, the ability of a country's government or major enterprises to assure overseas lenders of the safety of a loan, is a resource that can be used to attract or enhance other resources, such as jobs, technology, export market access and, more generally, economic development and political legitimacy. Island governments sustain imports in the face of lagging export earnings, and stimulate economic development, by borrowing abroad. Private sector enterprises also borrow. The total of public and private debt relative to the GDP, and the service payments on that debt relative to the export earnings of a country in a given year, are indicators of the burden of that debt.

Among South Pacific countries the debt burdens vary, from heavy in Papua New Guinea to light in Kiribati, Tonga and Vanuatu. In contrast to South America, no South Pacific country has defaulted on major overseas loans. Western Samoa was obliged to seek

Table 2.9　Contribution of aid to island economies, 1987

Country	Per capita (A$)	% of government expenditure
American Samoa	2 041	50.4
Cook Islands	921	40.9
Federated States of Micronesia	642[a]	70.0[c]
Fiji	34	5.0
French Polynesia	2 179	45.8
Guam	576	17.1
Kiribati	324	108.0
Marshall Islands	662[a]	81.6[b]
Nauru	9	0.1[c]
New Caledonia	738	21.3
Niue	2 902	71.6
Northern Mariana Islands	5 572	92.9
Palau (Belau)	2 486	108.8
Papua New Guinea	145	36.5
Pitcairn	2 980[a]	100.0[c]
Solomon Islands	120	35.5
Tokelau	1 746	92.8[b]
Tonga	194	47.1
Tuvalu	876	119.5
Vanuatu	249	48.8
Wallis and Futuna	1 980	64.7
Western Samoa	159	35.8

Notes: [a]1986　[b]1985　[c]estimate

Source: South Pacific Commission 1989a, pp. 12, 14.

rescheduling in 1980–82, and other countries have high debt/GDP ratios, but the debt service burdens remain low by Third World standards. This is because the creditworthiness of South Pacific countries remains high and they can secure concessionary interest loans with easy repayment terms from international agencies such as the Asian Development Bank (ADB) and the International Monetary Fund (IMF). Borrowing is limited not by the absence of lenders but by the limited absorptive capacity of small island economies. A summary of selected island countries' debt burdens is presented in Table 2.10.

Summary of liabilities and assets

Broadly speaking, the liabilities of the South Pacific states are economic in character and derive from small size and isolation (Fairbairn 1991, p. 39). They include:

Table 2.10 Overseas debt burdens of seven countries, 1987

Country	Debt/GDP ratio (%)	Debt service ratio (%)
Fiji	39.3	18.4
Kiribati	9.3	3.1
Papua New Guinea	68.3	19.8
Solomon Islands	73.9	6.5
Tonga	44.3	3.8
Vanuatu	6.8	2.9
Western Samoa	77.7	12.5

Source: Browne 1989, pp. 15–16 and passim.

- shallow natural-resource base, still exploited mainly by outsiders;
- uneven human-resource base, further weakened by emigration;
- narrow and inflexible manufacturing base, largely foreign owned;
- limited domestic market or investment attractiveness because of low purchasing power;
- weak private sector entrepreneurialism because of few incentives;
- few economies of scale;
- high costs of transportation and communications;
- vulnerability to fluctuating international economic conditions, especially prices;
- persistent deficits in budgets and trade balances, partly due to governmental extravagance;
- tardiness of information collation and dissemination because of administrative inexperience and overload; and
- substantial dependency on outside largesse and protection for survival.

On the other hand, South Pacific states have substantial political assets, which derive from harmonious relations within and between South Pacific states and a large measure of international goodwill (Fairbairn 1991, pp. 57, 65, 83). These assets, which help to offset the liabilities listed above, include:

- absence of a history of anti-colonial violence and, today, a close and mutually respectful relationship with the former colonial powers;
- shallowness of social and other schisms, low degree of political violence, high degree of political tolerance, and substantial legitimacy and responsibility of traditional elites, leading to a high degree of constitutional and legal regularity and a low degree of economic disruption;
- moderate competence of new administrators and leaders, trained by former colonial powers and able to attract and manage capital and technical assistance from abroad;
- impressive record of success in mobilising outside support for aid, loans, disaster relief and military protection;

- skilful regional cooperation in achieving international legal safeguards for oceanic environments and resources;
- constructive participation in the Commonwealth and in United Nations affiliated and other intergovernmental bodies, resulting in diplomatic access, support and services; and
- sympathetic posture by former colonial powers, not least because of the islands' evident needs, non-threatening postures and clear commitment to the West during the period of Soviet initiatives in the South Pacific.

With allowance for exceptions, which are detailed in the country chapters below, the above generalisations encapsulate the liabilities and assets of the South Pacific states. These endowments reflect the historical and geographical legacies with which island leaders must work as they pursue their countries' national interests and foreign policy goals.

However, governments' capacities are affected not only by history and geography but also by the presence of other governments, neighbours and outsiders. If island governments are to improve their countries' economic circumstances, and thus their own legitimacy and stability, by using international opportunities to offset local economic weaknesses, then they must acknowledge the help they can get from outside patrons and the self-help they can effect by banding together in regional organisations. The following two chapters outline the interests of extraregional governments in the South Pacific region and review the initiatives of South Pacific governments in forming regional organisations through which they gain bargaining power in relations with outsiders.

3   Extraregional governments

The progress from colonialism to independence in the South Pacific has not brought an end to the influence of the former colonial powers (Crocombe and Ali 1983b). First, nine territories or dependencies are still linked directly to an extraregional government, and two others are constrained in their foreign policies by the terms of their free association compacts. Second, the independent states are still affected by the political, security and economic policies of the extraregional powers. There is an overlap of interests between outsiders and islanders, which is likely to persist even as more island states become independent. This chapter sketches the extraregional governments' interests, policies and involvement and makes rough assessments of the relative scope, quality and outlook of the continuing interactions. Subsequent chapters will look at the interactions from the regional and individual island states' points of view.

Australia

Australia, following the independence of Nauru in 1968 and Papua New Guinea in 1975, has no dependencies in the South Pacific. The government of Australia has strong strategic interests in the region but also has substantial economic, humanitarian and environmental concerns. The current policy, as enunciated by the Minister for Foreign Affairs and Trade Senator Gareth Evans in 1989, is called Constructive Commitment and contains the following elements:

- promotion of close, confident and broadly based relations with all Pacific island countries on a basis that recognises their individual differences;
- fostering of effective regional cooperation, through the South Pacific Forum and its agencies, and the South Pacific Commission;
- recognition that, for the island countries, security hinges on economic and social development, and offering assistance to help them achieve both;
- respect for full sovereignty of the island states in relation to both their interests and their external affairs; but at the same time
- promotion of shared perceptions of the region's strategic and security interests, laying the basis for a regional approach to situations, either internal or external, that put regional stability at risk (Australia Government 1989e, p. 45; Fry 1991c).

The 1987 defence white paper identified Australia's area of primary strategic concern and direct military interest as an arc from Papua New Guinea to New Zealand including all the nearby countries of the Southwest Pacific (Australia Government 1987b, p. 2). The Department of Defence submission to a 1989 parliamentary inquiry stated that Australia had a direct interest in:

- limiting the extent and nature of major external military-power involvement in the region;
- fostering a strategic outlook that accords with Australia's strategic concerns;
- encouraging Pacific island countries to look to Australia for guidance on strategic and defence issues; and
- facilitating Australian Defence Force operations in the region (Australia Government 1989b, p. 146).

A close relationship is fostered by the most extensive diplomatic outreach of any outside government (see Table 3.1). Australia maintains missions staffed with diplomatic, trade, aid, immigration or military officials in each independent state and most dependencies. Regional organisations are encouraged by diplomatic support, cash aid, technical assistance and the secondment of specialist officers. Australia's aid programme, valued at nearly A\$400 million in 1989, was the largest in the region, if France's and the US's transfers to their six territories are counted as subsidies instead of aid (see Table 3.2). In 1987 over 55 per cent of Australian bilateral aid was directed to South Pacific countries, overwhelmingly to Papua New Guinea. Fiji, Solomon Islands, Vanuatu, Western Samoa and Tonga were also in the top twenty recipients, and all the other island states received some measure of Australian aid (Australia Government 1988, pp. 4, 9).

Table 3.1 Extraregional political links, 1991

Extraregional government	Dependencies or associated states	Diplomatic posts	Military links[b]
Australia	0	10	8
New Zealand	3	10	5
United States	6	6	4
France	3	3	3
Britain	1	6	0
Japan	0	4	0
China	0	4	0
Taiwan	0	4[a]	0
Indonesia	0	3	1
Malaysia	0	1	1
Soviet Union	0	1	0

[a] Includes two trade offices performing diplomatic functions.
[b] Substantial cooperation, training, supply or exercises.

Australia's exports to the region are about A$1 billion, and investments, particularly in Papua New Guinea, are substantial, and these economic links are valued by the government as mutually beneficial. Regional products are given free entry by the South Pacific Regional Trade and Economic Cooperation Agreement of 1980 and encouraged by the South Pacific Trade Commission, funded by the Australian government. Military exercises with Papua New Guinea, Tonga and, before 1987, Fiji, deployment to Vanuatu, civil action under the Defence Cooperation Programme, provision of boats through the Pacific patrol boat project, and sharing of air and maritime surveillance intelligence, all are examples of the defence activities in the region. At the same time, Australia has taken the lead in promoting the South Pacific Nuclear Free Zone Treaty and in environmental protection initiatives.

Australia's interests in the region are not limitless. South Pacific trade and investment constitute less than 5 per cent of Australia's global involvement. Australia regards itself as a middle-sized global player with its major economic interests in the northern hemisphere. Regarding strategy and defence, Southeast Asia is of greater concern than the Southwest Pacific (Babbage 1990). Australia will continue to play a major role in the South Pacific, but it is content to share the stage with New Zealand, France, the United States and Japan (Fry 1991b).

New Zealand

New Zealand identifies with the South Pacific more than any other outside country because of its relatively small size, insular geogra-

Table 3.2 Extraregional economic links, 1986–87

Extraregional country	Exports to South Pacific (A$ million) 1986	Imports from South Pacific (A$ million) 1986	Aid to South Pacific (A$ million) 1987	Visitors to South Pacific (000) 1987
Australia	1 026	371	348	124
New Zealand	318	77	47	52
United States	537	475	304[a]	212
France	954	200	527[a]	36
Great Britain	115	225	32	n.a.
Japan	527	516	78	601
Others	1 811	1 091	223	245
Total	5 822	2 955	1 559	1 270

[a] Mostly subsidies to dependent territories. US aid outside US flag territories was US$8.2 million; French aid outside French territories was US$1.4 million.

Source: South Pacific Commission 1989a, pp. 14, 19, 25.

phy, commitments to Cook Islands and Niue, and continued administration of Tokelau. Because approximately 15 per cent of its population is of Polynesian origin, racial, cultural and immigration policies are of major importance, and this is acknowledged by the establishment of the ministries of Maori Affairs and Pacific Island Affairs. New Zealand took the initiative in hosting the first South Pacific Forum in 1971 and has fostered South Pacific cultural activities, including radio and television time, regularly since then. The government promoted the South Pacific Nuclear Free Zone starting in 1975, the Pacific Islands Industrial Development Scheme in 1976, and the South Pacific Regional Trade and Economic Cooperation Agreement in 1980. It set up the South Pacific Trade Office in 1990 to help island exports. Over two-thirds of bilateral aid, the highest proportion of any donor, is directed to island countries or to South Pacific regional organisations, programmes and projects (Hoadley 1989, pp. 63–5; 1991b).

Since 1925 New Zealand has taken responsibility for the administration of Tokelau (population about 1600). The Administrator is the Deputy Secretary of External Relations and Trade, based in Wellington. The Official Secretary, based in Apia, is advised by five Tokelauan directors, and the Tokelau Public Service of 168 is staffed entirely by Tokelauans. Visiting missions from the United Nations Special Committee on Decolonisation have found little desire for independence or even greater self-government. Tokelauans are New Zealand citizens and more of them live in New Zealand now than in their home islands, and it appears to be in their interest to preserve this arrangement. Tokelau receives over NZ$2000 worth of aid and technical assistance per capita from New Zealand and a number of other donors and agencies. It is a member of the South Pacific Commission but otherwise plays no active role in South Pacific affairs.

In 1976 the Minister of Defence began reorienting New Zealand's strategy towards the South Pacific (Hoadley 1991a). The 1987 defence white paper included among the ten principal defence objectives the following:

- to preserve the security of New Zealand, its 200 mile (322 kilometre) Exclusive Economic Zone (EEZ) and the island states (Cook Islands, Niue and Tokelau) for which New Zealand has defence responsibilities;
- to mount an effective military response to any low-level contingency within New Zealand's area of direct strategic concern, defined as a broad arc stretching from Australia through Papua New Guinea, Kiribati in the north and across to Cook Islands in the east;
- to promote the security and stable development of the South Pacific by providing practical assistance in defence matters;
- to maintain close defence cooperation with Australia in the South Pacific; and
- to provide disaster relief assistance, resource protection, rescue and medical evacuation services to the South Pacific (New Zealand Government 1987b, p. 31).

A major South Pacific policy review was undertaken in 1990. The resulting 300 page report contained 62 recommendations covering diplomacy, economic relations, aid, cultural relations, the environment and defence and security issues (New Zealand Government 1990a). The thrust of the recommendations was New Zealand's indissoluble relationship with the South Pacific in all policy sectors and the government's duty to promote harmony both with and within the region. In spite of his criticism of his predecessor's parochialism the first visit abroad by the newly elected Minister of Foreign Affairs in 1991 was to the South Pacific. The new government's 1991 defence white paper reiterated the traditional commitment to South Pacific stability (New Zealand Government 1991, pp. 20–21, 33,45).

New Zealand is too small to have a profound impact on the region, but its presence is welcomed by local leaders because it is perceived as sympathetic and sensitive to island needs, in contrast with the larger powers. Papua New Guinea's invitation to the New Zealand Navy to assist in negotiating a ceasefire with the Bougainville rebels, called the Endeavour Accord, and the choice of Wellington for the signing of the South Pacific Forum-sponsored convention condemning driftnet fishing, are all indicators of the value of New

Zealand's constructive role. This role is acknowledged by the United States as an instance of burden sharing in spite of differences over nuclear-capable ship visits, and by Japan, which consults with New Zealand diplomats and aid officials on the nuances of small island countries.

United States

Strategic interests have dominated US perceptions of the region since the previous century (Bunge 1985; Dorrance 1990a; Smith and Pugh 1991). Guam was acquired, with the Philippines, as a prize of the Spanish–American War, and the annexation of Tutuila and Manua (now American Samoa) was part of a strategic balancing manoeuvre directed at Germany. For a time these islands were useful as coaling stations. Japanese aggression in 1942 using island staging points confirmed the necessity of a policy of strategic denial of the islands to hostile powers. This policy was advocated especially by the US Pacific Command in the post-World War II years. The US government had no economic interests and no developed policy in other respects, and 'benign neglect' from 1945 to the 1960s was the result.

The coming to independence of South Pacific colonies, and agitation by the United Nations and by local leaders in its dependencies, stimulated Washington to initiate moves towards self-government in its three dependencies and negotiations on the future status of the Trust Territory. Soviet initiatives and island declarations of 200 miles (322 kilometre) EEZs further attracted State Department attention. Funds for development and for the repair of damages done by nuclear testing were increased steeply.

Explicit policy towards the South Pacific was first articulated in 1978 by Richard Holbrook, Assistant Secretary of State for East Asian and Pacific Affairs. 'The region has been relatively overlooked but is now emerging into a new and important role in the world', said Holbrook. He continued 'there is a reservoir of great goodwill towards the United States among the peoples of the South Pacific and this enhances the prospects for cooperative relations'. He proceeded to outline elements of a new US policy, as follows:

- understanding and sympathy for the political aspirations of the South Pacific peoples;
- support for South Pacific regional cooperation;
- active US participation in regional organisations;
- larger and more effective US presence in the islands;

- pursuit of Micronesian status negotiations to an agreement on free association and termination of the trusteeship; and
- continued close cooperation with the other four metropolitan powers in the region in support of the progress of the South Pacific peoples (Kiste 1990, pp. 6–7).

These goals were refined in following years. In 1990 the State Department's Director of the Office of South Pacific Affairs stated that his government's three main policy objectives were:

- to strengthen democratic institutions;
- to promote economic growth and development; and
- to prevent the region from becoming an area of superpower rivalry (Mullin 1990).

In the 1980s the United States concluded friendship treaties with Kiribati, Tuvalu, Cook Islands and New Zealand (on behalf of Tokelau), and a fishing treaty with South Pacific Forum members. New diplomatic posts were opened in Marshall Islands, Federated States of Micronesia, Solomon Islands and Western Samoa, and posts in Fiji and Papua New Guinea were upgraded. An aid office was opened in Suva, bilateral aid programmes were initiated for Fiji and Papua New Guinea, and Peace Corps volunteers increased to about 400 for the region. High level officials attended the post-forum dialogues in Kiribati in 1989 and Vanuatu in 1990. The Wellington Convention condemning driftnet fishing, and the Convention for the Protection of the Natural Resources and Environment of the South Pacific Region, were signed.

Free association arrangements were concluded with Marshall Islands and Federated States of Micronesia and negotiated with Palau pending the resolution of constitutional problems. The federal government created an Office of Pacific Island Affairs and an Interagency Group under a Deputy Assistant Secretary of State to implement policy towards the freely associated and independent island states, and charged the Assistant Secretary of the Interior for Territorial and International Affairs with study, liaison and reporting duties in pursuit of solutions to social, economic and political problems in US flag territories.

In October 1990 President Bush invited island leaders to an unprecedented summit. There he stated that 'the United States has rededicated itself to lasting security in the region. A security which comes not so much from force of arms, but through nurturing of free people, free market and free economies' (East–West Center 1990, p. 8). The president then announced a number of initiatives:

- to limit the use of the chemical weapons disposal unit at Johnston Atoll;

Library of
Davidson College

- to establish a Joint Commercial Commission to consult on trade and commercial opportunities;
- to establish an Asia–Pacific Growth Fund and an Environmental Investment Fund;
- to encourage a mission of US investors to island countries;
- to extend the United States–South Pacific Regional Fisheries Treaty;
- to augment Agency of International Development private sector assistance for agriculture and marine resource development; and
- to extend three educational exchange programmes to the South Pacific.

Cook Islands Premier Geoffrey Henry, speaking for the eleven island states represented, said 'you have, by one single act [the summit], begun to replenish the pool of goodwill' (East–West Center 1990, p. 14).

However, implementation of the president's summit pledges proceeded slowly, and doubts were raised as to whether private sector initiatives would be effective in the isolated resource-poor micro-states. The president has ignored Congress's and South Pacific leaders' calls to sign the protocols of the South Pacific Nuclear Free Zone Treaty, and tacitly condoned continued French nuclear testing. The centre of Washington's attention and the bulk of US involvement remain north of the equator. The flag and freely associated states receive over 90 per cent of US aid, trade, tourists and investment. The United States sends fewer diplomats to the South Pacific, and gives less aid, than tiny New Zealand. Washington is willing to rely now, as in the past, on Australia, New Zealand, France and Britain to manage the diplomatic affairs south of the equator and on Japan and the European Community powers to provide growing amounts of aid and trade access.

France

France remains the major colonial power in the South Pacific nearly a century and a half after it first entered the region, having outlasted the departure of Germany and Japan and decolonisation by the other powers. As Britain, the United States, Australia and New Zealand brought their island colonies to independence in the past two decades, France in contrast integrated its overseas territories constitutionally, politically and economically with the metropol. New Caledonia, French Polynesia, and Wallis and Futuna are regarded as parts of the 'body of France' (Victor 1990, p. 345).

French interests in the South Pacific range from the symbolic and moral to the strategic and economic. Original French motives were a mix of strategic rivalry with Britain and a civilising mission among native peoples, in which strategists, administrators, missionaries and educators cooperated. Since the 1880s French internationalists have regarded the Pacific as the region of the future—an area of strategic centrality and economic growth potential in which France must participate to maintain its great power status (Aldrich 1988, p. 11). The three Pacific territories (and Vanuatu, until 1980) were thus France's entry points into this dynamic region, assuring that France would be a full participant in future developments.

To maintain great power status, the French government has developed an independent nuclear-weapons capability, and tests it to keep up its effectiveness and credibility. The possession of the Mururoa and Fangataufa test sites, and of the supporting facilities in Tahiti, are integral to France's global strategic role. Wallis and Futuna and New Caledonia also support the French Polynesia facilities. They, with the other eight overseas territories in the Indian and Atlantic oceans, the Caribbean and South America, are visible signs of France's global presence. The sun never sets on the French empire as it does now on Britain's; and more important, high altitude missiles and communications satellites are never out of line of sight from a French ground station, and the European Space Programme relies on French territories scattered around the world. New Caledonia contains the largest known nickel deposits in the world, and also chrome and cobalt—all ingredients of weapons grade steel and thus regarded as strategic resources by the government of France (Bates 1990, pp. 17–18). The seabeds surrounding French Polynesian and Wallis and Futuna are thought to be rich in polymetallic nodules and crusts that may become economic to mine in future.

In the 1980s the Institut du Pacifique in Paris projected scenarios in which France played a central moderating and balancing role between the giant rim powers of the United States, Japan and the Soviet Union, thus preventing hegemony and keeping the sea lanes open. France was portrayed as a protector of the smaller rim states and the island states. French exit would leave a vacuum of power resulting in destructive rivalry or in its place being taken by a radical 'Cuba of the South Pacific' (Aldrich 1989, pp. 93–4). France's moral obligation extended also to the territories' French citizens, many of whom have fled from Algeria, Indochina and Vanuatu and deserve a safe haven. Others who have migrated in good faith from France have invested their lives in the territories. Together, with segments of the oceanic population, they comprise majorities that consistently vote in democratic referenda for continued French presence.

France has been criticised by South Pacific leaders for failing to grant independence to its territories, suppressing indigenous independence movements, ignoring calls to stop nuclear testing, intervening in Vanuatu and New Zealand affairs, distorting territorial economies, soliciting votes with massive subsidies, and displaying insensitivity and arrogance generally. The French intellectual Jean Chesneaux criticised the French government for indulging in six 'geopolitical fantasies' as follows:

- The Pacific is a vacuum; so France can use it as it wishes.
- The Pacific is the new centre of the world; so France must be in it.
- The Pacific is an arena of East–West conflict; so France must volunteer its military and nuclear arms to guard Western values against the Soviet threat.
- The Pacific is the last battlefield between the Gauls and the Brits; so France must prevail here.
- The Pacific is a technological Eldorado; so France can lead in seabed minerals prospecting, the development of space communications networks and tropical bio-engineering research.
- The Pacific is threatened by hegemonists; so France will champion the rights of the peoples of the islands against US, Japanese and Australian encroachments (Chesneaux 1986, pp. 77).

The government of France believed these unflattering images were rooted in misunderstandings and responded by sponsoring closer links between its territories and neighbouring island states (Bates 1990, pp. 93–108). In 1987 Gaston Flosse, Tahitian-born Secretary of State for the South Pacific, undertook a two-part initiative. First, he began a round of visits and dialogues with South Pacific leaders to explain France's position and alleviate misperceptions; and second, he set up joint research programmes, education exchanges and aid funds to demonstrate France's ability to play a constructive role serving mutual interests in the region. Exchange visits and aid to Cook Islands, Tonga and Fiji were particularly visible and successful. In 1990 France signed an EEZ demarcation and air surveillance agreement with Cook Islands. French aid was restored to Vanuatu and directed increasingly to regional organisations such as the South Pacific Applied Geoscience Commission (SOPAC), with particular stress on education, research and telecommunications (Henningham 1990, pp. 146–9).

The annual meeting of high French officials held in Noumea in February 1988 adopted a new 'triple orientation':

- to open French South Pacific territories to a more dynamic cooperation with the region;
- to involve the territories more in the conduct of French foreign policy; and
- to integrate France more closely in the region.

The South Pacific Council of state and territorial leaders, meeting in Papeete in 1990, reiterated France's 'policy of cooperation and dialogue with South Pacific countries'. The Council's communiqué encouraged the elected governments of the territories to use their statutory capacities 'to participate in regional negotiations and sign international agreements on behalf of France', particularly regarding trade, cultural and educational exchange, oceanographic research, and environmental protection (Conseil du Pacific Sud 1990, p. 1).

These objectives were to entail intensified official consultations, cultural exchanges, dialogues with the South Pacific Forum, intraregional trade, aid and sharing of the nascent resources of the French University of the South Pacific and the scientific research of French institutes. Broadcasting, in English, was to be upgraded (France Government 1988; Martin 1991, p. 1). These initiatives, parallel to the granting of limited autonomy to French Polynesia in 1984 and the 1988 Matignon Accords that accommodated New Caledonian nationalism pending a referendum in 1998, found favour among island leaders and were supported by Australia and New Zealand.

Nevertheless, French aid, trade, military activity and political attention remain focused overwhelmingly on the three overseas territories. Generous financial transfers give the territories the highest standard of living in the South Pacific, but they dwarf the aid given to poorer neighbouring states. The urban economies of the territories are so integrated with that of France, and the variations of income so extreme between the expatriates and the island populations, that critics doubt the ability of the territories to survive economically even if they were to achieve autonomy politically. Future possibilities include: continuation of the present arrangements; or increasing self-government leading to free association on the Cook Islands or Marshall Islands model; or partition and retention by France of Tahiti, Mururoa, Fangataufa and Noumea and surrender of the rest; or total independence and abandonment of the South Pacific by France altogether. Self-government in free association, with France continuing to play a constructive role in the region with financial assistance and economic and technical cooperation, is the option most favoured by Pacific leaders.

Japan

Japan regards itself as a natural member of the island Pacific by virtue of its proximity, insular geography and historical involvement. Japanese settlement of Micronesia began in the 1880s, and in World War I Japan replaced Germany as a colonial power. Defeat in World War II expelled Japan from the occupation of any Pacific islands (save the nearby Ryukyus and Ogasawaras), and no future possessions can be foreseen. For three decades a state of 'amnesia' prevailed regarding policy on the South Pacific (Watanabe 1991, p. 4). The 'oil shocks' of 1973 alerted Japanese officials to a policy blind spot to the south and stimulated 'resource diplomacy' to secure minerals and timber from Papua New Guinea, Solomon Islands and New Caledonia. Independence and the proclamation of EEZs by island states obliged Japan to negotiate for fishing and trade access. Embassies were opened in Papua New Guinea in 1975 and Fiji in 1979, a modest aid programme was initiated and Japanese tourism and investment were increased. Soviet penetration starting in 1976 added a strategic dimension to Japanese policy: the prevention of Soviet or other hostile presence in the islands or astride the sea lanes through which essential raw materials travelled to Japan.

In 1980 the Japanese government aggregated its several interests in the concept 'comprehensive security', connoting the pursuit of security in a regional context by means of diplomatic, economic and cultural cooperation and the limiting of military means solely to the defence of the Japanese home islands (Yasutomo 1986). This concept was applied to the South Pacific by Foreign Minister Kuranari in 1987. The Kuranari Doctrine contains the following principles:

- respect for the independence and autonomy of small Pacific states;
- support of the South Pacific Forum and other regional arrangements;
- assistance to preserve the political stability of the region;
- improvement of the quantity and quality of aid and other channels of economic cooperation in pursuit of regional prosperity; and
- promotion of 'heart-to-heart' understanding by cultural exchange (Kanasugi 1988, p. 44–5).

An underlying strategic rationale was expressed in the phrase 'political stability'. It was reiterated by Kuranari in Suva in January 1987 when he said 'we cannot support the introduction of new tensions in this peaceful and untroubled region' (Horiguchi 1987, p. 43). Kuranari pledged an immediate US$2 million to a Special Pacific Islands Fund to supplement the several bilateral aid projects already in progress, and hinted of more to come. The Japan International Cooperation Agency (JICA) bolstered its field offices in South Pacific capitals, increased the number of Japan Overseas Cooperation Volunteers, and set up a small-scale grant assistance programme for which local bodies and non-government organisations were eligible. The administrative criterion that aid must be government-to-government was further loosened to provide aid to regional projects administered by the South Pacific Forum, the United Nations Development Programme (UNDP), the United Nations Economic and Social Commission for Asia and the Pacific (ESCAP) and the International Finance Corporation (IFC).

Figure 3.1 Maritime boundaries/EEZs of South Pacific states

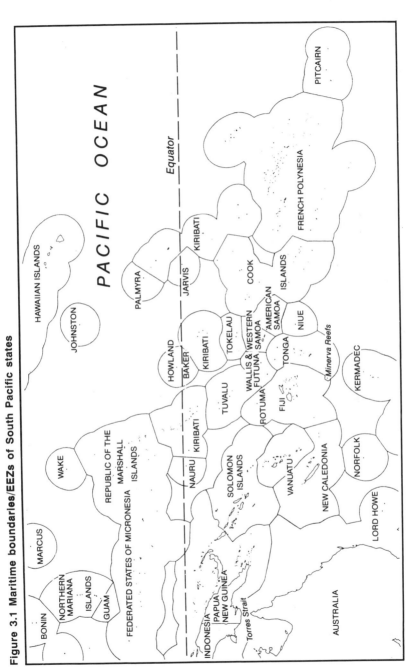

Disbursements rose rapidly, from US$55 million in 1986 to US$98 million in 1989 and over US$100 million in 1990, surpassing New Zealand aid and bringing Japan to second place among donors behind only Australia (Numata 1990, p. 10). The major recipients in 1988 were Papua New Guinea (US$41 million), Solomon Islands (US$14 million), Fiji (US$9 million) and Western Samoa (US$8 million)—each a significant source of raw material exports to Japan. Over US$1 million each was disbursed to Kiribati, Vanuatu, Tonga and the three Micronesian states associated with the United States and seven other island states, mostly in Polynesia, received smaller amounts. Sectors assigned high priority were fisheries and local industries, education and health, and transport and telecommunications.

The surge of aid facilitated closer contact not only with recipients but also with other donors, raising Japan's visibility in the region and contributing to diplomatic goals (Rix 1990, p. 42). Periodic consultations with New Zealand and the United States were initiated, and Japan went one step further with Australia to mount a joint study mission to Papua New Guinea and Fiji. Joint airport and schools projects in Western Samoa, Tonga and Vanuatu set precedents for Japanese administrative coordination with Australia, New Zealand, Canada and the United States.

In 1990 Japan's contacts extended to the South Pacific Commission (SPC). JICA funded a media centre and a women's radio project under commission auspices, and as a consequence Japan's ambassador to Papua New Guinea was invited to address the South Pacific Conference. Ambassador Noguchi indicated Japan's wish to become a member of the commission in due course, which 'would certainly make it easier for us to contribute more to the SPC financially and otherwise' (Noguchi 1990).

'Heart-to-heart' understanding was enhanced by inviting South Pacific leaders, experts and scholars to Tokyo (400 in 1988) and by sending officials, experts, students and cultural figures to South Pacific capitals. In 1989 Japan was invited by the South Pacific Forum to attend a post-forum ministerial dialogue, signalling that Japan had become a valued outside partner alongside Australia, New Zealand, the United States, Canada, France and China. At the 1990 forum dialogue Ambassador Togo raised Japan's image by announcing regional environmental research initiatives and pledging an end to Japanese driftnet fishing 1 year before the United Nations-imposed deadline (Togo 1990).

Throughout this period tourism and investment grew rapidly. Micronesia was the favoured destination for both because of proximity and historical association. Japanese tourists exceeded 600 000 by 1987, triple the number of US tourists.

Japan's diplomatic, trade and resource initiatives were described by some as self-interested, and its aid was criticised as tied to Japanese economic interests, experts and firms (Edo 1986). Nevertheless, Japanese economic, fishing and aid agreements have been completed and renewed without notable controversy, and the reputation and acceptance of Japan have steadily risen in the eyes of island leaders. The governments of New Zealand, Australia and the United States saw Japanese aid as helping to share the burden of maintaining economic stability in the region. Following the declaration of the Kuranari Doctrine, Prime Minister David Lange 'welcomed Japan's intention to play a greater role in the region and offered New Zealand's cooperation in exploring constructive avenues' (New Zealand Government 1987a, p. 22). Australia's ambassador to Japan said 'Australia welcomes Japan's increased interest in this region' (Australia Government 1987a, p. 47).

Japan appears to have had no grand design beyond keeping the Pacific island region politically and militarily tranquil, free for shipping, air travel and tourism, open for the purchase of fish, timber and minerals, and closed to the weapons and agents of hostile outside powers (Hoadley 1991c). South Pacific leaders have shared these goals and accepted Japan as a major player in the region.

Britain

Britain's role and interests have declined steeply since its colonies began to achieve independence, beginning with Fiji in 1970. Britain maintains diplomatic posts in Fiji, Papua New Guinea, Vanuatu, Solomon Islands, Kiribati and Tonga, and deals with other island states through cross-accredited high commissioners in Canberra or Wellington and visits by ministers and trade commissioners. Members of the Royal Family and units of the Royal Navy visit, but only infrequently, on ceremonial occasions.

Pitcairn, population less than 100, is Britain's last dependency in the region. It is administered by the High Commissioner to New Zealand. Local affairs are managed by the Island Council. Britain provides subsidies, grants and technical assistance to maintain basic services and is responsible for foreign affairs and defence. There is no agitation for, or realistic prospect of, independence, and Pitcairn plays no significant role in South Pacific affairs (Douglas and Douglas 1989, p. 484).

In 1986 British imports from the region had fallen to 7.6 per cent and exports to 1.9 per cent of the islands' trade and to less than 1 per cent of British global trade (South Pacific Commission 1989a, p. 19). In 1987 British aid slipped to seventh, overtaken by New

Zealand's, and constituted just 2 per cent of aid received by island states (South Pacific Commission 1989a, p. 14). Nevertheless, British aid remains significant in the small states of Kiribati and Tuvalu, and in the former colonies of Vanuatu and Solomon Islands, all of which receive irreplaceable technical assistance in the form of seconded experts, teachers and administrators, project aid for human resource development, and support of regional organisations (Britain Government 1989). Britain also contributes indirectly, through the Commission of the European Communities, to the European Development Fund (EDF) and to STABEX (export price stabilisation) grants under the Lome Convention.

European Community and Canada

The European Community collectively was the fifth-largest supplier of imports, the fourth-largest donor of aid and the largest customer for exports of the South Pacific region in 1986, surpassing even Japan in the latter two relationships (Commission of the European Communities 1989). The EC maintained liaison offices in Honiara, Suva, Port Vila and Port Moresby. The relationship does not extend far beyond trade and aid; and although the European Community presence is valued, it cannot be regarded as a major player in the region. The same may be said of individual European states, most of which have diplomatic posts in Fiji and Papua New Guinea, effecting a constructive but low key role.

Canada is emerging from the shadow of the United States and has projected its presence into the South Pacific, primarily to New Zealand and Australia, but also to the island states as a trade partner and an aid donor. Canada's emphasis is on fishing and maritime-related technical assistance. Its main clients are Kiribati, Tuvalu, Vanuatu and Solomon Islands, and the South Pacific Forum and Forum Fisheries Agency.

Soviet Union, Libya, China, Taiwan

Strategic rivalry with the United States as well as the search for acceptance, status and resource access stimulated Soviet offers of aid, trade, fishing agreements and diplomatic posts, starting in 1976 (Gill 1989; Dorrance 1990b). Spokesmen cited the explorations of von Bellingshausen and other Russians, and the global diplomatic and economic interests of a great power, to assert a legitimate Soviet presence in a previously Anglo-American sphere of influence. Offers of fishing port aid to Tonga in 1976 and oceanographic research to

SOPAC in 1980 were pre-empted by prompt counteroffers by Australia, New Zealand and the United States (Hegarty 1989a, p. 114). The Soviet Union gained a favourable image by signing the protocols of the South Pacific Nuclear Free Zone Treaty in 1986. Although the Soviet Union secured diplomatic recognition from a number of island states, closer contracts were resisted and it has not been invited to South Pacific Forum dialogues. Fishing agreements were finally signed with Kiribati in 1985 and Vanuatu in 1987, but they lapsed after 1 year each, and no further agreements followed. In 1990 the Soviets finally opened their first island post, in Port Moresby. Soviet trade and aid was virtually nil, and the once-feared naval presence and subversive activities have not materialised. The Soviet role in the South Pacific remains more anticipation than substance.

The appearance of Libyan People's Bureau representatives in Port Vila and news that ni-Vanuatu and Kanak nationalists had flown to Libya for 'political training seminars' in the mid 1980s stimulated concern that Libya would extend its revolutionary Islamic foreign policy to the South Pacific (Hegarty 1987). Already Libya had People's Bureaus in Kuala Lumpur and Canberra, and Colonel Gaddafi professed a Third World radicalism that threatened to encompass the island states and to stir opposition figures to violent action. However, a leadership struggle in Vanuatu and Australian government expulsion of Libyans brought the episode to an end by 1988, and neither Libya nor Cuba nor North Korea, all of which were recognised by Vanuatu in gestures of Third World solidarity, had any visible presence in the region by 1991.

Chinese trade with and migration to the islands during the colonial period gave the Chinese governments a more substantial interest in the South Pacific than the Soviets had. Beijing's interests extended also to protecting 'maritime sovereignty' from 'Soviet–American hegemony', using South Pacific waters for missile tests and prospecting for seabed minerals. Diplomatic rivalry between the People's Republic of China in Beijing and the Republic of China in Taipei intensified in the 1970s, and each sought diplomatic partners in the Third World including among the newly independent island states (Biddick 1989; Herr 1991a). Both were concerned to avoid being outflanked by the other, and by the Soviet Union. In the succeeding decade the People's Republic of China secured recognition from, and established diplomatic posts or conducted small aid programmes in, Western Samoa, Fiji, Vanuatu, Papua New Guinea, Kiribati, Marshall Islands and Federated States of Micronesia. The Republic of China in Taipei secured diplomatic recognition from, and established trade and aid ties with, Tonga, Solomon Islands, Nauru and Tuvalu. Taipei also opened trade offices in or provided aid to Papua

New Guinea, Fiji and Marshall Islands—countries that had official ties with its rival in Beijing. Beijing responded by negotiating a province-to-province relationship with Solomon Islands, whose national government recognises Taipei.

Party General Secretary Hu Yaobang visited the region in 1985 and articulated three principles that would guide China's policy:

- China fully respected the foreign and domestic policies of the South Pacific countries.
- China fully respected the existing close relations among the island countries.
- China fully respected the treaties the South Pacific countries had signed with the great powers (Biddick 1989, p. 812).

Beijing also signed the protocols of the South Pacific Nuclear Free Zone Treaty in 1987, and succeeded in projecting a benign image that the Tiananmen Square massacre has not entirely erased. Taipei in contrast has suffered because of poaching in island states' EEZs and extensive driftnet fishing in international waters by Taiwan-registered fishing boats, but has gained favour in Fiji by making low interest loans for military purchases when Fiji was embargoed by Australia, New Zealand and the United States. The two governments are likely to retain a presence in the region even after the Soviet threat vanishes because of their mutual rivalry and their respective ambitions to gain international stature commensurate with their size and economic strength. So far the rivalry has generated aid, loans, investment and market access, and the island states have benefited. However, island governments will be wary of any degeneration of the rivalry into economic manipulations, political interventions or subversive manoeuvres that may jeopardise their vulnerable political and economic systems.

Asian states

Several Southeast Asian states have a declared interest in the South Pacific (Pryor 1988; Thambipillai 1988; Dorrance 1990a, p. 52). Indonesia shares a common boundary and has experienced both strife and cooperation with Papua New Guinea. Indonesia's sense of entitlement to leadership have led to vigorous diplomatic activity and the establishment of posts in Fiji and New Caledonia as well as Papua New Guinea. In 1978 the National Congress mandated closer links with the South Pacific, and during 1980–88 the Technical Cooperation with Developing Countries programme included 177 island trainees: 98 from Papua New Guinea, 30 from Fiji, 26 from Western Samoa, 15 from Solomon Islands, and small numbers from Kiribati, Cook Islands, Tonga, Tuvalu and Vanuatu (Alatas 1988). The Ministry of Foreign Affairs sponsored research and teaching at Hasanuddin University and international seminars in 1988 and 1991 on Indonesian–South Pacific relations. Indonesia expressed support for Kanak and Polynesian independence and the South Pacific Nuclear Free Zone and initially condoned the Fijian military coups.

Indonesia's efforts in the early 1980s to sponsor links between the Association of Southeast Asian Nations (ASEAN) and the South Pacific Forum resulted in exchange visits by officials of the secretariats, discussion of mutual research possibilities, particularly in fishing, and a major publication and seminar on investment (Pryor 1988, pp. 64–6; South Pacific Forum 1987). In 1982 Indonesia encouraged Papua New Guinea to become an ASEAN observer and member of three affiliated committees, and in 1987 to participate in the Southeast Asia Human Resource Development programme and to accede to the ASEAN Treaty of Amity and Concord. Nevertheless, Indonesia's diplomatic, trade and aid activities are not prominent, and its visibility is not high except in Papua New Guinea, with which it conducts diplomacy and economic and cultural exchange and military consultations at their common border. In Vanuatu Indonesia is still regarded with suspicion because of its suppression of East Timorese and West Papuan nationalist aspirations.

Malaysia has taken a special interest in Fiji. Malaysia and Fiji experienced parallel British colonial immigration policies, similar tensions between indigenous and immigrant races, and comparable constitutional peculiarities. During the 1950s and 1960s Fijian soldiers assisted in suppressing communist insurgency and Indonesian infiltration in Malaysia. Malaysia viewed the 1987 coups and the rewriting of the constitution with some sympathy. Malaysia responded favourably to Fiji's appeals for trade agreements and technical and military training aid to replace those that lapsed with Australia and New Zealand, and established a diplomatic post in Suva. India also has taken an interest in Fijian affairs, mainly to condemn discrimination against Indian citizens and to block Fiji's re-entry into the Commonwealth.

The Philippines has an historical association, going back to the Spanish colonial period, with the islands of Micronesia. At present numerous Filipinos work in the Nauru phosphate industry, and Nauru in turn has invested money in the Philippines. If Guam gains control of immigration, it will look to skilled Philippine labourers, artisans, administrators and entertainers to staff its tourist and garment industries.

South Korean fishing, trade and diplomatic interests are becoming visible, and small aid and goodwill exchanges have followed, motivated partly by rivalry with North Korea. The Prime Minister of Singapore and the President of Israel have visited island countries in recent years. These contacts were made possible by visits to nearby Australia and New Zealand and were motivated more by curiosity and courtesy than by substantive business; they have not been followed up save for small trade agreements. Sporadic visits by these and other officials raised the visibility of their states marginally but did not respond to specific interests other than cultivating goodwill among South Pacific leaders, some of whom could influence United Nations deliberations and votes.

The Asian states are seen by some island leaders as alternatives to the six former colonial powers. Asian contacts offer new diplomatic perspectives, trade opportunities, investment and aid, and assist island representatives to gain access to the services of international organisations. Asian goodwill is welcome inasmuch as it builds confidence and promotes visibility. However, while Asian leaders stress peace and Third World solidarity, they are ultimately motivated by their own economic, political and security interests, mostly focused on their immediate neighbourhoods. Their countries' roots in the South Pacific are not yet deep, their involvement is not yet substantial, and their future commitment is uncertain. They are unlikely to displace the traditional powers as the leading players for the foreseeable future.

On the positive side, distance and lack of vital interests have also forestalled clashes among Asian states, or with the former colonial powers. Outside bloc rivalries and economic exploitation, decried by writers of the 1980s (Hayes 1986; Walker 1988), have remained muted, non-military and non-violent in the South Pacific. The varying interests of the several outsiders from Asia, Europe and North America have coexisted harmoniously with the fragile economic and political interests of the island states so far. Management of this coexistence has been facilitated considerably by South Pacific regional organisations, as described in the following chapter.

4 Regional organisations

States in the South Pacific constitute a loosely integrated regional functional system. International relations typologies derived from classical balance-of-power systems do not apply because island states have negligible capacity to project military power or to participate in alliances. Distance between countries insulates them from intrusions by each other, and the Western alliance system has shielded them from interventions by outsiders. Although they lean towards the West for reasons of cultural affinity and economic benefit, island states regard themselves as politically independent, not as members of a Western bloc in a bipolar world, and have established links with the Soviet Union, China and other communist states. The influence of outsiders—Western or Eastern—is increasingly counterbalanced by regional self-identity as leaders promote inter-island cooperation, both bilateral and multilateral.

Administrative and political functions

The most visible manifestation of South Pacific regionalism is the growth of regional intergovernmental organisations. These are rudimentary by comparison with those of the European Community but compare favourably with those of Southeast Asia and the Caribbean, making allowances for small scale. They are not steps on the way to political amalgamation, for island states vary in political outlook and nationalism remains strong. Rather, South Pacific organisations are voluntary and functional in nature, concentrating on trade,

Table 4.1 Evolution of specialised regional intergovernmental organisations, 1970–83

1970	University of the South Pacific
1970	Conference of South Pacific Chiefs of Police
1972	South Pacific Judicial Conference
1973	South Pacific Labour Ministers Conference
1973	South Pacific Regional Meeting on Telecommunications
1974	South Pacific Regional Shipping Council
1975	Cook Islands Niue New Zealand Joint Shipping Service
1975	Pacific Islands Tourism Development Council
1976	South Pacific Regional Civil Aviation Council
1979	Regional Committee on Trade
1980	Pacific Islands Conference
1980	Pacific Islands Development Program
1981	Pacific Law Officers Meeting
1981	South Pacific Board for Educational Assessment
1983	Tourism Council of the South Pacific

Source: Haas 1989, *passim*.

transportation, communications, health, education, maritime resources and the environment. With regard to their declared programmes they alert governments to problems and opportunities of common concern, provide a motive and channel for the exchange of information on specialised topics, and offer occasions for individuals in authority to forge consensus and to coordinate policies. This is particularly true of the specialised organisations listed in Table 4.1, which may be described as administrative in nature.

South Pacific intergovernmental organisations have implicit functions of a more political nature. They build confidence in island leaders' ability to meet and mix with foreigners, provide experience in political intercourse and international lobbying, and magnify the political influence of microstates in their dealings with large outside powers and international organisations. They also provide benign arenas for rivalry between governments, constructive outlets for the ambitions of strong-minded leaders, and channels for the containment of factional manoeuvre by groups of members. Their one-member, one-vote rules allow small island states equality with large neighbours. Because they include metropolitan powers such as Australia, New Zealand, Britain, France and the United States, they offer channels of information and aid from, and a communications link to, the wider community of the wealthy developed countries.

Intraorganisational cleavages

Neither common interests nor the ideal of The Pacific Way (tolerance and decisions by consensus) are sufficient to insure harmony between members. Disputes between Australia, Indonesia and France, and between New Zealand and the United States, on behalf of their island dependencies troubled relations until the 1980s, and the colonial period left in dispute the boundaries between Vanuatu and New Caledonia, Tonga and Fiji, Papua New Guinea and Solomon Islands, and American and Western Samoa (Prescott 1988).

Generally speaking, five structural cleavages have disturbed the consensus of the major South Pacific regional organisations in recent years (Neemia 1986, ch. 6; Fry 1981 and 1991a; Kite 1977). The first cleavage was between Fiji and the other members. The establishment in Suva of the South Pacific Forum Secretariat and a number of other regional bodies, such as the University of the South Pacific and offices of international agencies, has stimulated complaints by other members that Fiji is getting the lion's share of the educational and training opportunities, employment benefits, fees for services and taxes, relative to its share of the costs. Also, Fiji's Ratu Mara was suspected of arrogating to himself the role of natural leader of and spokesman for the South Pacific region in international circles.

The second cleavage was between the small states and the large states. The small states relied more on the intergovernmental organisations to bestow nominal equality of status and influence in regional affairs, and to provide aid and technical assistance. The South Pacific Forum Secretariat, whose secretary general has usually been a man from a small state (previously Tuvalu, now Kiribati), has been a source of considerable support. The small states tended also to turn to larger outside patrons, typically the former colonial power, for assistance. In contrast, the larger states, possessing natural resources and some industry, assumed a more self-sufficient nationalistic posture, to which the intergovernmental organisations were adjuncts rather than essential, and sometimes a nuisance.

The third cleavage overlapped the second and divided the Polynesian states from the Melanesian states. Polynesian states, gaining independence early such as Western Samoa, or assertive of a Polynesian identity leading to an economic entente such as Tonga, or confidently cosmopolitan such as Cook Islands, tended to be politically conservative. In contrast the Melanesian states, emerging later and after some strife from colonialism, asserted a critical, anti-colonial, pro-Third World doctrine sometimes called Melanesian socialism. The Melanesian states asserted their collective identity by forming the Melanesian Spearhead Group in 1986, while the Polynesian governments responded with the idea of a Polynesian Economic and Cultural Community (MacQueen 1990; Haas 1989, pp. 126–9).

Fourth, the island governments distinguished themselves not only from the extraregional powers of France, Britain and the United States but also from the intraregional metropolitan governments of Australia and New Zealand. The Melanesians, and Fiji in particular since 1987, suspected Australia of harbouring leadership ambitions not sufficiently sensitive to island interests. At the Port Vila forum in 1990, for example, Prime Minister Bob Hawke's support of US chemical-weapons destruction on Johnston Atoll provoked suggestions that the thirteen island members should caucus apart from the two metropolitan members. New Zealand, with its larger Polynesian population and close association with Cook Islands, Niue and Tokelau, has avoided most, but not all, of this criticism.

Fifth, the independent states distinguish themselves from territories which are still dependencies of the United States and France. This reinforces the island–cosmopolitan cleavage, and both cleavages manifest themselves in the rivalry between the South Pacific Forum and the South Pacific Commission (SPC). The single regional organisation concept put forward by Melanesian leaders in 1980, which would subordinate the commission to the forum, manifested itself again when the forum set up the South Pacific Organisations Coordinating Committee in 1988 under forum chairmanship and invited the commission to join. The commission, the metropolitan governments that channelled aid funds through it, and even Fiji and Western Samoa, resisted. Confrontation was avoided by compromises entailing a rotating chair, a rotating secretariat and a rotating venue (Fry 1989b, pp. 2–3).

Because the five cleavages do not coincide, but rather cancel each other out to some extent, sub-regional groupings have not dominated either the South Pacific Commission or the South Pacific Forum. The established regional organisations continue to enjoy substantial consensus and the confidence of their members and their outside aid patrons. Recently, attention has been given to problems of overlapping functions, administrative rivalries, featherbedding, and generally inefficiency that allegedly beset the bureaucracies of the South Pacific Commission and forum secretariat in the early 1980s. As outside aid funds became scarcer, and as donors demanded closer coordination and better administration of projects, the intraorganisational rivalries eased, replaced by management issues. Politics gave way to efforts to speed up delivery of benefits by means of integrated work programmes.

South Pacific Commission

During World War II the outside powers deliberated on how best to achieve security and stability in the South Pacific in the postwar period (Smith 1972, pp. 28–52). Australia and New Zealand in their 1944 Canberra Pact, as a complement to their declaration to establish a regional zone of defence, proposed also to set up a 'South Seas Regional Commission' to secure a common policy on the wellbeing and advancement of peoples in their territories (Kay 1972, p. 145). In 1947 Britain, France, the United States and the Netherlands joined the endeavour, and the six powers established the South Pacific Commission. Subsequently the Netherlands dropped out, and eight island states joined after they achieved independence: Western Samoa in 1965, Nauru in 1969, Fiji in 1971, Papua New Guinea in 1975, Solomon Islands and Tuvalu in 1978, and Cook Islands and Niue in 1980. In 1983 all the remaining governments and self-governing administrations of the region were accorded full membership in the commission.

At present 27 entities send delegates to the meetings of the South Pacific Commission, and also to the annual South Pacific Conference, which ratifies the commission's work programme and budgets, and to the conference's Committee of Representatives of Governments and Administrations, which functions as a committee of the whole, meeting twice yearly. Each member contributes to the commission budget according to the formula presented in Table 4.2. The commission is serviced by a secretariat of approximately 130 staff based in Noumea and in offices in Suva to administer the Community Education Training Centre, the Fisheries Training Programme, the Plant Protection Service and the Regional Media Centre.

The purposes of the commission, expressed in the 1947 Canberra Agreement as amended and abridged, are as follows:

- to provide a forum for island governments to be heard on equal terms;
- to be a vehicle for regionalism;
- to assist in meeting basic needs of the people of the region;
- to facilitate the flow of indigenous products, technical know-how and people;
- to be a catalyst in the development of regional resources;
- to serve as an aid-organising institution; and
- to collect and disseminate information on the region.

These objectives are manifested in the integrated work pro-

Table 4.2 South Pacific Commission members and contributions

Member	Year joined	Contribution (%)
Australia	1947	33.362
United States	1947	16.880
New Zealand	1947	16.185
France	1947	13.901
Britain	1947	12.214
American Samoa	1983	0.552
Fiji	1971	0.552
French Polynesia	1983	0.552
Guam	1983	0.552
New Caledonia	1983	0.552
Federated States of Micronesia	1983	0.394
Marshall Islands	1983	0.394
Northern Mariana Islands	1983	0.394
Palau (Belau)	1983	0.394
Papua New Guinea	1975	0.394
Cook Islands	1980	0.248
Kiribati	1983	0.248
Nauru	1969	0.248
Niue	1980	0.248
Solomon Islands	1978	0.248
Tokelau	1983	0.248
Tonga	1983	0.248
Tuvalu	1978	0.248
Vanuatu	1983	0.248
Wallis and Futuna	1983	0.248
Western Samoa	1965	0.248
Pitcairn	1983	0.000
Total		100.000

Source: South Pacific Commission 1990, pp. 1, 2, 23.

gramme, whose elements include the following: Food and Materials Programme (small-scale agriculture, plant diseases); Marine Resources Programme (fisheries development and training, fish processing, tuna and billfish assessment); Environment Management Programme; Rural Development and Technology Programme (traditional institutions, intermediate technology); Community Health Programme (water, sanitation, nutrition, dental health, epidemiology); Community Education Services (women, youth, communities, media); and Socio-economic Statistical Services (economics, demography, information dissemination). The commission also maintains a library and information service, subsidises visits and assists cultural events such as the Festival of Pacific Arts.

Projects within each programme are executed variously by permanent staff, contract staff, commissioned experts or beneficiary governments, and often jointly with other agencies such as the Forum Fisheries Agency, the South Pacific Applied Geoscience Commission (SOPAC), the University of the South Pacific, the United Nations Fund for Population Activities (UNFPA), the Economic and Social Commission for Asia and the Pacific (ESCAP) and the European Development Programme. For example, the South Pacific Regional Environmental Programme (SPREP) was run jointly by the South Pacific Forum Secretariat, the United Nations Environment Programme (UNEP) and ESCAP. In 1990 it became an autonomous regional organisation in its own right (Pearsal 1990). Programmes and projects are funded partly through the annual commission budget provided by member governments and partly by special grants made by member and non-member governments and by international aid agencies. In 1988 member governments contributed roughly A$5.6 million to the core budget; sixteen governments, five United Nations agencies, two Commonwealth agencies and a dozen other agencies ranging from the Asian Development Bank (ADB) to the World Wildlife Fund provided another A$5.3 million in extrabudgetary funds, for a total of A$10.9 million (South Pacific Commission 1989b, pp. 201–2). This total rose to A$15.4 million in 1990, of which 70 per cent was extrabudgetary grants (South Pacific Commission 1990, p. 17). As well, joint projects engage donors such as the Japan International Cooperation Agency (JICA), the US Agency for International Development and the European Development Fund (EDF).

The commission's guiding philosophy is 'service to its Island member countries and co-operation with other regional and international organisations, working to improve the economic, social and environmental qualities of the region' (South Pacific Commission 1990, p. 4). Its declared role is advisory and consultative; it is a conduit for aid funds and research initiatives from other sources and administers these in response to the wishes of the 22 island members of the South Pacific Conference and its Committee of Representatives of Governments and Administrations. The distribution of projects and of funds spent varies between the 22 island members, with New Caledonia and Fiji appearing to get the largest proportion in the early 1980s (Neemia 1986, pp. 75-8).

At mainly French insistence, political matters have been explicitly excluded from the commission's agenda since it was formed, the focus remaining on economic, technical and cultural development initiatives. The proscription of political issues such as nuclear testing and decolonisation led to dissatisfaction on the part of island leaders, particularly Fiji's Prime Minister Ratu Mara, and stimulated the formation of the South Pacific Forum where island leaders' political concerns could be aired (Fry 1981, p. 462). Radical Melanesian independence leaders viewed the commission as protective of the interests of the former colonial powers, administratively conservative and paternalistic, unresponsive to South Pacific political self-assertion, and oriented to the needs of the Polynesian members and, after 1983, of the self-governing territories that made up the majority. They proposed that the commission be subordinated to or absorbed by the forum.

By the late 1980s opposition had subsided as a result of reforms to make the commission's budget more transparent and its operations more responsive to the South Pacific Conference and its committee, and to distribute projects more widely. Also, rotation of annual conference venues to a widening circle of island capitals was initiated, and islanders were appointed as Secretary General, Director of Programmes and Deputy Director of Programmes—the top three position of the South Pacific Commission Secretariat. The commission's role as an indispensable conduit for aid was enhanced by growing European Community, French (particularly after the 1988 Matignon Accords), Japanese and US funding that would not otherwise have been forthcoming. It was appreciated even by critics that the commission was the only body that brought all the government leaders of the island Pacific states together, raising regional consciousness and giving to the indigenous leaders of the non-independent island territories voice and experience that they could gain nowhere else.

The 1989 South Pacific Conference broke new ground by hearing a call by Guam's governor for more autonomy and Fiji's criticism of Australia and New Zealand for reducing aid, and by passing a resolution condemning driftnet fishing by Japan and Taiwan, suggesting that the no politics rule could be interpreted flexibly (Fry 1989a, p. 28). By 1991 the South Pacific Forum had ceased its efforts to incorporate its rival and tacitly accepted the South Pacific Commission as a fixture—a politically constrained but economically, technically and culturally useful counterpart regional organisation (Herr 1991b).

South Pacific Forum

The initiative to set up an intergovernmental forum to discuss political issues that could not be aired in the South Pacific Commission was taken by Fiji's Prime Minister Ratu Mara, was backed by the prime ministers of Western Samoa and Cook Islands, and was subsequently supported by Australia, New Zealand, Nauru and Tonga (Fry 1981, p. 464). These became founder members of the South Pacific Forum at the inaugural meeting in Wellington in 1971. Island states were invited to join as they became independent (or self-governing in free association), and the entry of Marshall Islands and Federated States of Micronesia in 1987 brought membership to fifteen. Palau has inquired about observer status and is expected to become the sixteenth member in due course.

Forum members decided in 1989 to invite friendly outsiders, including France, Canada, Britain, Japan, China and the United States, to attend post-forum dialogue meetings each year. In 1990 a committee was set up to consider how such entities as the governments of the French and US territories, Taiwan, Germany, the Kanak independence party, the Association of Southeast Asian Nations (ASEAN) and the European Community could be linked to the forum. Membership and participation have been controversial issues. The Melanesian members have encouraged representatives of Kanaks to attend as unofficial observers. But they have resisted the inclusion of non-independent US or French island governments and have expressed scepticism even of Australia's and New Zealand's role. The Polynesian members have tended to the opposite view. In 1991 four members sponsored the Republic of China as a dialogue partner but four others which recognise the Peoples Republic of China urged caution so as not to jeopardise aid; the secretary general was then charged to devise a compromise for the 1992 forum meeting.

There is no charter or by-laws. Objectives and agendas are worked out by officials prior to forum summits. Forum meetings proceed by discussion and consensus-seeking and conclusions are announced in a communiqué. Past forums have condemned French nuclear testing and US tuna poaching, urged decolonisation of dependent territories, called for aid from Western donors, promoted consensus on the Law of the Sea and secured Japanese cessation of driftnet fishing. They have also resolved to set up a Regional Committee on Trade (1979), the South Pacific Regional Civil Aviation Council (1976), the South Pacific Regional Shipping Council (1974), the South Pacific Telecommunications Development Programme (1983) and the Forum Fisheries Agency (1977), and endorsed the establishment of the Pacific Forum Line, SPREP and SOPAC (Haas 1989, p. 95; *Far East and Australasia* 1989, p. 151).

In 1988 the forum set up the South Pacific Organisations Coordinating Committee (SPOCC) to bring coherence to the proliferation of regional bodies. Melanesian members viewed SPOCC as a mechanism to assert the forum's role as the premier regional organisation over the South Pacific Commission. However, the latter refused to join while the forum's secretary general was to chair meetings; so a rotating chair and venue were agreed to, and now the SPOCC brings representatives of regional organisations together annually on a basis of equality (Fry 1989b, pp. 2–3).

The 1990 forum meeting in Port Vila discussed five core issues: the environment (including the greenhouse effect, French nuclear testing and chemical weapons disposal at Johnston Atoll), fisheries management (including Japanese access and purse seine exploitation), decolonisation of New Caledonia, promotion of regional tourism and energy development, and arrangements for dialogue partners (New Zealand Government 1990b, p. 23). The forum also formally adopted the annual reports of its affiliated bodies the Forum Fisheries Agency, the Pacific Islands Development Program, SOPAC, SPREP and the University of the South Pacific. The difficult issues included the status to be accorded to the Kanak independence party, the racially biased draft constitution of Fiji, disposal of chemical weapons at Johnston Atoll, and subordination of the South Pacific Commission to the forum. According to media reports, the Melanesian members were at odds with Australia and New Zealand on each issue (Mangnall 1990a, pp. 10–15). In 1991 the Fiji oil monopoly and Taiwan's driftnet fishing and future link to the forum were vigorously debated. The final communiqués reflected only points of agreement; contentious matters were assigned to subcommittees or the forum secretariat, and were not made public.

Drafting pre-forum agendas and implementing post-forum decisions are the responsibilities of the Committee of Officials, which represents all members. The committee functions as a board of directors of the secretariat, which is the forum's administrative body. The secretariat, which was called the South Pacific Bureau for Economic Cooperation (SPEC) from its establishment in 1973 until 1988, is located in Suva. In 1991 it was staffed by 39 officers seconded by member countries and 32 clerical and support staff. Its secretary general is supported by a directorate and by eleven divisions and units including the ACP/EC and Petroleum units and the Civil Aviation, Economic Development, Energy, Finance, Legal and Political, Maritime, Telecommunications, Trade and Investment, and Administrative divisions.

The secretariat's operating budget is funded one-third each by Australia and New Zealand and one-third by the other thirteen members contributing 2.56 per cent each. Operating budget expenditure approved for 1991 was F$2 298 000. Extrabudgetary expenditure approved for special programmes and projects was F$9 422 000, funded by Australia, New Zealand, Britain, Japan, Germany, Canada and the United States and by international agencies including the United Nations Development Programme (UNDP), ESCAP, the European Community, the World Bank, the ADB and the Commonwealth Secretariat (South Pacific Forum 1991, p. 23). The forum secretariat's principal objective is to facilitate cooperation between island governments and collaboration with developed country governments. This is pursued by means of arranging and sponsoring intra- and extraregional consultations, producing project feasibility studies, proposals and cost estimates, and advising and liaising between member and non-member governments and international agencies.

Among the 200 projects with which it is involved at various stages is the South Pacific Telecommunications Development Programme. This programme encompasses nine projects in seven countries with a total value of US$7.5 million funded by the European Community with inputs also by United Nations agencies, the International Telecommunications Union (ITU) and member governments. The forum secretariat is the manager-coordinator of the projects on behalf of the donors and the recipients. Much of the work is done by specialists contracted and supervised by the secretariat. Several earlier secretariat programmes have grown to the point were they have been separated institutionally, such as the Pacific Forum Line and the Forum Fisheries Agency, but the secretariat continues to play general liaison and coordinating roles. The secretariat also did much of the preparatory work for the signing of the South Pacific Regional Trade and Economic Cooperation Agreement in 1980.

Forum Fisheries Agency

The United Nations Conference on the Law of the Sea, which endorsed the concept of 200 mile (322 kilometre) zones of economic management, stimulated island governments to consider how best to manage their potential fisheries resources. The 1976 South Pacific Forum's Nauru Declaration highlighted 'prospects for joint action and regional cooperation in matters such as surveillance and policing', possibly by means of an intergovernmental agency (Gubon 1987, p. 246). Subsequent forums split on whether to include distant-water fishing nations such as the United States in the proposed agency, with the Polynesian governments favouring inclusive membership. Australia and New Zealand, allied to the United States, did not wish openly to argue against US membership. The Melanesian governments objected that inclusion of the distant fishing states would dilute the agency's regional unity and weaken its bargaining position vis-à-vis the outside powers on asserting ownership of migratory tuna. The larger island states hoped to exploit the fish themselves, while smaller states aspired only to earning royalties from foreign fishing nations (Neemia 1986, pp. 34–5). Symbolic assertion of local control over regional resources was implicit in the Melanesian argument, and it prevailed.

In 1979 the then twelve members of the South Pacific Forum acceded to a convention to establish the Forum Fisheries Agency. At present the agency is located in Honiara, Solomon Islands, and is staffed by nineteen professional and twenty support officials (Forum Fisheries Agency 1990, p. B–17). Its director reports annually to the South Pacific Forum and coordinates his activities with the forum Committee of Officials, the forum secretariat and SPOCC. Annual meetings of member officials are preceded by a caucus by the Nauru Group, which represents interests in tuna management by two Melanesian and five Micronesian states (Doulman 1987c). The agency's operations are funded by members similarly to the forum secretariat funding formula, and also by contributions and special grants by Canada, Japan, the Commonwealth Fund for Technical Cooperation, the EDF, the Food and Agriculture Organisation (FAO) and the UNDP (Haas 1989, p. 117). Expenditures budgeted for 1991 were US$ 2 009 797 (Forum Fisheries Agency 1990, p. B–3). The South Pacific Commission has observer status and provides assistance as well, and the University of the South Pacific's Institute of Marine Resources contributes technical reviews.

The Forum Fisheries Agency's functions include:

- collecting, analysing, evaluating and disseminating statistical and biological information;
- focusing on management procedures, legislation and agreements adopted by other countries both within and outside the region;
- collecting and disseminating relevant information on prices, shipping, processing and marketing of fish and fish products; and
- providing technical assistance in the development of fisheries policies and in negotiations on the issue of licences, the collection of fees or matters pertaining to surveillance (Herr 1990).

The agency has been particularly active in advising member countries on the legal technicalities of delimiting their maritime boundaries and drafting appropriate legislation to protect them. In 1987 the agency negotiated the United States–South Pacific Regional Fisheries Treaty. The agency receives an aid package of US$4 million annually from the United States and also distributes US$7 million in US access fees to members in proportion to where the US tunaboats make their catches. In 1989 the agency helped to draw up the Convention for the Prohibition of Fishing with Long Driftnets in the South Pacific. This, in combination with forum and

Table 4.3 Forum Fisheries Agency assistance in negotiations, 1983–91

Negotiating partners	Year of assistance
Australia–Japan	1983–85
Cook Islands–Korea	1984–91
Cook Islands–Niue–Tuvalu–Western Samoa–New Zealand–American Tunaboat Association	1983–85
Cook Islands–Taiwan	1987–88
Federated States of Micronesia–Japan	1984–91
Federated States of Micronesia–Korea	1990–91
Federated States of Micronesia–Kiribati–Palau–American Tunaboat Association	1983–86
Kiribati–Japan 1984–85	1984–91
Kiribati–Korea	1983–91
Kiribati–Soviet Union	1985–87
Kiribati–Taiwan	1990–91
Marshall Islands–Japan	1984–5, 1989–90
Palau–Japan	1983–91
Papua New Guinea–Japan	1983–91
Papua New Guinea–Taiwan	1987–88
Solomon Islands–Japan	1983–89
Solomon Islands–Taiwan	1983–84, 1989–90
Tuvalu–Japan	1983–89
Tuvalu–Korea	1990–91
Tuvalu–Taiwan	1989–91
Vanuatu–Soviet Union	1986–89
Forum Fisheries Agency members–Japan	1988–90
Forum Fisheries Agency members–United States	1984–89

Source: Bugotu 1990, p.11.

United Nations declarations, was instrumental in inducing Japan, South Korea and Taiwan to stop driftnet fishing by 1992. The agency has assisted members to draw up bilateral agreements with distant fishing governments (see Table 4.3). Its Honiara office maintains a database on catches, and receives, collates and disseminates information collected by New Zealand and Australian military air and sea surveillance on fishing activities. (See also Figure 3.1.)

Pacific Forum Line

Distance, low volumes, union disputes and rising costs on South Pacific routes have driven many extraregional commercial shipping lines to discontinue operations. Regularity and quality of shipping services have declined, hampering the export of island produce and import of provisions, particularly in outlying island groups. The inaugural South Pacific Forum meeting in 1971 gave prominence to these problems, and subsequent forums stimulated the formation of a South Pacific Regional Shipping Council in 1974. Failures of the Tongan Shipping Service and Nauru's *Enna G* venture, and the limits of the Cook Islands–Niue–New Zealand Joint Shipping Service, focused council members' attentions on a wider cooperative arrangement to gain a stable financial base and economies of scale (Haas 1989, pp. 84–92). Reducing dependency by asserting the indigenous control of regional transportation was an additional motive for regional collaboration (Neemia 1986, p. 29).

In 1977 nine island states and New Zealand established the Pacific Forum Line, whose objectives as set out in its establishment memorandum were:

- to operate a regular and viable shipping service;
- to establish rationalised shipping services;
- to contain escalating freight costs;
- to meet special requirements of particular areas;
- to provide essential services on non-commercial routes;
- to promote the export trade of the South Pacific region; and
- to encourage the economic development of the region (Neemia 1986, pp. 30–2).

After operating at a loss for several years, subsidised mainly by New Zealand and Australia, its member states in 1982 pledged substantial capital, which, added to a loan from the European Investment Bank (EIB), enabled the purchase of 1500 containers, rolling stock and other assets (see Table 4.4). Routes, rates and quality of service stabilised, and the line turned a profit in 1985 and has operated in the black most years since then. Throughout the 1980s the Pacific Forum Line operated four ships chartered from South Pacific corporations or governments: three on profitable routes and the fourth operating at a loss but providing an essential service to outlying member countries. In 1989 the line purchased the *Forum New Zealand II* from the New Zealand Shipping Corporation.

In structure the Pacific Forum Line is a corporate joint venture with ten shareholders. Its policy is set by the ministers of transportation of member countries meeting annually. A board of directors chosen by member governments oversees operations and reports to the ministers and also to the South Pacific Regional Shipping Council and other supporting organisations and donors. Professional management staff located in Apia conduct day-to-day activities.

South Pacific Applied Geoscience Commission

Hoping to locate new sources of foreign exchange, Fiji in 1970

Table 4.4 Pacific Forum Line members and shareholding, 1982

Member	Initial shares (WS$)	Refinance shares (WS$)
Cook Islands	10 000	54 917
Fiji	10 000	4 731 359
Kiribati	10 000	660 665
Nauru	10 000	n.a.
New Zealand	10 000	4 318 000
Papua New Guinea	10 000	5 975 024
Solomon Islands	10 000	53 930
Tonga	10 000	1 199 456
Tuvalu	10 000	1 480 326
Western Samoa	10 000	1 480 326

Source: Haas 1989, p. 91.

proposed the establishment of a Committee for Coordination of Joint Prospecting for Mineral Resources in South Pacific Offshore Areas (subsequently known as CCOP/SOPAC), similar to the one set up for Asia 4 years previously (Haas 1989, p. 151). Support was forthcoming from the governments of New Zealand, Papua New Guinea, Solomon Islands, Tonga and Western Samoa, and they established a working committee under Economic Commission for Asia and the Far East (ECAFE) auspices, operating from ECAFE's Bangkok office, in 1972. Cook Islands joined in 1973, Kiribati in 1975, Vanuatu in 1978 and Australia in 1986. Nauru and Guam and other US dependencies became observers. Activities of the committee shifted increasingly to the Technical Secretariat of thirteen professional staff and sixteen support staff located in Suva, Fiji, and in 1984 CCOP/SOPAC became an autonomous regional organisation. In 1989 it was renamed the South Pacific Applied Geoscience Commission, but the acronym SOPAC was retained for recognition. SOPAC is a member of the South Pacific Organisations Coordinating Committee is its own right but makes an annual report to the South Pacific Forum Secretariat.

SOPAC's declared aims are:

- to provide information on the physical environment of coastal and nearshore areas;
- to assist with resource and environmental management, hazard evaluation, coastal protection works, and coastal-development project planning and implementation;
- to search for coastal, nearshore and offshore minerals such as phosphates, manganese nodules and precious corals;
- to assess and promote hydrocarbon and wave energy potential;
- to coordinate marine geological and geophysical research;
- to curate and distribute marine geophysical research; and

- to train nationals in the implementation of their own work programmes (New Zealand Government 1990b, p. 7).

Each member government sends a delegate to annual committee meetings to set policy guidelines, review past and future work programmes, and approve the budget, all in coordination with the Technical Advisory Group of donor representatives. The Technical Advisory Group Secretariat then executes the work programme, typically by engaging prospecting firms on contract and coordinating scientific experts seconded by donors for analysis, reporting or training.

Considerable offshore resource mapping has been completed, and deposits of minerals, hydrocarbons, clays and corals have been located and assayed. By 1986, 38 person-years of training had been conducted and a course instituted leading to the Certificate of Earth Science and Marine Geology. SOPAC projects are funded primarily by the UNDP; the European Community, Canada and the United States also make substantial project grants. Each member state contributes 9.1 per cent to the operating budget, save Australia (12.8 per cent), Kiribati (2.3 per cent) and Tuvalu (6.8 per cent) (Haas 1989, p. 154).

South Pacific Regional Environmental Programme

As they became independent, island governments became aware of the need to manage the environments of the vulnerable islands and waters in their care. In 1973 the South Pacific Conference approved the recruitment of an ecologist to the staff of the South Pacific Commission. Consultations between the commission, the newly founded UNEP, ESCAP and the South Pacific Forum Secretariat (then SPEC) led in 1978 to the approval of a Comprehensive Environmental Management Programme. Rivalry between the commission and the forum secretariat for control was eased by their agreeing on a joint initiative, the first of its kind (Pearsal 1990, p. 7). International funding was arranged, the name was altered, and the South Pacific Regional Environmental Programme (SPREP) was formally inaugurated in January 1980 by means of a contract signed by the two regional bodies and the two international funding agencies.

A SPREP Secretariat was set up in and funded by the South Pacific Commission. The secretariat's work was to be supervised by a coordinating group of delegates of the four principals chaired by the South Pacific Forum Secretariat delegate. The work programme and budget were submitted to the annual South Pacific

Table 4.5 SPREP operational budget, 1987

Source	US$	%
United Nations Environmental Programme	357 358	43.8
Island countries	241 273	29.6
Outside countries	131 587	16.1
South Pacific Commission	60 692	7.5
Economic and Social Commission for Asia and the Pacific	12 418	1.5
Others[a]	11 857	1.5
Total	815 185	100.0

[a] World Wildlife Fund

Source: Pearsal 1990, p.11.

Conference for approval. In addition to this oversight role, each member government and territory was entitled to liaise with the SPREP Secretariat through a 'SPREP focal point'—its own official designated for this purpose. The SPREP operations budget is funded as shown in Table 4.5; in addition, special projects are funded separately.

SPREP's milestones included agreement in 1983 on an Action Plan for Managing the Natural Resources and Environment of the South Pacific Region and adoption in 1986 of the Convention for the Protection of Natural Resources and Environment of the South Pacific Region. The convention includes protocols prohibiting dumping radioactive wastes at sea and testing nuclear explosive devices. An ongoing programme of workshops, training sessions, research, planning, consultations and grants-in-aid is conducted by contracted specialists in response to applications for assistance by member governments. Focal points include climate change, watershed and water quality management, pesticide hazards, protected areas and species, natural resources management and pollution control.

In 1988, in response to criticism that the South Pacific Commission exerted too much influence on the SPREP Secretariat, SPREP's coordinating group was replaced by a steering committee with one representative each from Melanesia, Micronesia, Polynesia, Australia or New Zealand, and Britain or France or the United States. The 1990 forum set up a committee to study how to strengthen the capacity and efficiency of SPREP. Upon the forum's recommendation, SPREP was established as an autonomous regional organisation with its headquarters in Apia. Its activities continue to be coordinated through other regional bodies and SPOCC.

Pacific Islands Development Program

The Pacific Islands Development Program (PIDP) was set up in 1980. Its parent body is the South Pacific Conference of heads of government which meets every five years, which it serves as a secretariat and research, publishing, policy advice, and training arm. Its Standing Committee and Program Planning Committee are comprised of Pacific island leaders. Polynesian island state leaders have been its most active supporters and some have tried to coopt PIDP resources to serve their own countries' development needs, pleading weak human capital bases; these initiatives have been resisted by Melanesian leaders. Its location in the East–West Center, Honolulu, draws Hawaii into the South Pacific network. PIDP is funded by international agencies and metropolitan governments including the United States and Australia, with smaller contributions by the South Pacific governments. Its budget is approximately US$1 million annually. Recent policy-relevant research has centred on disaster preparedness, energy, indigenous private sector development, administrative and management reform, and regional cooperation (Fairbairn 1991, p.163).

South Pacific Organisations Coordinating Committee

The South Pacific Organisations Coordinating Committee (SPOCC) was set up in 1988. Taking account of the rivalry between the South Pacific Commission and the South Pacific Forum, and recognising that the proliferation of organisations could lead to friction, waste, and criticism, South Pacific leaders charged SPOCC with studying and making recommendations on a rational division of labour between the seven principal regional intergovernmental organisations. SOPCC meets annually with a rotating venue and rotating chair. It has no powers, no budget, and no standing administration. The South Pacific Forum has instructed the Secretary General of the forum secretariat to support SPOCC activities. Nevertheless, the initiative has been judged successful in defusing clashes between powerful personalities and between conservative and radical states, easing fears of poor states that another expensive bureaucracy would mushroom, and securing the confidence of outside donors that aid would be apportioned and used efficiently throughout the region. The current conception is one of a South Pacific wheel with the established regional organisations seen as seven spokes rotating smoothly around the SPOCC hub.

Table 4.6 International organisations in the South Pacific, 1987

African, Caribbean and Pacific Group
Asian Development Bank
Commonwealth Secretariat and Fund for Technical Cooperation
Food and Agriculture Organization
International Monetary Fund
International Labour Organisation
International Finance Corporation
International Telecommunication Union
International Maritime Organization
International Civil Aviation Organization
International Fund for Agricultural Development
International Development Association
Lome Convention
United Nations Development Programme
United Nations Educational, Scientific and Cultural Organization
United Nations General Assembly
Universal Postal Union
World Bank
World Health Organization
World Meteorological Organization

Source: Banks 1987, pp. 823–26.

International intergovernmental organisations

South Pacific states also participate in international intergovernmental organisations. These range from specialised functional agencies such as the Universal Postal Union (UPU) through financial and aid bodies such as the World Bank, to general purpose organisations such as the United Nations General Assembly. Fiji, Papua New Guinea and the larger island states belong to all or most of the international organisations listed in Table 4.6. Some states host branch offices, such as those of the UNDP in Suva and ESCAP in Port Vila and the European Community in both. The smaller states have joined more selectively, conscious of the cost of membership and of travel to attend meetings. Some island states are associate members or observers, but all of them receive services, technical assistance and aid from the international organisations, either directly or through the regional organisations. The extent of membership of each South Pacific state is indicated in Table 4.7.

In sum, international organisations are valuable links to the international community, reducing the isolation and raising the standards

Table 4.7 Membership in international organisations, 1989

Country	Categories A to D	Categories A to F
American Samoa	1	7
Cook Islands	6	27
Federated States of Micronesia	2	11
French Polynesia	2	7
Fiji	26	113
Guam	1	12
Kiribati	9	53
Marshall Islands	1	10
Nauru	7	40
New Caledonia	2	8
Niue	2	16
Northern Mariana Islands	1	9
Palau (Belau)	2	10
Papua New Guinea	33	127
Solomon Islands	16	85
Tonga	12	73
Tuvalu	3	38
Vanuatu	2	61
Western Samoa	13	78
Australia	61	224
New Zealand	37	168

Note: Categories A to D include global, intercontinental, and regional intergovernmental organisations. Categories A to F include A to D plus semi-autonomous agencies, foundations, funds and programmes.

Source: Union of International Associations 1988, table 4.

of the island countries and providing opportunities for island participation in world affairs.

5   Cook Islands and Niue

Cook Islands and Niue remain outside the United Nations General Assembly and the Commonwealth and are not recognised as fully independent states by Japan. Local leaders occasionally complain of post-colonial restraints on their sovereignty. Yet their unique arrangements with the former colonial power, New Zealand, have provided a precedent for US decolonisation of the Trust Territory of the Pacific Islands and may soon provide a model for self-government of the French island territories of New Caledonia, French Polynesia, and Wallis and Futuna. For newly independent microstates of the Pacific and elsewhere the free association model, applied flexibly, has several advantages and few disadvantages.

The establishment of free association

The establishment of a relationship of free association requires the following conditions to be satisfied:

- a colonial government willing to fulfil its obligations under the United Nations Charter and comply with General Assembly Resolutions 742, 1514 and 1541 of 1960 and United Nations Fourth Committee recommendations to conduct an orderly process of decolonisation;
- a post-colonial government willing to provide protection and resources, and to extend tolerance, to its former territory over an extended period of decades;
- a colonised society without a history of violent anti-colonial struggle,

an administrative capacity for self-governance, and a continuing rapport and willingness to work with the former colonial government; and
• an expression of self-determination involving the enfranchised population, acceptable to the United Nations.

These requirements were met in Cook Islands' and Niue's long and harmonious colonial relationship with New Zealand, extending the better part of seven decades, in the careful preparations that preceded self-government, and in the orderliness and effectiveness with which the fledgling island governments took on functions gradually devolved by New Zealand. The way was pointed by General Assembly Resolution 1514 passed on 21 December 1960, which listed not only integration and independence but also free association as acceptable means of bringing colonial territories to self-government. Principle VII of the resolution stipulated four requirements: that the process be voluntary and democratic; that the individuality and culture of the associated people be respected; that the associated people determine their state's internal constitutional arrangements; and that the associated state be free to opt for independence through democratic and constitutional processes (United Nations 1964). These requirements were met in negotiations over a period of years and provided a model of free association for former US territories in the Pacific (Ghai 1988, pp. 25 ff). The transfer of authority was accomplished without overassertiveness or impatience on the island side or undue haste or reluctance on the New Zealand side.

The essence of the associated state relationship was the exercise of free choice by the governments of Cook Islands in 1965 and Niue in 1974 to entrust New Zealand with foreign affairs and defence functions while retaining the right to make final decisions in these two policy spheres (see Table 9.1). It is a widely held misconception that New Zealand makes foreign and defence policy for Cook Islands and Niue. In fact the island governments make their own foreign policy and, to the extent they can afford it, execute it as well (Short 1983, pp. 186–7).

The island governments may turn to the New Zealand government for expertise, contacts, outreach, support and assistance, which New Zealand extends in compliance with the Cook Islands Constitution Act of 1964 as amended in 1965 and the Niue Constitution Act of 1974. The Cook Islands Constitution Act affirms 'the responsibilities of New Zealand for the external affairs and defence of the Cook Islands, those responsibilities to be discharged after consultation by the Prime Minister of New Zealand with the Premier of the Cook Islands' and the Niue Constitution Act carries similar phrases (Clark and Blaustein 1985, p. 9). An exchange of letters by the prime ministers in May 1973 reaffirmed that 'the special relationship between the Cook Islands and New Zealand is on both sides a voluntary arrangement which depends on shared interests and shared sympathies' (Asia Pacific Research Unit 1982a, p. 4). None of these instruments specifies the functions New Zealand is to perform or the level of aid to be given; this is a matter for negotiation between the governments on a basis of trust and mutual benefit.

This imprecision has allowed some criticism to arise from outside parties pursuing a radical decolonisation programme and from island leaders constrained by their own law (modelled on New Zealand law) or irritated by the New Zealand government's resistance to further demands for aid. The New Zealand response on such occasions is that both island governments are sovereign in every practical respect and thus free to terminate the 'special relationship' at any time (Clark and Blaustein 1985, pp. 109–10). The New Zealand government has sponsored the associated states for bilateral recognition and for membership in international organisations, arguing that they have full legislative powers and are thus sovereign. Objections that they are not independent because they share foreign affairs activities and citizenship with New Zealand are countered with observations of complete United Nations Fourth Committee satisfaction with the arrangements and by noting that the associated states can undertake international agreements more freely than the Micronesian states in the compacts of free association with the United States. Cook Islands and Niue have entered into bilateral treaties with the United States and South Korea, have signed the United Nations Convention on the Law of the Sea, have joined numerous international and regional intergovernmental bodies, and are treated as sovereign states in fact if not in name by all their various partners, including Japan.

Cook Islands

Cook Islands is a parliamentary democracy recognising the Queen, represented formerly by the Governor General of New Zealand but now by an elected Queen's Representative as titular head of state. It has its own High Court with provision for appeals to the Privy Council in London. It is governed by a prime minister, a cabinet of seven ministers, and a parliament of 24 members. The present prime minister since 1989, Geoffrey Henry, is leader of the Cook Islands Party, which, once headed by his uncle Albert Henry, led Cook Islands to self-government a quarter-century ago. The seat of government and administration is in Avarua on the most populous island, Rarotonga. It lies 1633 nautical miles (3024 kilometres) from

Auckland—the nearest metropolis. The population of 17 100 (in 1987) is spread over fifteen islands totalling 240 square kilometres in area and commanding 1 839 000 square kilometres of sea area in its Exclusive Economic Zone (EEZ) (South Pacific Commission 1989a, p. 4).

Relations with New Zealand

Cook Islands foreign affairs have evolved in close association with New Zealand, first as a source of missionaries and trade, then as a colonial administrator, and most recently as a multifaceted patron (see Table 5.1; Bellam, 1980, *passim*). Cook Islands law, education, currency and professional practices are modelled on their New Zealand counterparts, and English is widely spoken with a New Zealand accent. Administration and the judiciary rely on seconded New Zealand officers, and 16 per cent of the budget is financed by New Zealand aid (Cook Islands Government 1989, p. 12). New Zealand is the source of finance, construction capacity and managerial expertise for the country's major infrastructure, communications and transportation amenities, including telecommunications (New Zealand Telecom) and air and sea transportation (Air New Zealand and the New Zealand Shipping Corporation), and is the destination of the bulk of exports and the source of the most tourists. Under the free association arrangements Cook Islanders are also New Zealand citizens and can migrate freely. In 1986 it was estimated that over 30 000 Cook Islanders lived in New Zealand—twice as many as remained at home (Bedford 1991, p. 155).

Table 5.1 Evolution of Cook Islands foreign affairs

1200s Migrants from Tahiti and Samoa mixed with earlier arrivals from the Marquesas to form the present population, which is related to the New Zealand Maori.

1606–20 European explorers Quiros, Cook, Bligh and others made infrequent landings.

1821–88 Rarotonga *ariki* (chiefs) accepted Reverend John Williams and his London Missionary Society followers and adopted some Christian and European customs. Trade with New Zealand began.

1888 On the urging of the New Zealand government fearful of French expansion, and with the agreement of the Rarotonga *mahea* (queen) and the *ariki*, the British Foreign Office established a protectorate over the southern group of islands.

1901 The New Zealand government, with British and *ariki* approval, annexed Rarotonga and the northern islands, establishing the present boundaries of the Cook Islands.

1915 Law was codified by the Cook Islands Act of the New Zealand Parliament.

Rudimentary improvements in consultation, administration, infrastructure, health and education, prototypes of modern economic aid, were made under the supervision of the Ministry of Native (later Island) Affairs during the following decades.

1946 The New Zealand government subscribed to United Nations principles foreshadowing the decolonisation of dependencies. A union set up by Cook Islanders in Auckland and Avarua by Albert Henry struck for more representation and assistance. New Zealand set up a legislative council, which evolved into the present Cook Islands Parliament.

1962 Urged by the United Nations Committee on Decolonisation, New Zealand announced that the Cook Islands would have internal self-government in 3 years.

1964 The New Zealand Parliament passed the Cook Islands Constitution Act providing four options including independence.

1965 Consequent upon a decision by the newly elected government of Albert Henry and his Cook Islands Party, Cook Islands chose to become a sovereign self-governing state in free association with New Zealand on 4 August 1965. The New Zealand government assumed responsibility for foreign affairs, defence and economic assistance and extended citizenship and unrestricted immigration to all Cook Islanders. The Queen, represented by the Governor General of New Zealand, became titular head of state.

1971 Cook Islands became a founder member of the South Pacific Forum.

1973 The prime ministers exchanged letters clarifying that free association with New Zealand in no way restricted Cook Islands' freedom to pursue its own policies and interests in the field of foreign relations and defence and that any New Zealand initiatives impinging on Cook Islands would be subject to consultations with the Cook Islands Prime Minister.

1978 Prime Minister Albert Henry was found guilty of wrongfully using public monies to fly his party's voters home from Auckland and subverting the electoral process. He was barred from office, and the opposition Democratic Party led by Dr Tom Davis came to power.

1980 The Cook Islands Constitution was amended to abolish the power of the Governor General of New Zealand to make regulations and to substitute the Cook Islands Court of Appeal for the New Zealand High Court. The New Zealand High Commissioner was redesignated the New Zealand Representative. An 'overseas constituency' was created to enfranchise Cook Islanders living in New Zealand and became the largest of the single-seat electoral districts.

1980 Cook Islands joined the South Pacific Commission.

1982 A locally chosen Queen's Representative replaced the New Zealand Governor General.

1983 The US Senate ratified a Treaty of Friendship giving up claims to the Northern Cooks.

1986 The number of Cook Islanders living abroad was estimated to be double the number living at home.

Source: Bedford 1991, p. 155; Craig and King 1989, pp. 43–5; New Zealand Government 1984, p. 20; Clark 1985; 'Cook Islands' 1986.

Foreign relations

The Cook Islands government conducts diplomacy and foreign relations generally by three means. First, cabinet ministers and officials travel abroad frequently to make direct contact with their counterparts in other states and international organisations. Foreign officials visiting Cook Islands invariably have access to a counterpart. The representative in Wellington argues that this is as effective and more economical than maintaining expensive embassies abroad, although he acknowledges that overseas trips by officials are decried by the opposition (Short 1983, pp. 183–4).

Second, the Ministry of Foreign Affairs staffs and maintains missions in key countries. Cook Islands is permanently represented by the following officers: a representative in Wellington; a consul in Auckland; a consul in Sydney; a procurement officer in Canberra; a representative in Papeete; an honorary consul general in Honolulu; and an honorary consul general in Oslo.

Third, the Cook Islands government can request the New Zealand Ministry of External Relations and Trade to assist in a variety of ways, such as convey messages from ministers, collect background information, write position papers, conduct negotiations, and provide consular services for Cook Islanders travelling abroad and for foreigners wishing to travel to Cook Islands. New Zealand maintains a representative in Rarotonga through which routine diplomacy is conducted.

Japan's reluctance to recognise Cook Islands as a sovereign state is an exception, and a dozen governments have accredited a nearby ambassador, usually in Wellington, to Cook Islands. These include Australia, Britain, Canada, China, Fiji, France, Germany, Malaysia, Nauru, Netherlands, Norway, South Korea and the United States. Cook Islands is a member of the World Health Organisation (WHO), the Food and Agriculture Organisation (FAO), and the Lome Convention and an associate member of the Economic and Social Council (ECOSOC). It deals with a variety of other international organisations as an independent legal entity, often through the mediation of New Zealand. In South Pacific regional bodies Cook Islands is fully accepted and participates vigorously as a member of the South Pacific Forum and its affiliated bodies, and the South Pacific Commission. It participates also in such specialised bodies as the South Pacific Applied Geoscience Commission (SOPAC), the South Pacific Regional Environmental Programme (SPREP), and all those listed in Table 4.1.

Diplomatic activity abroad is supported by the Cook Islands Ministry of Foreign Affairs. The ministry is headed by the Minister of Foreign Affairs who is sometimes the prime minister, a permanent secretary, four division heads responsible for international affairs, regional affairs, protocol, and finance and administration, and a supporting staff numbering approximately fifteen officers and clerks.

Economic relations

Cook Islands foreign policy is oriented to economic development. In a nutshell, the principal goals are to attract capital to raise productivity so as to enable exports to earn foreign currency to pay for imports and social amenities. Aid is the key to stimulating and sustaining the process. Thirty-five per cent of the government's capital and operating budget is provided by aid receipts from five countries and two international organisation (see Table 5.2). In 1987 France advanced a NZ$13.7 million loan and subsequently contributed to hurricane relief and project aid in small but growing amounts. Other donors of cash, kind or technical assistance noted by the Minister of Finance included Korea, Japan, Britain, Malaysia, WHO, FAO and the Commonwealth Fund for Technical Cooperation (Cook Islands Government 1989, p. 12).

One of the purposes of aid is to provide infrastructure, facilities and administrative and legal stability to attract productive capital from abroad so as to stimulate exports. The objectives as laid down by the Development Investment Act 1977 are to encourage partnerships and local participation with overseas enterprises and to encourage foreign investment in capital-intensive sectors with potential for overseas sales. Advantages offered to investors include political stability, a common-law legal system, good communica-

Table 5.2 Cook Islands aid donors and receipts, 1987

Donor	A$000
New Zealand	11 563
Australia	1 313
Germany	47
United States	29
Canada	10
Asian Development Bank	2 555
United Nations Development Programme	28
Others	200
Total	15 745

Source: South Pacific Commission 1989a, p. 14.

tions via satellite transmission, international air services, freedom from exchange control regulations or disclosure requirements, modern company law, and low fees, taxes and tariffs. Other attractions include proficiency in English and liberal access to the New Zealand and Australian markets under the South Pacific Regional Trade and Economic Cooperation Agreement for products with at least 50 per cent Cook Islands content.

The New Zealand government offers subsidies and privileges to New Zealand private-sector investors by means of the Pacific Islands Industrial Development Scheme, and Cook Islands has attracted companies engaged in sheetmetal forming, fibreglass manufacturing, aluminium joinery, sawmilling, ballet shoe manufacturing and milk reconstituting. Other industries are based mainly on processing citrus, pineapple, bananas, copra, vegetables and other tropical produce. Efforts are being made to stimulate private sector entrepreneurship (Fairbairn 1987). Postage stamps and coins are significant overseas currency earners. The export earnings of these products are shown in Table 5.3. New Zealand takes about 80 per cent of exports and provides 60 per cent of imports. Australia, the United States and French Polynesia also are significant trade partners (Douglas 1989, p. 40).

Export earnings offset less than a fifth of imports (South Pacific Commission 1989a, p. 15). Low profitability, undercapitalisation, limited entrepreneurial skills, uneven labour supply, small domestic-market base, limited natural resources, transportation uncertainties and costs, and unpredictable demand and prices abroad, all conspire to hold production and export receipts down while rising consumer expectations tend to push imports up. The shortfall is made up by invisible earnings, principally tourism, and aid, remittances and fees on financial transactions.

Tourism has been the largest source of overseas earnings for a decade. Assuming that each of the 33 886 visitors who arrived in 1988 spent A$300 each, the country may have earned approximately

Table 5.3 Cook Islands export earnings by product, 1986

Product	A$000	%
Clothing and footwear	2 372	49.8
Fruits and vegetables	1 341	28.1
Corals and shells	578	12.1
Copra	160	3.4
Others	315	6.6
Total	4 766	100.0

Source: South Pacific Commission 1989a, pp. 16–17.

A\$10 million—nearly twice the merchandise export earnings. Of these arrivals, 36 per cent came from New Zealand, 16 per cent from Australia, 16 per cent from Europe, 10 per cent from the United States and 6 per cent from Canada; others came from Japan and neighbouring islands states (Cook Islands Government 1989, p. 7). Recognising the importance of this sector, the government in 1989 streamlined the Tourist Authority and budgeted NZ\$1 million for marketing and promotion.

Limited opportunities at home have induced two out of every three Cook Islanders to emigrate, mainly to New Zealand (30 000) but also to the United States (2000) and Australia (1400) (Bedford 1991, p. 155). These emigrants tend to keep in touch with relatives and to visit occasionally and sometimes to retire in the islands. Their remittances in cash and in goods and services were estimated to total NZ\$3.4 million in 1984 and over NZ\$5 million in 1987—sums comparable to merchandise export earnings (Douglas and Douglas 1989, p. 41; Loomis 1990, p. 50).

The Off-Shore Banking Act 1981, the International Companies Act 1982 and the Trustee Companies Act 1982 allow foreign enterprises to incorporate and financial institutions to do business without incurring tax charges. In 1991 Hong Kong financiers approved Cook Islands as an offshore domicile for companies participating in the colony's stock exchange, and new incorporations are expected. These offshore enterprises, numbering about 2000 in 1991, pay an annual fee, rent or build facilities, and hire local staff, all of which contribute to the invisible earnings of the Cook Islands.

Foreign policy issues

The three principal parties in the parliament are loosely organised and do not structure debate on foreign policy. Debate arises from constituency differences, with representatives supporting foreign aid and investment projects that will benefit their own island. Other differences revolve around personal clashes and political rivalries.

The current government of Prime Minister Geoffrey Henry has elevated several issues to prominence since its election in 1989. First, while recognising that new investment, particularly in tourism, was the quickest way to stimulate the economy, Henry noted that foreign investors controlled 80 per cent of Cook Islands tourism. An independent study confirmed that locals receive fewer benefits than foreigners from the investments (Milne 1987). He indicated that investors must be prepared to bear more of the costs of providing roads, water and electricity, and foreshadowed tightening up the code of the Development Investment Act (*New Zealand*

Herald 14 April 1990). The financial collapse of the Italian con-struction company SICEL delayed the completion of the 200 bed Sheraton resort until 1992 and put in jeopardy the government's NZ$51 million share (*New Zealand Herald* 22 November 1990).

Second, in 1990, with the help of an ADB loan and an Australian grant, the Henry government entered into a joint venture with New Zealand Telecom for a high-tech satellite-relayed international and interisland telephone service, and also initiated television transmis-sion in association with Television New Zealand. Cable and Wire-less, whose assets were nationalised to make way for New Zealand Telecom, claimed NZ$20 million in compensation and Cook Islands' credibility in honouring overseas contracts suffered (Keith-Reid 1991, p. 16). These initiatives were intended to link Cook Islands with global networks but carried risks of cost, indebtedness, foreign influence and accelerated emigration. The public debt approached NZ$100 million and servicing it will require either inflation or taxation, neither encouraging to business interests.

Third, fishing and aquaculture (cultivation of pearls and giant clams) have been given higher priority as a potential export earner. This has entailed negotiations with Japan and the United States for technical assistance, bringing Japanese and US influence deeper into the South Pacific. Cook Islands licenses fishing in its EEZ by Korea, Japan and the United States, but poaching is thought to cost the country millions of dollars annually. Australia offered one of its Pacific patrol boats to provide surveillance, but fuel, maintenance and basing costs proved prohibitive. Prime Minister Henry suc-ceeded in 1989 in persuading Australia to pay for 1250 hours' worth of fuel and maintenance out of a recommended 1650 hours of patrolling per year, and to build a base for the boat on the island of Penrhyn (*New Zealand Herald* 24 July 1989). The Royal New Zealand Navy provided training for local crews. In November 1990 the patrol boat apprehended two Taiwanese poachers and fined them. In addition, negotiations were undertaken with France for demarca-tion and joint patrolling of common borders and air force surveil-lance, the latter to supplement patrols by the Royal New Zealand and Royal Australian Air Force Orions (*New Zealand Herald* 6 February 1991). Despite this assistance, fisheries development will still be costly if done thoroughly and strict EEZ policing has implications potentially clashing with the interests of aid donors and other partners.

Fourth, disputes with the United States over nineteenth-century claims to small islands of the Northern Group, and interpretations of the Law of the Sea Convention of 1976 regarding the ownership of migratory tuna in EEZs, have been settled amicably by the 1982 Treaty of Friendship and subsequent negotiations (Hoyle 1985, pp. 77–9). Cook Islands is a party to the 1987 United States–South Pacific Regional Fisheries Treaty, and the current government is active in promoting good relations with the United States. Cook Islands leaders in the past have been irritated by New Zealand's criticism of their questionable use of budgetary aid, New Zealand's refusal to allow nuclear ships to visit leading to a breakdown of the ANZUS (Australia, New Zealand and United States Security Treaty) relationship, and New Zealand's limited capacity to provide maritime surveillance and other defence-related services. The United States, and more recently France, have begun to appear as alternative investors and suppliers of aid. For example, a French company based in Tahiti has been awarded a NZ$7 million contract, whose financial terms bordered on the concessionary, to upgrade Rarotonga's electrical power supply. Also, the Davis government took seriously the idea of a Polynesian Economic and Cultural Community that would include the government of French Polynesia, and promised land on which to build a headquarters, to be financed by France. The scheme collapsed when Davis, Flosse and Chirac left office, but could be revived. These initiatives were rational insofar as they diversified Cook Islands' sources of support, but they carried risks of alienating traditional partners.

Fifth, critics of the fact that Cook Islands does not enjoy sovereign status in the eyes of Japan, the United Nations and the Commonwealth, or may be vulnerable to political interference by New Zealand (Crocombe 1980, *passim*), sometimes raise the prospect of declaring independence. This would entail severing the special relationship with New Zealand and could be done unilaterally by constitutional amendment. New Zealand's official response has been that this is a matter for Cook Islanders to decide; the unofficial response has veered closer to 'good riddance'. A succession of Cook Island prime ministers has attempted, with New Zealand's backing, to diversify trade, aid and economic diplomacy to ease the frictions of dependence. At the same time moderate leaders on both sides recognise that there is no practical alternative to the present arrangements in the near term. The issue is likely to arise again in times of stress, and leaders will be obliged to look beyond the short term irritants to base their policies on the long term mutual interests of the two countries.

Niue

Niue is a single raised coral island of 258 square kilometres of land area commanding 390 000 square kilometres of maritime EEZ (South Pacific Commission 1989a, p. 4). Niue is governed by a premier and three other ministers chosen from a popularly elected

Legislative Assembly of twenty members. It has evolved from and continues to enjoy a close relationship with New Zealand (see Table 5.4). The titular head of state is the Queen, represented by the Governor General of New Zealand. The court of appeal is the New Zealand Supreme Court (Douglas 1989, p. 378). The Niue Constitution Act 1974 vests responsibility for foreign affairs and defence in New Zealand subject to consultation between the two prime ministers (Niue 1986, p. 284). Niue is free to amend its constitution

Table 5.4 Evolution of Niue's foreign affairs

1000s Niue was settled by eastern Polynesians, Samoans and, more recently, Tongans.

1774 Captain James Cook was the first European to visit Niue and nicknamed it 'Savage Island'.

1830–54 After several attempts the London Missionary Society succeeded in converting the population to Christianity.

1860s Niueans began leaving, some carried off as slaves, others voluntarily as indentured labourers. Small trading began.

1898 Mataio (King) Fataaiki petitioned Queen Victoria for protection.

1900 Niue was declared a British protectorate.

1901 New Zealand annexed Niue as part of Cook Islands.

1904 Niue gained separate administration, a resident administrator and an island council.

1960 New Zealand, in the spirit of progress towards self-government in nearby Cook Islands and Western Samoa, set up the first elected Niue Assembly and began delegating to it the resident commissioner's powers.

1974 The Niue Constitution Act, passed by the New Zealand Parliament, came into force. Niue became a self-governing state in free association with New Zealand. The Governor General of New Zealand became the titular head of state. The Act provided that New Zealand would take responsibility for Niue's foreign affairs and defence, on consultation with the Premier of Niue, provide economic and technical assistance, and allow continued citizenship and unrestricted immigration.

1975 Niue joined the South Pacific Forum.

1980 Niue joined the South Pacific Commission.

1981 The Niue Consular Office was established in Auckland—a counterpart of the Office of the New Zealand Representative in Alofi.

1986 Niue ratified the South Pacific Nuclear Free Zone Treaty. Five times as many Niueans were estimated to be living abroad, mainly in Auckland, as in Niue.

Source: Bedford 1991, p. 155; Craig and King 1981, pp. 207–8; Douglas and Douglas 1989, pp. 384–5; Asia–Pacific Research Unit 1982d, pp. 4–5

and dissolve the relationship at any time (Chapman 1976). Niueans are also New Zealand citizens with unrestricted right of entry. An estimated 10 500 Niueans live in New Zealand—four times the number remaining on the island (Bedford 1991, p. 155). New Zealand currency is used.

Staple exports in recent years have been coconut cream, root crops, passionfruit and lime products, and handicrafts, much of it going to expatriate Niueans and other South Pacific communities abroad. In 1985 some 90 per cent of exports went to New Zealand, 7 per cent to Cook Islands, and the balance to Fiji and Australia. In spite of free access to the New Zealand and Australian markets under the South Pacific Regional Trade and Economic Cooperation Agreement, exports have fallen badly in recent years due to hurricane damage, deterioration of facilities and erratic transport.

In 1985, 60 per cent of imports came from New Zealand, 20 per cent from Fiji, 13 per cent from Japan, 3 per cent from Western Samoa and 2 per cent from Australia (Douglas 1989, pp. 382–3). Imports exceeded exports by a ratio of 20 to 1 in 1986. The shortfall in export earnings was made up by aid from New Zealand (A$6 874 000), Australia (A$260 000) and the United States (A$121 000), which represented about two-thirds of the government's budget (South Pacific Commission 1989, p. 14).

Niue's only diplomatic representative abroad is the consular affairs officer in Auckland. His terms of reference, which reflect Niue's foreign policy goals, are:

- to promote trade, tourism and investment;
- to recruit for the Niue Public Service (which employs four-fifths of the workforce);
- to counsel Niuean students;
- to send back information of interest to Niueans at home;
- to encourage Niueans abroad to return home; and
- to liaise with the New Zealand Ministry of External Relations and Trade.

Direct foreign contacts are effected by ministerial visits and hosting foreign visitors in Niue. New Zealand diplomats represent Niue in most countries and in international organisations. Niue conducts relations with Australia, the United States, the Netherlands and numerous others for functional purposes, but is not recognised as sovereign by Japan. Niue is not a member of the United Nations General Assembly or the Commonwealth, but is an associate member of the Economic and Social Commission for Asia and the Pacific (ESCAP) and a member of numerous regional organisations, including the South Pacific Forum and its affiliates, the South Pacific

Commission, and the functional organisations listed in Table 4.1 (Haas 1989, *passim*).

Foreign policy issues revolve around different emphases by members of the cabinet, political parties being too rudimentary to define issue positions. Most issues involve whether to retain the present relationship with New Zealand, favoured by the present long-serving Premier Robert Rex, or to loosen the ties, and the implications of each course for more aid, investment, tourism and the retention of population. In 1989 a select committee considered appointing a Niuean Queen's Representative in place of the New Zealand Governor General (*New Zealand Herald* 24 June 1989). This followed an audit report critical of the government's accounting for New Zealand's 3 year $33 million grant-in-aid—particularly the failure to use the money to stimulate private sector development (*New Zealand Herald* 13 April 1989). New Zealand politicians, most recently the Minister of External Relations and Trade in January 1991, periodically query whether aid is being used effectively (Barber 1991, p. 8). In early 1990 Finance Minister Sani Lakatani questioned the validity of the Westminster parliamentary system and advocated more independent contacts by Niue with potential donors, to diversify and increase aid and solicit tourism, which, with the collapse of tropical fruit exports, offers the best hope for income earnings (Guest 1990a, p. 59). Later he criticised the Rex Cabinet's lack of initiatives in expanding private sector business activities, mainly in tourism (Guest 1990b, p. 29). The premier was unconvinced and sacked Lakatani.

The issue of attracting tourism and investment was also linked with civil air transport. When Niue's weekly air service was interrupted in 1988 by the New Zealand civil aviation authority's refusal to license Air Nauru flights to Auckland, the government supported the establishment of a new private line: Niue Airlines. However, low loadings and managerial disputes put the venture in jeopardy. Critics queried the wisdom of spending another US$33 000 to install runway lights in view of Hanan Airport's underutilisation, but the government responded that upgraded facilities would attract more air services and thus stimulate more tourism and export opportunities. Drilling by a Sydney company for uranium and precious metals 600 metres beneath the volcanic island holds out the promise of royalties, but probably not before the turn of the century (*Pacific Islands Monthly* March 1991a, p. 35).

A Hong Kong entrepreneur's proposal to set up a clothing factory that would employ 500 Niue workers was encouraged by the government, particularly former Finance Minister Lakatani, but criticised by Assemblyman Young Vivian because it would entail bringing in 1000 Hong Kong workers, disrupting the way of life of the 2000 Niueans. A French offer of NZ$800 000 in 1987 to set up a communications satellite ground station was criticised by the Niue People's Action Party as 'just trying to buy friendship' to offset the bad image that nuclear testing had given to France, and the Auckland chairman of the party asserted 'we must try and stop the French getting in'. Political criticism, and the government's unwillingness to meet French conditions such as routing traffic through Tahiti, killed the project; a New Zealand firm was then contracted to provide the service. Government Secretary Terry Chapman summed up Niue's vulnerable position when he reportedly said, only half joking, that the ultimate reason why New Zealand should continue to subsidise Niue was that it was 'an empty island awaiting a more threatening occupant' (*New Zealand Herald* 30 January 1990).

6 Fiji

Fiji's two large and 800 small islands support the South Pacific's second-largest population of over 700 000 in relative comfort. Fijian culture, arts and economy flourished in the islands for over 2000 years before the first Europeans arrived (see Table 6.1). However, the confluence of Melanesian and Polynesian migrations and struggle with ambitious Tongan leaders produced endemic wars and a sustained rivalry between the eastern Lau Islands and the western islands. European trade, missionary education and weapons favoured the eastern Bau area chiefs, from whom Ratu Sir Kamisese Mara and other post-independence paramount chiefs are descended, leaving the western chiefs, of whom the late Prime Minister Dr Timoci Bavadra and his widow Adi Kuini are the best known descendants, at a political disadvantage.

Political evolution

Benign British colonialism from 1874 to 1970 left a legacy of peace, law, government institutions and economic infrastructure. The rising standard of living was a consequence of the introduction of Indian indentured labourers to cultivate sugar for export. Taxes from this and other foreign-oriented enterprises financed public works, health and education facilities. In the face of European settler opposition, British governors pursued an indigenisation policy, protecting and subsidising chiefly and communal institutions and inducting educated Fijians into the colonial government service.

Table 6.1 Fiji's political evolution

1290BC Carbon-dated Lapita pottery provides evidence of complex civilisation evolving from a confluence of Melanesian and Polynesian migrations. Regional and tribal wars were endemic.

1643 Dutch explorer Tasman was the first European to see Fiji.

1700s English explorers Cook, Bligh and Wilson sighted various Fijian islands.

1800–14 The chief of the Bau area assisted European traders' exploitation of sandalwood and hosted the first European settlement.

1820–40 The Russian explorer von Bellingshausen, the French explorer d'Urville, and the American explorer Wilkes examined various islands, the latter making the first reliable charts.

1822 US ships began calling to buy *bêche-de-mer* (sea slug) for the China market.

1830–35 Wesleyan evangelists established churches and schools, bringing Christianity and English and an alphabet to the Fijian language.

1840 The United States appointed a vice consul in Levuka.

1844 Marist missionaries commenced evangelising, raising the possibility of French penetration.

1854 Cakobau, Chief of Bau, converted to Christianity and appealed to Britain for assistance in his wars with rivals, including a Tongan chief.

1858 Britain appointed a consul who assisted Chief Cakobau to fend off Tongan, French and US intervention.

1871 Cakobau established a national monarchy. Blackbirding, alienation of land and commercial swindling by Europeans led him and the paramount chiefs to seek British protection.

1874 Cakobau and eleven paramount chiefs signed a deed of cession to Britain in return for a pledge of protection of Fijian rights, privileges and welfare. Tribal wars and land alienation were halted, and British law was established.

1879–1920 The Australian Colonial Sugar Refining Company imported about 60 000 indentured Indian labourers to build the sugar industry. Their descendants remained to become tenant farmers, petty businessmen and numerically the largest ethnic group.

1929 The first Indians were elected to the colonial Legislative Council.

1937 The revised Legislative Council assigned equal numbers of seats to European, Fijians and Indians.

1960 The National Federation Party, representing Indian voters, was established.

1964 Universal adult suffrage on the basis of racially separate rolls began.

1966 The Alliance, representing mainly Fijians, was established. Its leader, Ratu Sir Kamisese Mara, became the first chief minister under the self-government constitution of 1966.

1970 A new constitution was adopted, and Fiji attained independence on 10 October, 96 years after cession. Fiji joined the Commonwealth and United Nations General Assembly. Ratu Mara led the Alliance to victory in the elections of 1972,

1977 and 1982 and served as prime minister and Minister of Foreign Affairs for 17 years.

1971 Fiji joined the South Pacific Commission—the third Pacific island state to do so.

1972 Fiji led the movement to establish the South Pacific Forum as an independent political counterpart to the South Pacific Commission. Suva became the venue for the forum secretariat, other regional and international organisations, and the University of the South Pacific.

1978 Fiji contributed troops to the United Nations Interim Force in Lebanon (UNIFIL) and later to the Multinational Force and Observers (MFO) in the Sinai.

1980 Fiji joined the South Pacific Regional Trade and Economic Cooperation agreement (SPARTECA).

1987 The Federation/Labour Party coalition won the election, and its Fijian leader Dr Timoci Bavadra became prime minister. Colonel Sitiveni Rabuka led two army coups and declared Fiji a republic. Former Governor General Ratu Sir Penaia Ganilau became president and appointed an interim government led by Ratu Mara as prime minister. Fiji's Commonwealth membership lapsed. Western countries cut off military aid and suspended economic aid. Tourism and trade slumped.

1988 Fiji turned to France, China, Taiwan and Malaysia for new military and economic aid and markets. Australia restored ministerial level contact.

1990 The government closed the Embassy of India in retaliation for India's lobbying against the readmission of Fiji into the Commonwealth.

1991 A new constitution biased in favour of Fijians was adopted, and elections were scheduled for 1992. New Zealand and the United States restored ministerial level contact and some aspects of defence cooperation.

Source: Ali 1982, pp. 138–54; Craig and King 1981, pp. 84–8; Douglas and Douglas 1989, pp. 125–9; Low-O'Sullivan 1989, pp. 32–40.

After independence, friendly neighbours, ample markets, experienced Fijian political and administrative leadership, and energetic Indian entrepreneurship and labour encouraged optimism about prospects for development. However, Fiji emerged also as the region's most racially divided society and became the first to retreat from democratic government into military rule, bringing upon itself economic reverses as tourists and aid donors temporarily ostracised it after 1987. The flight of Indian capital, both financial and human, has slowed commerce, left gaps in the public service and the professions, and obliged the government to open the economy to foreigners who may not have a long term interest in the country.

In the 1990s Fiji's leaders face the task of legitimising their racially biased form of parliamentary government and rebuilding confidence in their economy. This in turn requires strengthening external relations with old partners and fashioning new ones so as to attract the international support, aid and resources necessary to underpin long term development. The plea by Ratu Mara to the United Nations General Assembly on the eve of independence is still applicable today: 'The setting of standards must not assume that there are universal solutions to problems in all parts of the world. In our small land of Fiji with its multi-racial society . . . we have had to work out our own particular solution and political framework' (Fiji 1977, p 104).

Foreign relations

Fiji is regarded as the most active South Pacific island state in international affairs (Low-O'Sullivan 1989, p 32). From 1970 to 1975 it was the first and only Pacific island member of the United Nations General Assembly. Fiji gained prominence through active membership of the Economic and Social Council and its regional arm the Economic and Social Commission for Asia and the Pacific and the Special Committee on Decolonisation (Committee of Twenty-four). In the late 1970s and early 1980s Fiji took an especial interest in the United Nations Law of the Sea Preparatory Committee and the negotiations leading to the Law of the Sea Convention. Fiji was the first to establish an armed forces and to contribute troops to peacekeeping operations, first to the United Nations Interim Force in Lebanon (UNIFIL) and in the 1980s to the Multinational Force and Observers (MFO) in the Sinai and in 1991 to the Kuwait–Iraq buffer force. The United Nations Development Programme (UNDP), International Labour Organisation (ILO) and World Health Organisation (WHO) have established regional offices in Suva. Other United Nations affiliated agencies in which Fiji is active are listed in Table 6.2.

The harmonious colonial relationship with Britain led Fiji on independence to join the Commonwealth and to participate actively in such institutions as the biennial Commonwealth Heads of Government Meetings and to contribute to, and benefit from, the Commonwealth Secretariat, the Commonwealth Youth Programme and the Commonwealth Fund for Technical Cooperation. In 1982 the Queen addressed the Great Council of Chiefs at Bau and noted, 'The contribution of your people to the Commonwealth and world affairs has been far out of proportion to your relatively small population' (*Fiji Focus* 1982, p. 16).

During the period of self-government prior to independence, Fiji became the leading member of the Pacific Island Producers' Association and the venue of the University of the South Pacific. In 1970 Ratu Mara, with the Commonwealth Heads of Government Meetings model in mind, and apprehensive about the metropolitan bias of the

Table 6.2 Fiji's membership in international organisations

United Nations organs and programmes

Commission on Transnational Corporations

Economic and Social Commission for Asia and the Pacific

Economic and Social Council

Law of the Sea Preparatory Committee

Special Committee on Decolonisation (Committee of Twenty-four)

United Nations Conference on Trade and Development

United Nations Development Programme

United Nations Educational, Scientific and Cultural Organisation

United Nations Fund for Population Activities

United Nations General Assembly

United Nations Industrial Development Organisation

United Nations Interim Force in the Lebanon

Organisations affiliated to the United Nations system

Food and Agriculture Organisation

International Civil Aviation Organisation

International Fund for Agricultural Development

International Labour Organisation

International Maritime Organisation

International Telecommunication Union

Universal Postal Union

World Health Organisation

World Intellectual Property Organisation

World Meteorological Organisation

Banking and financial organisations

Asian Development Bank

International Bank for Reconstruction and Development

International Finance Corporation

International Monetary Fund

Source: New Zealand Government 1987c, *passim.*

South Pacific Commission, conceived a new South Pacific regional organisation to bring together the recently independent island states' leaders for consultation and mutual support. On Ratu Mara's initiative, and with New Zealand's assistance, the South Pacific Forum's first meeting was held in Wellington in 1971. In the subsequent two decades Fiji has supported the establishment of the forum secretariat, located in Suva, and specialised bodies for cooperation on fishing, civil aviation, shipping, telecommunications, mineral prospecting and the environment (Haas 1989, pp. 8–9).

Bilateral diplomacy grew alongside international and multilateral diplomacy. At present Fiji has diplomatic relations with over 60 states (see Table 6.3). Contacts are maintained by means of nine Fijian embassies and three honorary consulates abroad and sixteen foreign embassies and fourteen foreign honorary consulates located in Suva. A number of other states have accredited their diplomats in other capitals to Fiji, and vice versa, and these links, plus visits by ministers and senior official and informal contacts at meetings of international agencies, keep Fiji in touch with events abroad.

Table 6.3 Fiji's diplomatic links

Fiji diplomatic missions overseas
Australia (Canberra), embassy (also accredited to the Philippines and Singapore)
Australia (Sydney), consulate general
Belgium (Brussels), embassy (also accredited to France, Italy, Luxembourg, the Netherlands and the Commission of the European Communities)
Britain (London), embassy (also accredited to Germany, Israel, Egypt and the Holy See)
Japan (Tokyo), embassy (also accredited to the People's Republic of China and the Republic of Korea)
Malaysia (Kuala Lumpur), embassy
New Zealand (Wellington), embassy
United Nations (New York), permanent mission (also accredited to Canada)
United States (Washington), embassy

Honorary consuls for Fiji overseas
Canada (Ottawa)
Indonesia (Jakarta)
Papua New Guinea (Port Moresby)

Foreign embassies in Fiji
Australia
Britain
Federated States of Micronesia
France
India (closed 1990)
Israel
Japan
Malaysia
Marshall Islands
New Zealand
Papua New Guinea
People's Republic of China
Republic of China (Taiwan), trade mission
Republic of Korea
Tuvalu
United States

Countries with honorary consuls in Fiji
Belgium
Canada
Denmark
Mexico
Nauru
Netherlands

Finland
Greece
Israel
Italy

Norway
Pakistan
Philippines
Sweden

Countries with missions elsewhere accredited to Fiji

Bangladesh
Chile
Cyprus
Indonesia
Iraq
Nepal
Nigeria
Peru
Singapore
Soviet Union

Spain
Sri Lanka
Switzerland
Thailand
Turkey
Tuvalu
Venezuela
Western Samoa
Yugoslavia

Other countries with which Fiji has official relations

Albania
Argentina
Bahamas
Bulgaria
Burma
Colombia
Cook Islands
Kiribati
Lebanon
Libya

Maldives
Mexico
Mongolia
Nauru
Niue
Norway
Romania
Senegal
Tonga
Vanuatu

Source: Fiji Government 1990a.

Fiji was the first island state to set up a separate Ministry of Foreign Affairs. The establishment, procedures and practices were modelled on the British precedent with modifications for small scale and more recent experience. The ministry is headed by the Minister for Foreign Affairs and directed by a permanent secretary with the assistance of an under secretary, a chief assistant secretary, and assistant secretaries for the four divisions of: Trade, Aid and Regional Affairs; Political Relations and Treaties; Protocol (including information and research); and Administration. The first is the largest, reflecting Fiji's high priority on economic development. The number of principal officers serving in Government Buildings exclusive of clerical staff is approximately fourteen, and approximately twenty diplomats serve in missions in ten capitals abroad. Foreign policy and practice reflect the views of Ratu Mara, who set up the ministry and has served as an active minister for the bulk of the period since 1970. Until recently the roles of other ministers of the Cabinet, and of the permanent secretaries, have been clearly subordinate, although the Minister for Finance and Economic Planning and the Minister for Trade and Commerce and their secretaries are influential players in the foreign policy process as regards economic affairs.

Economic relations

Trade, aid and investment flows from Britain were predominant during the 1960s but have declined relatively as Fiji has diversified its economic relations with other bilateral and international partners. Table 6.4 shows that exports to Britain have declined from 56 per cent to 29 per cent in the period 1975–90, replaced by rising exports to Australia (19 per cent), New Zealand (17 per cent), the United States (10 per cent) and Japan (6 per cent). Rising exports to Australia and New Zealand indicate some success for the South Pacific Regional Trade and Economic Cooperation Agreement (SPARTECA) since its inception in 1980, and the post-coup government's deliberate search for alternative markets seems to have borne fruit inasmuch as Malaysia, previously a very minor market, took 7.7 per cent of exports in 1989. However, Fiji's initiatives in soliciting French, German and other European Community markets, and in fostering trade with Pacific island neighbours with some successes in Kiribati, Vanuatu and New Caledonia, have not made a significant impact on overall trade statistics. Regarding imports, sources of supply have shifted away from Britain and towards New Zealand, the United States and Asian suppliers, notably Singapore, Malaysia, South Korea, Hong Kong, China and Taiwan.

Fiji's international economic policies are geared to its national development objectives, which stress:

- growth of production and jobs;
- equitable distribution;
- improved social conditions;
- financial stability; and
- unity between ethnic groups.

In the 1980s these priorities generated a strategy based on the development of resource-based sectors of the economy for import substitution and export promotion, increase in domestic savings to reduce external borrowing and aid dependence, encouragement to overseas private investment, and the enhancement of tourism (Fiji Government 1985, pp. 8–10).

Traditionally, Fiji's most valuable resource has been sugar, generating up to three-fourths of export earnings, followed by coconut products and gold, generating up to half the remainder (Fiji Government 1985, appendix D). The government's policies of diversification and industrialisation have modified the pattern by raising fish products from zero in 1970 to 6 per cent in 1990, and timber products from less than 1 per cent to 5 per cent, and by exporting new manufactured goods such as cement, paint and boats. Garment

Table 6.4 Fiji's trade partners, 1975 and 1990 (%)

Destination of exports	1975	1990
Britain	55.9	29.2
Australia	9.2	18.8
New Zealand	8.3	17.0
Japan	0.3	5.5
Asia	6.7	5.4
United States	1.9	10.3
Pacific islands	8.9	—[a]
Others	9.1	11.4
Total	100.0	100.0
Source of imports	1975	1990
Britain	13.4	3.1
Australia	28.9	28.4
New Zealand	12.1	16.7
Japan	15.7	11.3
Asia	16.7	20.0
United States	4.0	13.3
Pacific islands	0.2	—[a]
Others	9.0	4.7
Total	100.0	100.0

[a] Included in Others.

Source: Fiji Government 1985, appendix D; Fiji Government 1990b, pp. 59, 63; Fiji Government 1991b, p. 5.

exports doubled and redoubled in the 1980s to reach 24 per cent by 1990. Nevertheless, sugar and sugar products such as molasses remained predominant at 38 per cent of exports in 1990, and gold comprised another 10 per cent; so it was premature to conclude that Fiji's economy had made a fundamental shift from primary to secondary production (Fiji Government 1991b, p. 1).

The drive to diversification and processing entailed the import of capital equipment, machinery and fuel, and the rising standard of living generated demand for foreign goods. Consequently the rising import bill raced ahead of export earnings, and the balance of merchandise payments remained stubbornly negative throughout the 1980s, with export earnings covering only 80.5 per cent of import costs in 1990 and the deficit running over 15 per cent of gross domestic product (GDP) in 1989 (Fiji Government 1990b, p. 54). In 1987 the external debt rose to 39.3 per cent of GDP, and debt service consumed the equivalent of 18.4 per cent of overseas earnings. From 1987 to 1989 gross external reserves fell by over 30 per cent measured in terms of months of imports (Browne 1989, pp. 58–9; Kubuabola 1990, chart 13). The post-coup government reduced its official borrowing, but in deregulating and privatising it stimulated overseas borrowing by private banks and enterprises at high rates of interest and repayment (Fiji Government 1990b, p. 53). The investment promotion drive brought in further private capital, mainly from Australia, New Zealand and Taiwan, preventing a gross imbalance of the current account. Other income was generated by fees and the sale of transportation services at Nadi International Airport and the ports (F$94.7 million), tourism and travel (F$212.5 million), aid and other transfers to the government (F$51.3 million), and fees earned by the Fiji Military Forces in peacekeeping duties in the Middle East (F$38.5 million). Together, these earnings in services totalled F$397 million and compensated for the merchandise trade deficit of F$358.9 million (Fiji Government 1990b, pp. 53–4).

Earnings from tourism have grown steadily since independence. In 1982 tourism earnings exceeded sugar exports to become Fiji's leading source of foreign currency, and in the 1980s tourism accounted for approximately 15 per cent of GDP and employed over 16 000 people directly or indirectly—over 7 per cent of the labour force (Fiji Government 1985, p. 88). The government has recognised this by investing in transportation, communications and tourist services, notably the flag carrier Air Pacific, Nadi International Airport and the cruise ship ports, the Hotel Aid Act, the Fiji Visitors Bureau and the international promotion campaign headlined 'Fiji, the way the world ought to be'. Foreign investors have been invited to develop facilities: QANTAS, Air New Zealand and EIE (Japan) have shares in Air Pacific; EIE is developing a multimillion-dollar resort complex at Denarau; Malaysian interests injected new capital into the Mocambo and Fijian Hotels; and the South Cross Hotel came under South Korean control.

Arrivals—which fell from an historic high of 256 824 in 1986 to 189 866 in 1987 because of the political disturbances, a hijacking attempt at Nadi International Airport and Japan Air Lines' decision to overfly Fiji—recovered to reach 250 565 in 1989 and 278 996 in 1990 (Fiji Government 1991c, p. 1). Australia and New Zealand are the source for half the arrivals, the United States accounts for another one-seventh, and Japan is approaching British and European visitor levels (see Table 6.5).

Fiji's dependence on aid is lower than that of most island countries, but is significant nonetheless, underwriting up to half the development budget in some years. Aid receipts in 1986, the last pre-coup year, are listed in Table 6.6, showing that Australia and New Zealand provided 61 per cent of all aid—a predominance that assumed great significance when these two donors suspended aid as a result of the coups of 1987. Aid receipts declined sharply after

Table 6.5 Source of visitor arrivals to Fiji, 1990

Country of residence	Arrivals	%
Australia	103 535	37.1
New Zealand	29 432	10.5
United States	36 928	13.2
Canada	18 438	6.5
Britain	16 773	6.0
Europe	27 221	9.7
Japan	21 619	7.7
Asia	6 255	2.3
Pacific islands	17 528	6.3
Others	1 277	0.5
Total	278 996	100.0

Source: Fiji Government 1991c, table 3.

1987, but consolidated figures are not available. Income from remittances was negligible in Fiji, in contrast to the smaller Polynesian countries, and the remittance flow became strongly negative in 1987 and afterwards as Indians attempted to invest their funds elsewhere or to support sons and daughters in gaining higher education and establishing themselves abroad.

Post-coup changes

Following the displacement at gunpoint of the elected Bavadra Cabinet in May 1987, Fiji suffered an immediate cessation of military aid, exercise and secondment arrangements, and a temporary suspension of most economic-assistance programmes. Trade was not embargoed, but a preferential sugar-purchasing agreement with New Zealand lapsed, and New Zealand and Australian waterside unions threatened to boycott goods from Fiji. The Australian, New Zealand and Indian governments voiced strong criticism, called their high commissioners home for consultations, and instructed officials not to attend meetings called by the coup leader Colonel Rabuka or, later, to engage in any ministerial-level contact. Other governments such as the United States and Britain expressed regret, took various actions to signal disapproval of the coup, and urged prompt restoration of a constitutional government.

Following the second coup, after Rabuka declared Fiji a republic, the Commonwealth Heads of Government Meeting, urged by the Indian and New Zealand prime ministers, declared that Fiji's membership had lapsed. Commonwealth aid and technical assistance programmes worth millions of dollars were not renewed. Tourism

Table 6.6 Fiji's aid donors and receipts, 1986

Donor	A$000	%
Australia	19 945	49.0
New Zealand	4 883	12.0
Japan	10 905	26.8
Britain	2 237	5.5
Germany	789	1.9
United Nations Development Programme	628	1.8
Others	1 296	3.2
Total	40 683	100.0

Source: South Pacific Commission 1989a, p. 13.

and exports fell as a result of turbulence in Fiji, which included sporadic Indian union refusals to work in the sugarcane industry.

The interim government responded with an omnibus initiative drafted by Minister of Foreign Affairs Filipe Bole in October 1987. The foreign policy objectives of the new republic were to be:

- to promote recognition of the republic and the government;
- to promote and establish new patterns of trade;
- to develop new campaigns for restoring the tourist industry; and
- to attract foreign investment and technical assistance *from sources other than Australia and New Zealand* (Fiji 1987, p.1).

The main targets of the new republic's diplomatic initiatives to secure recognition were to be the neighbouring Melanesian and Polynesian island states, Southeast Asian states and other Third World states. Visits or representations were to be made to the states of the South Pacific Forum, the Commonwealth, the European Community and the United Nations, and particularly to Malaysia, Indonesia, Singapore, South Korea, Taiwan, China and the United States 'to seek their understanding and support' (Fiji Government 1987, p. 3). Other sections of the Ministry of Foreign Affairs release proposed turning away from Australia and New Zealand to Malaysia, Indonesia, Singapore, South Korea, Taiwan and Hong Kong for cheaper and more reliable imports and for sources of new capital investment and aid.

The success of Fiji's post-coup policies has been mixed. No state broke off diplomatic relations with Fiji save India, whose mission in Suva was expelled in 1990. Relations with international organisations not affiliated with the Commonwealth continued uninterrupted. The island state leaders of the South Pacific Forum were disinclined to put Fiji's deviation from constitutional government on the forum agenda, regarding this as a domestic not a regional issue, and Tonga, Marshall Islands and the Melanesian states early stated their intention to work with the new government in spite of Australia and New Zealand's disapproval. Southeast and East Asian governments likewise dealt with Fiji pragmatically. By the end of 1987 Indonesian and Malaysian delegations had visited and entered into negotiations to enhance trade and economic cooperation with Fiji, leading in 1991 to links between the Fiji National Petroleum Company and Malaysia's Petronas, for example. Fijian leaders visited China and Taiwan, securing loans and aid (Low-O'Sullivan 1990, p. 37; Biddick 1989, pp. 808–10). Australia, to avoid giving a clear field to France, restored ministerial contacts. The promulgation of the new constitution in 1990 and the prospect of elections in 1992 persuaded New Zealand to restore economic aid and ministerial contact. Australia, New Zealand and the United States continued to withhold military cooperation.

In years past Fijian troops assisted the British forces in World War II and in the Malayan Emergency. Fiji was a welcome partner in the Australian Defence Cooperation Programme and the New Zealand Mutual Assistance Programme and in occasional small-scale cooperation with British and US forces. The coup precipitated the cutoff of these traditional defence contacts. Australia cancelled the delivery of three vessels promised under its Pacific patrol boat project. Fiji was obliged to seek new military assistance from France and Asian countries. Fiji succeeded in soliciting F\$12 million from France to fund a maintenance facility for army vehicles and a helicopter and advice on the setting up of an air wing, and also negotiated a maritime surveillance arrangement (Bates 1990, p. 123). Fiji borrowed F\$2 million from Taiwan at low interest for the purchase of army vehicles and secured credit to purchase four patrol boats from Israel, with associated training. Ratu Mara and Major General Rabuka visited Beijing, and an army source claimed that China would extend 'full military cooperation' (*New Zealand Herald* 10 May 1990). It was reported that officers had been invited to Malaysia for training.

The new aid was not sufficient for Fiji's needs, however, and the government relied mainly on its own defence budget (F\$25 million in 1989, up from F\$15 million in 1986) to fund a new air wing, expand its naval arm, and set up its own officers' training school (Fiji Government 1990b, p. 33). This was partly offset by earnings from participation in Middle East peacekeeping forces, which were uninterrupted.

Economic policy issues

The political realignment provided an opportunity to reconsider

Fiji's economic policies, characterised by government conservatism, to liberalise them along the lines of the successful Newly Industrialising Countries (NICs) of Asia (Kaspar 1988; World Bank 1987). Perhaps the most visible change was the active solicitation of new industrial capital through the Tax Free Zone/Tax Free Factory scheme. Announced in December 1987, the new policy entailed the granting of generous tax holidays and allowances and unrestricted capital and profit repatriation to export-oriented factories. The Fiji Trade and Investment Board, created by the Economic Development Act 1980, was revitalised. In 1989 and 1990 it conducted visits, seminars or other promotional activities in Australia, Italy, Germany, Spain, Belgium, Britain, Japan, Hong Kong, Singapore, Malaysia, Indonesia and seven Pacific island countries, and facilitated contacts with or visits by business people from New Zealand, South Korea and China (Fiji Government 1989, pp. 7–8; Fiji Government 1990c, *Trade News* 1990c, pp. 13–26).

In addition to capital infusions in traditional enterprises, investors were encouraged to use Fiji's cheap labour (labour unions are restricted under the new government), good infrastructure, and privileged access to Western markets under the South Pacific Regional Trade and Economic Cooperation Agreement and the Lome Agreement, to set up Tax Free Factories to manufacture and export new products. In the period 1987–89, 70 new Tax Free Factories were set up with capital from investors from Australia (24), New Zealand (24), China (8), Taiwan (4), Singapore (2), and Canada, Hong Kong, Vanuatu, South Korea, Italy, Germany, South Africa and the United States (1 each) (Fiji Government 1989, p. 15).

By 1991 the new factories numbered 104, had attracted F\$50 million in new investment, employed an estimated 9169 workers, and had begun production of garments, wood and furniture, leather and footwear, food and other products. They and the established factories boosted exports of manufactured goods to F\$169.8 million or 25.9 per cent of total domestic exports in 1990. Textile and garment exports grew to F\$159 million, up from only F\$8.8 million in 1987 (Fiji Government 1991b). This success stimulated criticism in Australia, New Zealand and the United States, where domestic producers complained that 'sweatshop conditions' were generating unfair competition, and the raising of trade barriers particularly by the United States became a possibility. In 1991 Australia reallocated its SPARTECA textile quota to encourage imports from other island countries, and this, added to declining price advantage as Australia and New Zealand cut their global tariff rates, tended to slow Fiji's export growth rate (*Pacific Islands Monthly* 1991c, p. 32).

From independence Fiji imposed licensing and high tariffs on imports in pursuit of its declared policy to promote import substi-

tution industries (World Bank 1987, pp. 31–47). Behind these protective barriers, nurtured by indirect subsidies enjoyed by Indian
entrepreneurs in collusion with Fijian chiefly elites in government,
a number of manufacturing and retailing firms have prospered.
However, efficiency and international competitiveness have
remained low and prices to Fijian consumers high. The distortions
induced by protection became especially visible during 1987, when
foreign exchange controls were temporarily imposed to stem the
flight of capital as an estimated 10 000 Indians left the country
temporarily or permanently.

The new government brought to prominence younger officials less
aligned with the traditional elites, notably Secretary of Trade and
Commerce Navitalai Naisoro, who was associated with the commoner Fijian *taukei* movement. Naisoro and others argued for less
government intervention and lower import barriers as a counterpart
to the Tax Free Factory scheme. This would bring Fiji into con-
formity with the spirit of the General Agreement on Tariffs and
Trade (GATT) and forestall international criticism and possible
retaliation by bilateral trade partners, they argued. They were backed
by Robert Lee, holder of economics degrees from Auckland and
Harvard universities, Chairman of Lees Trading Company, and a
past President of the Fiji–New Zealand Business Council. Lee
argued that it was local Indian monopolists who lobbied for protection and thus avoided competition and drove prices up and quality
down, in flour milling for example (Sharma 1991, p. 18).

The traditionalists' sceptical response to the new policy was voiced
by the Presidents of the Fiji Manufacturers' Association and the Ba
Chamber of Commerce and Industries. They argued that the export
stimulation model could not be transferred from the large NICs to
small Fiji and that its application would drive local enterprises to
bankruptcy and throw their employees out of work. Indian miller
Hari Punja asserted that local mills could not compete against
unrestricted imports from the Australian giants (Sharma 1991, p. 17).

Naisoro's position was that workers in protected import substitution industries were few compared with the growing numbers in the
new export-oriented factories, and that the latter could absorb the
former. He asserted that Fiji would be better off without import
substitution industries because the elimination of licensing and the
reduction of tariffs below 40 per cent, which he proposed, would
bring consumers cheaper goods from overseas, and workers would
not need higher wages to gain a higher standard of living (*Fiji Times*
29 September, 2 October, 8 October 1990). At the end of 1990
Naisoro was transferred to the Ministry of Tourism, Civil Aviation
and Energy, and then sent to the Australian National University for
study leave.

In 1991 unease was expressed by some investors that the government had failed to confirm in legislation promises of tax holidays, the provision of electrical power and freedom to import specialised workers. The Ministry of Trade and Commerce reaffirmed its promises (*New Zealand Herald* 19 March 1991; *New Zealand Herald* 27 March 1991). In early 1991 the government's Fiji National Petroleum Company linked up with Esso Singapore to supply Malaysian oil products to local distributors on a monopoly basis, cutting out three established foreign suppliers, BP, Mobil and Shell (*Trade News* 1991, pp. 1–3). These moves eroded the credibility of the government's policies to free up the economy and shift from import substitution to export stimulation.

The long term future of the Indo-Fijian community is a controversial question among the Fijian elite, which also has foreign policy implications. Soon after the coup Colonel Rabuka expressed the opinion that Indians should emigrate and be replaced by Chinese immigrants, who would work harder and be less politically contentious. Australia and New Zealand experienced a surge of Indian applicants for immigration, some of whom sought asylum from alleged political persecution. Fiji's investment promotion policy targeted Asian states to encourage Chinese investors to set up Tax Free Factories or strengthen the tourist industry, and offered them residency privileges through the Business Immigration Scheme. However, the rumoured arrival of several hundred poor Chinese seeking employment or petty business opportunities such as restaurants and retail shops, some the victim of passport frauds, precipitated a reassessment by Fijian leaders, doubtless backed by established Indian businessmen. In March 1990 the interim government tightened visiting and immigration policies and required business immigrants to bring a minimum investment of F$500 000. The Cabinet also reserved commerce, importing and retail trades to Fijian citizens and lengthened the residence period from 5 to 7 years to qualify for citizenship (*New Zealand Herald* 10 March 1990). These episodes illustrate how the debate between conservative and liberal trade policies has become complicated by tensions between progressive and traditional Fijians in government and their Indian associates in business, and by a resurgence of economic nationalism.

Assessment

The political turbulence of the late 1980s has affected Fiji's foreign relations, but not fundamentally. Fiji's bilateral relations and multilateral relations continued virtually unchanged except for those with India, Australia, New Zealand and the United States and after a cool period these too began to warm. The search for new partners brought some new markets and sources of aid and investment from Japan, France, Malaysia and Taiwan, but the traditional partners continued to predominate in the overall statistics. New investment policies accelerated Fiji's shift from primary to secondary production and exporting but did not approach complete transition. Political disruption caused an economic downturn, but that proved temporary, and predictions of poverty remain as unfulfilled as predictions of civil war or outside intervention.

The return to constitutional and elected government anticipated in 1992 salvaged Fiji's standing in the eyes of democratic partners, and raised its chances of reinstatement in the Commonwealth; but barring an unlikely electoral victory by the Indian opposition parties, the return to democracy will not noticeably alter the conduct of diplomacy or economic relations. Fiji will continue to be a significant trader, a desirable venue for international organisations, an important hub for regional transportation and a strong player in South Pacific foreign affairs.

7   Kiribati and Tuvalu

Located in the central Pacific at the intersection of the equator and the International Date Line, these two island states are distant from centres of population and commerce, off the air and sea trunk routes, and little touched by the currents of development except in their capitals. They possess no mineral resources save the possibility of seabed manganese nodules, few other resources save fish, and limited potable water. Their small atolls are under pressure from rising population and rising sea levels. Yet their cultures retain integrity, their governments are stable and effective, and their politics are democratic and lively. Their prospects for survival as microstates are enhanced by vigorous foreign policies that have attracted support from old and new international partners and established Kiribati and Tuvalu in the international system.

Political evolution

First seen by Spanish explorers in the sixteenth century, the islands had been inhabited since before 1000 BC, peopled by migrants from Tonga, Samoa and Fiji (Craig and King 1981, pp. 147–9, 299–305; Douglas and Douglas 1989, pp. 298–301). The culture of present day Kiribati (formerly Gilbert Islands) is Micronesian, while that of Tuvalu (formerly Ellice Islands) is Polynesian. In both cases their societies were organised around dispersed clans, villages and islands, with a few chiefs in the north, when European whalers, traders and missionaries arrived in the nineteenth century (Talu

1979; Macdonald 1982). US, Hawaiian, Samoan and British missionaries brought Protestantism to Tuvalu and southern Kiribati and Catholicism to northern Kiribati, set up the first schools, which led to a high degree of literacy, and encouraged settlement in villages for physical improvements and economic cooperation. Anglo-German rivalry, pressure to end blackbirding and other European misbehaviour, and civil wars in Kiribati led the British to declare the Gilbert and Ellice Islands Protectorate in 1892. Gilbert and Ellice Islands became a colony in 1916 and absorbed Christmas Island in 1919, the Phoenix Islands in 1937 and the Line Islands in 1972. The Tokelau Islands were included until 1926 when they were transferred to New Zealand.

British residents and district officers were posted to the more populated islands, local councils were set up, and British law was introduced, modified considerably to take account of local mores. Improvements in health were made, but education was left to the missionaries, and infrastructure development was neglected save on Banaba (Ocean) Island (annexed in 1900) where phosphate mining became the leading source of revenue and employment. Occupation by the United States in 1943–45 after a harsh Japanese interregnum brought wage employment and consumer goods and an abortive request for US annexation. Preparations for self-government began when the British set up an Advisory Council in 1963, followed by a House of Representatives in 1967, an elected Legislative Council in 1973, and an elected House of Assembly with ministerial government in 1974.

The advent of representative government brought the differences between the Gilbert Islanders and Ellice Islanders to the surface. Ellice Islanders enjoyed a higher educational standard, in part because schooling was uninterrupted during World War II, and the British staffed half of the local civil service with them, a ratio five times greater than their proportion of the population. This was resented by Gilbert Islanders, particularly on Tarawa, the capital, who formed the Gilbertese National Party in 1965 to protect their interests. The Ellice Islanders for their part resented the higher numbers of seats in the House held by Gilbert Islanders and demanded an equal number to compensate for and reverse the tendency of the British to spend development funds in the more populous Gilberts, particularly Tarawa (Isala 1983, pp. 154–87; Macdonald 1982, pp. 244–61). The British held a referendum in 1974, supervised by a United Nations visiting mission, which found 92 per cent of voters supporting separation of the Ellice Islands administration. In 1975 the government and civil service were reorganised to separate the Ellice components and personnel, and in 1978 the Ellice Islands, now called Tuvalu, became independent.

A call by Banaba Islanders for secession under the protection of Fiji was turned down by the British, and a claim for compensation for phosphate earnings was dismissed by the courts (Douglas and Douglas 1989, pp. 301–2). The Banaban survivors of deportation and massacre during the Japanese occupation had been resettled in Fiji on Rabi Island and were considered Fijian subjects. Intervention on their behalf by the Fijian Prime Minister was regarded by the Gilbert Islands Chief Minister as unwarranted interference; the dispute also delayed Gilbert Islands independence and had the effect of creating resentment against both Britain and Fiji (Teiwaki 1988a, pp. 12–13).

Self-government for the Gilberts was achieved in early 1977, a pre-independence election was held in 1978, and the new state of 56 452 citizens, now called Kiribati, became independent on 12 July 1979 (Iuta 1980). Kiribati chose Commonwealth membership but is the only former British South Pacific colony to reject a parliamentary system of government in favour of a modified presidential system, in part a consequence of the Gilberts' admiration of the United States and frictions with Britain, and in part an assertion of independence. The president is elected nationally from among candidates chosen by the elected House of Assembly (Maneaba), and the president then chooses a Cabinet from among House members. Ieremia Tabai, a southern island Protestant educated in New Zealand, led Kiribati into independence and served as president until 1991. His successor was Teateo Teannaki, who won support from southern and outer islands. The opposition, largely Catholics from the northern islands, caucused in the Christian Democratic Party to complain about the alleged domination of government by the southern island Protestants, to support union opposition to the decentralisation of government corporations, and to express anxiety about the 1985 fishing treaty with the Soviet Union (Teiwaki 1988a, pp. 32–6). Otherwise political parties played little role. Electoral choices, Maneaba debates and public discussion were structured by the divides between the Catholic northern islands and the Protestant southern islands, between the developed capital island of Tarawa and the less developed outer islands, and between union members and the government. Personalities and local issues predominated over national or international issues or ideologies.

Kiribati foreign affairs

On independence, Kiribati joined the Commonwealth and made contact with agencies such as the Commonwealth Secretariat, Commonwealth Foundation and Commonwealth Fund for Technical Cooperation, from which aid and advice have been received, and the

Commonwealth Heads of Government Meetings, where the president has met world leaders biennially. Kiribati joined the United Nations General Assembly, the Economic and Social Commission for Asia and the Pacific (ESCAP) (associate member), the International Telecommunication Union (ITU), the Universal Postal Union (UPU) and the World Health Organization (WHO), and solicited aid and loans from the World Bank, Asian Development Bank (ADB), International Development Association (IDA), International Finance Corporation (IFC), International Monetary Fund (IMF) and United Nations Development Programme (UNDP). It also joined the South Pacific Commission, and the South Pacific Forum and all its affiliated bodies, which puts its president in annual contact with all the other South Pacific leaders. Kiribati hosted the Twentieth South Pacific Forum in Tarawa in 1989. To gain trade access Kiribati participated in the South Pacific Regional Trade and Economic Cooperation Agreement and the Lome Convention.

To conserve funds Kiribati has opened no overseas diplomatic posts but has designated its Secretary of Foreign Affairs and other officials as roving envoys, who, supplementing contacts made by the president, visit foreign capitals and attend international meetings to present Kiribati's views. Britain, which provides budgetary support, project aid and specialised personnel, also represents Kiribati in its missions around the world and provides consular services. Early diplomatic relations were established with the United States, Australia, New Zealand, Canada, Japan and the European Community. Britain, Australia, New Zealand and the People's Republic of China have resident missions in Tarawa, and Kiribati has appointed honorary consuls in Auckland, Hamburg, Honolulu, London, Port Moresby, Seoul, Sydney and Tokyo. Other countries have accredited their ambassadors in Suva, Port Moresby, Wellington or Canberra to Kiribati.

The Ministry of Foreign Affairs numbers nine senior and support staff under the Minister of Foreign Affairs, who is also the president. There is no defence establishment, the first Tabai government having rejected a proposal by its predecessor to establish one. However, Kiribati receives some civil aid and maritime reconnaissance intelligence through the Australian Defence Cooperation Programme and the New Zealand Defence Mutual Assistance Programme.

Maritime diplomacy

The exhaustion of Banaba phosphate in 1979 deprived Kiribati of approximately 6 per cent of its paid employment, 45 per cent of its gross national product (GNP) and 55 per cent of government revenue (Asia Pacific Research Unit 1982b, p. 8). Its only other resources, aside from people and coconuts, lay in the sea in the form of seabed manganese nodules and fish. Thus securing its maritime boundaries in competition with other states' claims became a foreign policy imperative.

Among the new government's first tasks was to secure its claims to fourteen islands of the Line and Phoenix groups also claimed by the United States under the Guano Act of 1856. With Britain's help a Treaty of Friendship was negotiated in 1979 and, after delay occasioned by conservative US senators, ratified in 1983, whereby all claims were dropped. Kiribati pledged at the time to seek US agreement before allowing military activities by other states on Canton, Enderbury and Hull islands and to consult in the cases of the other eleven islands (Douglas and Douglas 1989, p. 301; Teiwaki 1988b, pp. 224–6). Officials now doubt the legality of this limitation on Kiribati sovereignty and hope to renegotiate it; meanwhile the islands are being administered as full Kiribati possessions.

Kiribati's views have also diverged from those of the United States on opposition to US (and French) nuclear activities in the South Pacific, its support of US (and French) decolonisation, frictions over American Tunaboat Association poachers in the 200 mile (332 kilometre) Exclusive Economic Zone (EEZ), and its negotiations with the Soviet Union for a fishing agreement in 1985. US aid to Kiribati has been negligible relative to the large amounts spent in the former trust-territory states to the north; so this instrument of better relations has remained undeveloped, and relations between the two states remain good but not cordial.

The South Pacific Forum in 1976 and 1977, endorsing recommendations by the United Nations Conference on the Law of the Sea, recommended that member states legislate to claim 200 mile (332 kilometre) EEZs. The government of Kiribati did not have the personnel or financial resources to participate in the conference but accepted British and South Pacific Forum views in the interim. It proclaimed a 200 mile protected fisheries zone around the Gilberts in 1978 and around the Line and Phoenix Islands in 1980, and formalised the declarations in the Marine Zones (Declaration) Act 1983. This provided a zone of 770 000 square nautical miles (2 641 000 square kilometres) with an estimated potential fish catch of 100 000 tonnes (Teiwaki 1988b, p. 76).

However, this zone intersected those proclaimed by Tuvalu, Nauru, Tokelau, Cook Islands, Marshall Islands and the United States. Demarcation of the respective zones is important for several reasons: the apportionment of royalties from bilateral and multilateral fishing agreements, the management of disputes with the United States over proposed nuclear-waste dumping, and that country's non-acceptance of the Law of the Sea's provisions on the ownership of migratory species and seabed resources. Also, Tuvalu and Cook Islands fishermen make use of uninhabited islands of the Line and Phoenix groups across the boundary. Kiribati has proclaimed the equidistance principle and its willingness to comply with International Court of Justice rulings, but lacks the experts or funds to hire consultants to effect the demarcation or to assess other states' claims. The Canadian government is funding the International Centre for Ocean Development to work with the Forum Fisheries Agency to demarcate provisional boundaries and so preserve inter-island harmony in the meantime (North 1990, pp. 24–5).

Fishing agreement initiatives commenced in 1978 with the governments of Japan and South Korea and subsequently with the United States and the Soviet Union, as shown in Table 7.1. Income from fees was dependent on formulas and catches, was supplemented by aid in kind and had to be renegotiated periodically, making government budgeting and industry development planning difficult. For example, fishing royalties rose slowly to 9.0 per cent of central government revenue (exclusive of aid) in 1981, slumped to 7.4 per cent in 1983, rose rapidly to 13.2 per cent in 1986, and dropped below 10 per cent when the Soviet deal was terminated (Browne 1989, p. 73).

Negotiations with the Soviet Union attracted criticism from Catholics and the opposition Christian Democratic Party at home and from partner governments abroad, particularly those of Australia, New Zealand and the United States. Nevertheless, the Tabai government saw the Soviet offer as an opportunity to end dependence on budgetary assistance from Britain, which had to be requested annually, was granted subject to conditions, and was 'tied to punitive terms and conditions, much to the inconvenience and displeasure of the Kiribati government' (Teiwaki 1988b, p. 96). The sum agreed on, US$1.5 million, was equivalent to almost 2 years of British budgetary aid, approaching the equivalent of 10 per cent of the gross domestic product (GDP) and 15 per cent of government revenue in 1986. Anxiety about Soviet takeover or subversion was relieved by refusal to grant the fourteen boats permanent shore facilities or even landing rights except in emergency. In 1986 the Soviets declined to renew the agreement, claiming poor catches, and subsequently made a more advantageous agreement with Vanuatu; they have not shown much interest in Kiribati since then.

Aside from the welcome cash, the most significant effects of the Soviet agreement were to stimulate increased aid from Australia, New Zealand and China, and to galvanise the United States into a new fishing treaty (Doulman 1987b, p. 33). American Tunaboat Association poaching had resulted in the seizure of boats by Papua

Table 7.1 Kiribati receipts from fishing agreements, 1978–91

Fishing country	Year	(US$000) Fee	(US$000) Aid
Japan	1978	600	150
	1979	600	150
	1980	600	150
	1981/82	1 100	1 110
	1983/84	1 100	2 400
	1985	1 027	1 962
	1986	562	3 600
	1987	413	3 120
	1988	391	720
South Korea	1979	185	0
	1980	185	0
	1981	185	0
	1982	—[a]	0
	1984/85	200	0
	1986	344	0
	1987	551	0
	1988	491	0
	1991	1 000	0
United States	1983/84	Pro rata[b]	Boat
	1985	—[a]	0
	1986	230	0
	1987	279	Indirect [c]
	1988	203	16
Soviet Union	1985/86	1 500	0
	1987	—[a]	0

[a] No agreement. [b] US$55 per ton (US$54.13 per tonne) of catch. [c] A portion of US$4 million annually to the Forum Fisheries Agency.

Source: Teiwaki 1988b, p. 103; Kiribati Government 1988, pp. 43, 88; *Pacific Islands Monthly* 1991d, p. 35.

New Guinea and Solomon Islands and increasing irritation among South Pacific governments, at a time when the United States was trying to rally allies against Soviet expansion into the Pacific and to contain the effects of the Treaty of Rarotonga and New Zealand's and Vanuatu's strict antinuclear policies. Kiribati had joined the Forum Fisheries Agency in 1979 and signed the Nauru Agreement with three Melanesian and three Micronesian states in 1982 and a further agreement with Palau and Federated States of Micronesia in 1986 to strengthen their bargaining position vis-à-vis the powerful distant fishing states. The Nauru Group functioned as caucus within the Forum Fisheries Agency, focusing attention on tuna management. Fears that the issue would split the agency, or that outside fishing states would be allowed to play island states against one another, were not realised. On the contrary, the several island-state initiatives, plus the antipathy to Soviet penetration, created a political climate that induced the United States to conclude the United States–South Pacific Regional Fisheries Treaty in 1987. This ended American Tunaboat Association poaching and provided for an annual fee of US$7 million to be distributed according to venue of catches, plus a regional fisheries aid and technical assistance package to the Forum Fisheries Agency and its members worth US$4 million annually. Kiribati is now protected by this treaty and receives up to US$2 million annually in fees, and various aid projects, as a result of it and other fishing agreements.

Of all island states' EEZs, Kiribati's appears to have the greatest potential for mining seabed manganese nodules, cobalt-rich manganese crusts and polymetallic sulphides (Teiwaki 1988b, pp. 119–40). Kiribati relies on advice from the South Pacific Applied Geoscience Commission (SOPAC) on mineral resources, legal rights and development options. The government asserts that the Law of the Sea Convention assigns Kiribati clear ownership of minerals found in its EEZ. Exploitation options now under consideration are limited by the lack of government capital to finance national mining; so the formation of a joint venture enterprise is the next best option, followed by auctioning sites to multiple bidders or licensing a single foreign enterprise and charging fees or royalties.

Regarding minerals outside the EEZ, Kiribati inclines to the notion that they are the 'common heritage of mankind' as asserted in the Law of the Sea Convention, and that their exploitation should be managed by an international authority and profits distributed to the poorer countries. This puts Kiribati at odds with the United States, Britain and Japan—the most likely mining countries—which assert that non-EEZ seabeds are comparable to international waters, open to any mining enterprise within the limits of international laws and environmental prudence. So far Kiribati has earned no income from minerals, but it is thought that serious prospecting could generate revenues by the end of the 1990s.

Kiribati economic relations

Kiribati earns foreign currency also by exporting goods and services and by soliciting aid. The major export earner is copra, valued at A$4.2 million or 62.9 per cent of total exports in 1988. Second is fish and fish products, valued at A$1.6 million or 23.9 per cent of exports in 1988, earned by the government enterprise Te Mautari Ltd, which supplies fresh fish to Fiji and Hawaii and hopes to tap Asian markets in future. Total export earnings were only A$6.6 million, or 23.9 per cent of the import bill of A$28.2 million, spent mainly on food, machinery and fuel (*Pacific Economic Bulletin* 1990a, p. 58). Kiribati's major customers in 1988 were the Netherlands (69.3 per cent of total exports, virtually all the copra crop), Fiji (23.2 per cent, mostly fresh fish), the United States (4.2 per cent) and Tonga (2.5 per cent). Its main sources of imports were Australia (43.8 per cent), Fiji (15.3 per cent), Japan (10.9 per cent), China (5.2 per cent), New Zealand (4.9 per cent) and the United States (4.8 per cent). Imports from Britain have declined from 8.0 per cent to 1.5 per cent since independence (Kiribati 1989, pp. 22, 25).

Investment to expand local production and exports and reduce import dependency is encouraged by a 5 year tax holiday, tariff protection, import duty relief, government equity participation, and employee training at the Tarawa Technical Institute and the Marine Training School (New Zealand Government 1988; United Nations Industrial 1986, pp. 191–203). Priority sectors are the processing of fish, seaweed and coconut timber, light assembly work and tourism. Restrictions apply only to handicrafts and other sectors already served by I-Kiribati (natives of Kiribati) and to projects jeopardising the natural or social environment. The Melbourne Omex offer of US$2.5 million to dump Australian and European waste on Banaba Island is to be considered only after independent assessment (*Trade News* 1990b, p. 35). Enterprises more than 30 per cent overseas-owned need Foreign Investment Commission approval. Policy guidelines are found in the Foreign Investment Act 1985 and the Foreign Investment Regulations 1986.

Other sources of income necessary to balance the current account are services including fishing royalties and airport and port charges, remittances by I-Kiribati working in the phosphate mines at Nauru and on foreign ships, and aid, as shown in Table 7.2.

Also, the Phosphate Reserve Fund, set up by Britain from royalties from Banaban phosphate exports prior to 1979, stood at A$179

Table 7.2 Kiribati current account, 1988

Item	A$000
Merchandise trade	−20.9
Fishing and port fees	+4.0
Remittances	−3.4
Aid and interest earnings	+21.1
Interest, capital transfer	−5.5
Balance	+3.0

Source: Pacific Economic Bulletin 1990a, p. 57.

Table 7.3 Kiribati aid donors and receipts, 1988

Donor	A$000	%
Britain	8 761	40.1
Australia	3 000	13.7
New Zealand	3 000	13.7
Japan	1 200	5.5
Germany	450	2.1
United States	400	1.8
Canada	250	1.1
European Community	2 859	13.1
United Nations Development Programme and other United Nations	1 000	4.6
World Health Organisation	450	2.6
Asian Development Bank	50	0.4
Others	420	1.9
Total	21 840	100.0

Source: Kiribati Government 1989, p. 43.

million and earned A$5.2 million in interest in 1986 and A$11.7 million in 1988, allowing a transfer to increase the size of the fund. Borrowing is light and at concessionary rates because Kiribati is classified by the World Bank as a Least Developed Country (LDC); debt was only 9.3 per cent of GDP and the debt–service ratio only 3.1 per cent of goods and services earnings in 1986 (Browne 1989, pp. 73, 81). Earnings from tourism are negligible; most arrivals are aid officials, business people or family visitors. Earnings from stamp sales reached a peak of over A$1 million in 1982 but fell to a negligible figure by 1986.

Aid remained a major requirement, underwriting 5.4 per cent of total government revenues in 1988 (*Pacific Economic Bulletin* 1990a, p. 56). In the year following independence Britain shouldered 72.6 per cent of the burden of aid. By 1988 a number of other countries and international agencies had lifted their assistance, reducing the British share to 40.1 per cent, as shown in Table 7.3. British aid tended to take the form of advisors and seconded personnel after budgetary support stopped in 1986; Australia contributed water and sewerage projects; Japan concentrated on fishing aid and the Betio causeway; and the European Community concentrated on telecommunications facilities. China, stimulated by the Soviet fishing deal, offered small projects and in 1990 provided an interest-free loan of NZ$5.6 million to upgrade the international airport and build the new parliament building (*New Zealand Herald* 25 May 1990).

Tuvalu foreign affairs

On 1 October 1978 Tuvalu, a microstate of 7349 inhabitants on nine islands, achieved independence. It adopted a simplified parliamentary-democracy form of government composed of a parliament of twelve elected members headed by a prime minister, a Cabinet of five ministers, and a Tuvaluan governor general representing the Queen as titular head of state. Tuvalu became a 'special member' of the Commonwealth, eligible for benefits from its functional affiliates but not required to attend Commonwealth Heads of Government Meetings. Tuvalu joined the South Pacific Forum and its affiliated agencies and the South Pacific Commission. It hosted the Fourteenth South Pacific Forum in its capital, Funafuti, in 1984. However, its lack of funds and trained personnel precluded participation in international organisations outside the South Pacific except as a recipient of aid, advisory services, information and concessionary trade access such as the Lome Convention as a member of the ACP (African, Caribbean and Pacific) group.

Diplomacy was conducted largely by the prime minister, who was also Minister for Foreign Affairs, when he visited capitals and international meetings abroad. He was assisted by four officials attached to the Prime Minister's Office. Tuvalu established one diplomatic mission abroad, a high commission in Suva, and accredited the high commissioner to a number of other states whose ambassadors were resident there. There were also honorary consuls in Auckland, Sydney, Hong Kong, Tokyo and Germany. The British Foreign Office through its embassies provided liaison and consular services for Tuvalu. By 1982 Tuvalu had established diplomatic relations with fifteen states including: neighbouring Pacific island states; leading Pacific-rim states such as the United States, Japan, South Korea, the Republic of China (Taiwan) and Hong Kong; and Britain, France and Germany. Contacts by Soviet Union envoys in 1985 for fishing access were rejected. Relations with Kiribati, cool during the period of self-assertion, have now warmed, and the two atoll states find that they have many interests in common.

In foreign policy Tuvalu avoided extreme positions and preferred to move in the mainstream, guided by the South Pacific Forum consensus. Its leaders shared other island states' aversion to French nuclear testing and colonialism and refused a French warship visit in 1986; its prime minister also signed the South Pacific Nuclear Free Zone Treaty and criticised US chemical-weapons disposal at Johnston Atoll. Tuvalu was especially concerned with regional environmental cooperation in assessing the 'greenhouse effect' since, if the more alarmist forecasts came true, Tuvalu and most of neighbouring Kiribati would disappear beneath the rising sea level

116   THE SOUTH PACIFIC FOREIGN AFFAIRS HANDBOOK

within a generation. However, foreign policy issues were not a
concern for the majority of the population which lived at subsistence
level on the atolls outside Funafuti. The major concern of political
leaders and top officials was finding sources of income to under-
write government salaries, which generated half the GDP.

Tuvalu economic affairs

The Fourth Development Plan 1988–91 called for 'the strengthening
and diversification of the economy through the encouragement of
co-operative and private sector development and the greater independence of income-generating sectors' (Australia Government
1990b, p. 4). However, the realisation of this goal was constrained
by the basic character of the country: small land area with low
fertility and little rainfall, narrow resource and capital base, dispersed population, growing pressure on scarce land, small domestic
market, and remoteness from world markets and tourist routes.
Substantial tourism earnings could not be expected, and exporting
would be difficult in spite of free access to markets through the
South Pacific Regional Trade and Economic Cooperation Agreement, the Lome Convention and provisions by the General Agreement on Tariffs and Trade (GATT) for tariff relief for LDCs.
  Tuvalu's primary export earners in 1983 were stamps
(A$587 000), fish (A$250 000) and copra (A$61 000), but stamp
and fish sales declined in subsequent years (Douglas and Douglas
1989, p. 580; *Far East and Australasia* 1989, p. 814). Imports,
mainly of food, machinery, fuel and manufactured goods, mainly
from Australia, exceeded exports by a factor of ten or more. In
1985, for example, exports earned A$526 000 but imports cost
A$4 126 000 (Australia Government 1990b, p. 20). The gap was
filled by fishing fees, remittances, aid and investment income.
  In 1979 the government negotiated a Treaty of Friendship whereby
the United States renounced claims to four southern atolls but
required consultation if any outside government was to use them.
This secured Tuvalu's EEZ of 900 000 square kilometres and a
potential source of income from fish and seabed minerals (Teiwaki
1988b, chapter 6). Subsequently, fishing agreements were negotiated
with Taiwan, South Korea, Japan and the United States, which
earned the government A$516 617 in access fees in 1985 and
A$384 000 in 1986 (Douglas and Douglas 1989, p. 579). Tuvalu
signed the US–South Pacific Regional Fishing Agreement of 1987
and hopes to realise increased income from fees paid by the United
States through the Forum Fisheries Agency. Tuvalu also hopes to
follow Cook Islands and Fiji in cultivating and exporting trochus

shells and shellfish meat, and in 1989 persuaded the Royal New Zealand Air Force to seed several lagoons by airdrop.

In 1985 remittances from several hundred Tuvaluans working in the phosphate mines of Nauru or aboard British or German ships were estimated at A$830 000, well in excess of merchandise export earnings (Fisk and Mellor 1986, p. 56). The Tuvalu Maritime School, set up by the new government in 1979, had placed more than 170 graduates on foreign ships by 1989 and was recognised as a major economic asset by donors such as Australia and New Zealand (New Zealand Government 1989, p. 7).

The single largest source of overseas funds is aid. Tuvalu is one of the world's most aid-dependent economies. In 1985 aid receipts were equivalent in value to 91 per cent of the GDP and 96 per cent of government expenditure. Leading donors were Britain focusing on the secondment of experts and officers after the end of budgetary support in 1986, New Zealand focusing on health and human resources, Australia focusing on education and transportation infra-structure, and Japan concentrating on fisheries-related projects. Con-tributions in 1987 are shown in Table 7.4. Japan normally ranks a strong fourth place but diverted its aid to the Tuvalu Trust Fund in 1987.

An innovation that may be emulated by other island states is the Tuvalu Trust Fund. The price of Tuvalu's separation from Kiribati in 1975 was the surrender of claims to the Phosphate Reserve Fund, which has earned tens of millions of dollars of interest for Kiribati in succeeding years. To compensate Tuvalu, Britain provided budg-etary support, but this required time-consuming and irritating annual

Table 7.4 Tuvalu aid donors and receipts, 1987

Donor	A$000	%
Britain	3 723	50.1
New Zealand	1 451	19.5
Australia	863	11.6
United States	214	2.9
Canada	74	1.0
Japan	25	0.3
United Nations Development Programme	558	7.5
European Community	120	1.6
Others[a]	410	5.5
Total	7 438	100.0

a Food and Agriculture Organization, World Health Organization, United Nations Fund for Population Activities.

Source: Australia Government 1990b, p. 21.

negotiation and was viewed as demeaning charity by Tuvalu leaders. The government asked Britain, then Australia and New Zealand—the three members of the British Phosphate Commission, which had exploited Banaba Island—for a lump sum payment to pay off growing debts and make Tuvalu solvent. The novelty of the concept and reluctance to set a precedent of paying for colonial damages delayed its acceptance. The Tuvalu government persisted and refined the concept as an alternative that would simplify the annual aid negotiations and reduce administrative overheads. Australia commissioned a study in 1986, which showed its viability (Fisk and Mellor 1986). After further refinement by UNDP experts, the concept was accepted and the governments of Tuvalu, Britain, Australia and New Zealand signed an agreement establishing the International Trust Fund for Tuvalu. Britain contributed A$8 499 980, Australia A$8 000 000, New Zealand A$8 281 791, Japan A$694 830 and South Korea A$30 000 (Tuvalu Government 1990, p. 12). Donor and recipient governments formed a board, and Westpac Investment Management Pty Ltd, Sydney, was appointed manager. In 1990 the government of Tuvalu received in interest A$1 351 000—an amount comparable to fishing fees plus remittances.

8   Northern Marianas, Guam, American Samoa

The Mariana, Caroline and Marshall archipelagos were settled over 3000 years ago, probably by migrant Southeast Asian peoples. Population movements, intermarriage, trade and warfare led to ethnic characteristics and cultural patterns now recognised as Micronesian. However, the scattered island and atoll environment dictated the evolution of a multiplicity of languages and small self-sufficient social–political groupings led by local chiefs. Save for the relatively large island of Guam, colonised by Spain in 1668, European intrusion was sporadic, late and superficial in impact because of isolation from population, resource and trade centres. Spanish explorers entered the region in the sixteenth century and dominated the Marianas, and they were followed by infrequent British and Russian explorers in the next two centuries. In 1817 the Russian von Kotzebue surveyed the Marshall Islands, and in 1824 and 1828 the Frenchman Duperrey and the Russian Lütke surveyed the Caroline Islands, opening the way to more frequent visits by whalers, traders and evangelists, many from the United States, by mid century.

Colonialism

By the 1860s German traders had established posts, and in 1878 Germany negotiated with Jaluit chiefs for a coaling station and sent a consul. With Britain's concurrence in return for a free hand elsewhere, Germany in 1886 declared a protectorate over the Marshall Islands. Spain, whose galleons transited the region on the trade route between the Philippines and the Americas, responded by reasserting longstanding claims, occupying Pohnpei and Yap and sponsoring the establishment of Catholic missions elsewhere in the Caroline Islands. After losing the Philippines in the Spanish–American War, Spain sold its claims and possessions to Germany in 1899. Guam became a US possession. Germany introduced improvements in sanitation and some wage labour in coconut plantations and phosphate mines. The Spanish and the Germans met some local resistance, which was characteristic of relations between Micronesians and outsiders; the history of the archipelagos features a number of massacres of European and, later, Japanese visitors.

The imperial government of Japan, whose subjects began trading in Truk in 1887, took increasing interest in the island chains stretching southwards through the Bonin and Mariana islands to the Carolines and Marshalls, and in 1914 declared war on Germany and quickly occupied all its insular possessions (Peattie 1988, pp. 16–41). Japan secured a League of Nations mandate for the Mariana, Caroline and Marshall islands in 1921 and thereafter administered them as part of its empire, sending numerous administrators and migrants, improving the infrastructure, recruiting local labour, and developing the mining, copra, palm oil, tapioca and fishing industries for export to Japan.

World War II ended in US occupation, and then the administration of all Japanese Micronesian islands as the Trust Territory of the Pacific Islands under United Nations supervision from 1947. The trust territory was designated a strategic trust, under the supervision of the United Nations Security Council, as urged by the United States in accordance with articles 82 and 83 of the United Nations Charter. This was in contrast to the Papua New Guinea and Western Samoa trusts, which were placed under Trusteeship Council supervision (Smith and Pugh, p. 1991). Until 1952 the trust territory was under the jurisdiction of the US Navy and administered from Hawaii. It was then transferred to the US Department of the Interior save the Marianas, which remained under navy jurisdiction until 1962. Stretching from the International Date Line nearly to the Philippines, and from the equator to the Tropic of Cancer, this region of over 2000 islands in 3 million square miles (7.8 million square kilometres) of ocean was regarded legally as a single entity but divided into six administrative districts including Marshall Islands, Northern Mariana Islands, and four Caroline districts including Palau, Yap, Truk and Pohnpei. Kosrae was given district status in 1977. Guam, never part of the trust territory, was made an unincorporated territory of the United States in 1950, under Department of the Interior jurisdiction.

Self-government

Neither the Spanish nor German nor Japanese administration allowed participation by the island inhabitants. Chiefs in villages and outlying islands continued in their traditional roles while foreign administrators managed affairs in the larger island centres and economic enterprises. Each outside power monopolised and guided economic activity for its own benefit. Education was minimal and largely conducted by religious schools. US occupation altered this pattern by funding education and facilitating political participation. However, economic development was neglected. The 1947 Trusteeship Agreement undertaking to 'promote the economic advancement and self-sufficiency of the inhabitants' was honoured inasmuch as the United States established basic services and amenities, but aid remained minimal, US private enterprise desultory and foreign enterprise excluded for security reasons. The objective of the navy was to secure forward bases and surrounding seas and to facilitate nuclear testing; the Department of the Interior's objective was to discharge its unfamiliar duties with as little cost or controversy as possible. The period was characterised as one of 'benign neglect' (McHenry 1975).

Nevertheless, the US pledge in the Trusteeship Agreement to 'foster development of political institutions' and 'promote self-government or independence' was honoured, although within narrow limits justified by the qualifying phrases 'as are suited to the trust territory' and 'as may be appropriate to the particular circumstances', referring to the alleged political inexperience of the inhabitants (Ranney 1985, p. 10). District legislatures were established in Palau in 1947, in Marshall Islands in 1950, in the Caroline districts in 1957–59 and in the Marianas in 1963, empowered to conduct local affairs and advise on external matters.

The United Nations General Assembly Resolutions 1514 and 1541 on Decolonisation in 1960, and a critical report by a United Nations mission in 1961, galvanised the district legislatures to appoint commissions to negotiate with the United States over their future status. The Kennedy administration responded with a dual policy of facilitating self-government and winning Micronesian allegiance (Weisgall 1985, pp. 47–8). The federal government increased the trust territory budget from US$5 million in 1960 to US$15 million in 1963 and further to US$100 million by the late 1970s, initiated or expanded programmes in education, health, community development, food subsidies and elderly housing and 150 other programmes, and introduced the Peace Corps. In 1964 a territory-wide Congress of Micronesia was elected and took office in 1965. It provided a forum for self-expression and experience that encouraged not consensus on merger with the United States as expected, but district level nationalism and separatism. In 1969 the congress asserted that sovereignty resided in the people of Micronesia and their governments and that they had the right to self-determination under their own constitutions. The United States offered territorial status, then commonwealth status modelled on the Puerto Rico precedent, to each district government. The governments of Palau, Yap, Truk, Pohnpei, Kosrae and Marshall Islands rejected the overtures and pursued instead the option of free association; their subsequent political evolution and foreign policies will be described in the next chapter.

Northern Mariana Islands

The Northern Marianas district government, anxious to retain the privilege of migration to Guam and the United States and to retain other economic benefits including the US military presence, responded favourably. In 1975, observed by United Nations representatives, 78 per cent of voters approved the Covenant to Establish a Commonwealth of the Northern Mariana Islands in Political Union with the United States of America (Ranney 1985, p. 17). In 1978 the interim commonwealth constitution established an elected bicameral legislature and a popularly elected governor with full powers of internal self-government. Politics since then has been free and lively; recent issues have included tax and land laws, corruption, a proposed casino, relationships with the US Department of Defense, Filipino and Korean guest workers, and control over the 200 mile (332 kilometre) Exclusive Economic Zone (EEZ) (McPhetres 1988).

Responsibility for foreign affairs and defence were vested in the United States, and the judiciary was placed under US district-court jurisdiction. All land is locally owned, but the Department of Defense has long term leases in Saipan and Tinian; these have been decried by island nationalists. US federal law applies unless changed by the commonwealth legislature. Northern Mariana Islands has been compared to one of the 50 states in its semi-autonomous relationship to the federal government. In December 1990 the United Nations Security Council formally ended the trusteeship of the Northern Marianas, whereupon the covenant and the constitution became fully effective in international law and the inhabitants became full citizens of the United States.

The primary sources of Northern Marianas government revenue are covenant funds, federal programme funds and internal revenue. In 1986 direct covenant grants for government operations and capital improvements totalled US$27.7 million (Douglas and Douglas 1989, p. 407–8). Federal programme grants from fifteen departments and agencies came to about US$15 million, and there were additional benefits from Medicaid, Food Stamps and the Needy Families Food Program. Locally raised revenue from taxation, fees and utilities earnings was US$15.7 million, or about a quarter of total revenues; the other three-quarters came from Washington. Residents pay no income tax to the federal government. Mean household income is over US$10 000. The three commercial banks are the Bank of Guam, the Bank of Hawaii and the California First Bank and the currency is the US dollar.

Northern Marianas has no department of foreign affairs, but its Commerce and Labour Department encourages investment from overseas, particularly from Japan, and it maintains liaison and trade offices in Guam, Honolulu and Washington. Primary air links are via Continental Air Lines and Japan Air Lines, with secondary links via Air Micronesia and Air Nauru. Tourism is regarded as particularly promising to attract investment and generate local revenue and jobs. In 1987, 79 per cent of visitors came from Japan, 17 per cent from the United States and 4 per cent from elsewhere, for a total of 194 242—the third-highest figure for Pacific island countries. (South Pacific Commission 1989a, p. 25). Tourism rose to 333 277 arrivals by 1990 and was estimated to provide one-fifth of government revenue and to generate one-half of the gross domestic product (GDP) (North 1991, pp. 13, 15).

Northern Marianas in 1985 imported 61.8 per cent of its needs—mainly processed foods, building materials, fuel and consumer goods—from the United States, 23.5 per cent from Japan, 2.9 per cent from Australia and 11.7 per cent from other countries (Douglas and Douglas 1989, pp. 408–9). It exported fresh foods to Guam worth about a quarter of the value of imports. Growing rapidly is the garment assembly industry, capitalised by Japan and worked by guest labourers from neighbouring Micronesian states, who make up a large proportion of the Northern Marianas population (North 1991, pp. 13, 18). Northern Mariana Islands has some potential for exploitation of its EEZ, but domestic fishing remains undeveloped and most fishing is done by Japanese and South Korean vessels under licence. Fish cold storage and transshipment services for US tunaboats are growing steadily.

Guam

This unincorporated territory of 120 500 predominantly Chamorro inhabitants lagged relative to the surrounding trust territory in political rights and self-government. Petitions for full citizenship were submitted by Chamorro leaders in 1925, 1933 and 1936, but citizenship was not achieved until the passage of the Guam Organic Act 1950 (Commission on Self-Determination 1988, p. 6). Until 1962 movement into and out of Guam, by Guamanians and Mariana islanders as well as mainland Americans and foreigners, was restricted by the US Navy. A locally drafted constitution in 1969 was ignored by Washington, and a second constitution was rejected in a plebiscite because it was irrelevant to local aspirations. In 1971 a locally elected governor was installed, and in 1972 a Guamanian delegate to the US House of Representatives was elected. In the Legislature elected in 1986 there were thirteen democrats and eight republicans. The Legislature has jurisdiction over local matters (subject to the governor's veto) and has provided experience, confidence and a public forum to a new generation of local political leaders. A local court system is headed by the Guam Federal Court and ultimately the US Supreme Court in Washington; federal law applies unless modified by the Guam Legislature.

However, the development of governing institutions has been secondary to the question of Guam's ultimate status. A plebiscite in 1977 rejected independence. A plebiscite in 1982 found free association chosen by 4 per cent, incorporation chosen by 5 per cent, and the status quo supported by 10 per cent, so none of these was a serious option. The leading two options were tested in a second plebiscite in 1982, and it was found that commonwealth status was supported by 73 per cent, compared with 27 per cent support for statehood. A further poll in 1988 showed a strong desire for Chamorro self-determination.

Governor Joseph Ada led the Guam Commission on Self Determination to Washington for talks in February 1991, where he presented the concept of 'mutual consent'. This concept would entrench the proposed Guam Commonwealth Act, once passed by the US Congress, much as the Cook Islands Constitution Act and Niue Constitution Act are beyond the legal power of New Zealand to alter without the consent of the Cook Islands or Niue government. Ada further proposed that Guam be empowered to admit guest workers as Northern Marianas has done, thus serving the growing tourist and textile industries and keeping wage costs down, without giving the immigrants any rights to citizenship. Guam also wants easier access to the US Supreme Court, assistance in setting up trade promotion offices overseas and taking advantage of US tax regulations, and more funds for Guam's poor (*Pacific Islands Monthly* March 1991b, pp. 52–3). Guam has also claimed Wake Island, a US possession claimed by Marshall Islands as well.

Federal officials are sceptical about the wisdom of granting these requests until the administration and courts of Guam gain more experience and immigration policies can be rationalised. If negotiations are protracted, which seems likely, nationalism and impatience among Guamanians will grow, and the intergovernmental relationship will become strained.

The financial resources of the Guam government derive largely from the United States. Federal subsidies, grants and programmes comprised 21 per cent of direct government revenue in the mid 1980s. Federal income taxes collected in Guam from federal employees comprised another 15 per cent of revenues. Additional revenues were derived from fees and the indirect taxation of expenditures by US military personnel and their dependents, who numbered 23 355 in 1987 (Douglas and Douglas 1989, pp. 211–13). The military employed about 20 per cent of the local workforce, the federal government another 17 per cent, and the government of Guam 24 per cent.

Three-fifths of Guam's export earnings are from transshipments from the United States to neighbouring Northern Marianas and Federated States of Micronesia, and another fifth is from transshipments to US bases in Asia. Domestic exports are mainly fish to the mainland United States, Japan and Hong Kong. Garment assembly is a growing industry with prospects for exports to markets in the US mainland, Japan and Australia, if local content can be raised to 50 per cent and costs kept down by the importation of cheap labour. Imports exceed exports in value more than 10 to 1; they are purchased mainly from Saudi Arabia (fuel), the United States (food), and Japan and Hong Kong (manufactured goods), with smaller quantities from Taiwan, the Philippines, Australia and New Zealand. Export of services in the form of tourism is a major and still growing earner. In 1987 Guam received the highest number of visitors, 483 954, of any island country, of which 85 per cent were from Japan, 6 per cent from the United States, 5 per cent from other Micronesian countries, and 3 per cent from other Asian and European countries (South Pacific Commission 1989a, p. 25). Tourists spent an estimated US$373 million in Guam in 1988—a sum equivalent to one-half of the import bill or eight times the value of direct US subsidies (North 1991, p. 13). Tourism has attracted Japanese investment in hotels, golf courses and other amenities, but it has also pushed up the cost of labour and land.

Guam enjoys some attributes of a semi-autonomous state. It trades with, and solicits investment and tourism from neighbouring states. It hosts foreign diplomatic missions from Japan, Korea, Taiwan, the Philippines, Nauru, Northern Marianas, Federated States of Micronesia and Palau. Yet it labours under restraints that local leaders find onerous and will attempt to remove as Guam moves to commonwealth status. Among the objectives likely to be sought by Guam's government in its negotiations with the United States are:

- curtailment of special rights enjoyed by US servicemen and emergency powers vested in US commanders;
- access to lands now leased by the Department of Defense such as Agana Naval Air Station;
- jurisdiction over the resources of the 200 mile (332 kilometre) EEZ;
- ability to grant landing and shipping rights to non-US air and sea carriers;
- control over immigration from the US mainland and from neighbouring island countries;
- liberalised access to the US mainland market; and
- fewer restrictions on trade with and investment from Asian countries (Taitano 1988, p. 159–60).

However, in Washington's view these various demands are potentially incompatible with each other and with demands for commonwealth or free association status, and the government of Guam will face hard choices regarding which economic privileges to forgo in order to gain greater political autonomy.

American Samoa

Ceded to the United States by Tutuila and Manua chiefs in 1900–04, American Samoa was administered by the US Navy until 1951, whereupon it was transferred to the Department of the Interior and the navy presence phased out. Only a coastguard station remains. In 1960 a convention of Samoan leaders approved a constitution setting up a territorial legislature, granting a bill of rights and entrenching federal government policy 'to protect persons of Samoan ancestry against alienation of their lands and the destruction of the Samoan way of life' (Douglas and Douglas 1989, p. 27). The governor and the House of Representatives are popularly elected, and the Senate is chosen by the *matai* (chiefs); together they are empowered to make laws for the territory subject to federal law, US Supreme Court rulings and decisions of the Secretary of the Interior ('American Samoa' 1986). A non-voting representative is elected to sit in the US Congress in Washington.

American Samoans are 'US nationals'; that is, they have unrestricted entry into the mainland United States but cannot vote for the president or other federal candidates until they qualify for US citizenship by serving in the US armed forces or meeting residence and other qualifications. It is estimated that 85 000 Samoans were living in Hawaii and the West Coast as compared with only 36 260 living in American Samoa in 1986 (Douglas and Douglas 1989, p. 11).

The per capital income of American Samoans is one of the highest in the South Pacific as a result of income from remittances sent by emigrants working abroad and federal government programme expenditures in the territory. The territorial government derived only 49 per cent of its revenues from local sources in 1984; of the balance, half came from the Department of the Interior, and the other half came from other US agencies in the form of subsidies, grants and other benefit programmes (Douglas and Douglas 1989, p. 22). Imposition of a 5 per cent import tax raised the proportion of local revenue to over 50 per cent in 1991.

Twenty per cent of tax revenues and 90 per cent of export earnings are derived from the operations of the Star-Kist and Van Camp canneries at Pago Pago. The canneries employed 27 per cent of the labour force in 1985, a fifth of whom were migrant workers from Western Samoa and other island countries (Schug 1987, pp. 195, 199). Exports earned A$373.1 million and imports cost A$460.7 million in 1986—a creditable near-balance compared with many other island countries (South Pacific Commission 1989a, p. 15). Exports are directed to the United States and Japan; imports come from the United States, Japan, Western Samoa and New Zealand.

Tourism is a smaller but significant earner. Visitors in 1987 totalled 45 127, putting American Samoa third in the South Pacific behind Guam and Northern Marianas on a visitor-per-capita basis. However, the bulk of the visitors came from Western Samoa, and only 17 per cent from the United States, 6 per cent from New Zealand and 10 per cent from other countries. This, plus the fact that 53 per cent of visitors cited reasons other than business or pleasure for visiting, suggests that most visitors were not tourists but Samoans visiting relatives; so earnings from tourism were not proportionate to the number of visitors (South Pacific Commission 1989a, pp. 25–6).

The elected governor, Peter Tali Coleman, in 1991 encouraged a review of constitutional links with the United States. Coleman's immediate objectives were to insulate American Samoa from Secretary of the Interior interference in legislation, appropriation, spending and appointments, and to explore the possibility of membership in regional bodies such as the South Pacific Forum. The long term objective was to negotiate a commonwealth status similar to Northern Marianas with additional freedoms and privileges similar to those enjoyed by Cook Islands in its relationship with New Zealand (Ritova 1991, p. 31). Persuading the US federal government to maintain protection, subsidies and immigration privileges while surrendering the power to supervise American Samoan administration and expenditures is likely to engage the energies of the American Samoa territorial government for some years to come.

9 Marshall Islands, Federated States of Micronesia, Palau

In 1978 the voters of Marshall Islands and Palau rejected a proposed Micronesian constitution providing for commonwealth status for the Trust Territory of the Pacific Islands. Their governments pressed the United States for an alternative arrangement, based on the concept of free association. This arrangement had been pioneered by Cook Islands and Niue in their post-colonial relationships with New Zealand, as described in Chapter 5. It fulfilled the guidelines laid down by the United Nations Charter and Resolutions 1514 and 1541 of 1960 as interpreted by the Trusteeship Council and the Special Committee on Decolonisation (Committee of Twenty-four), and was working to the satisfaction of all governments concerned.

American free association

The Marshall and Micronesian governments sought a similar middle ground that avoided US federal government rights of eminent domain to requisition land for defence purposes as entailed by commonwealth status on the one hand, and separation and loss of economic benefits on the other, as shown in Table 9.1. Free association permitted self-government, including control over law and land and the autonomous conduct of foreign affairs. But it also entailed an obligation to avoid foreign policy initiatives contrary to US interests as determined by joint consultations, and assigned responsibility for defence to the federal government. The Marshall

Table 9.1 Comparison of commonwealth status, free association and independence

Commonwealth	Free association	Independence
Political		
Micronesia has local government but is under the US Constitution, Congress and law forever. The United States conducts foreign policy. Micronesians are US citizens and have non-voting congressmen in Washington.	Micronesia is self-governing under its own constitution and conducts its own foreign policy within the limits of US interests. Micronesians can work in the United States but not become citizens without qualifying. Micronesia can leave the free association at any time.	Micronesia is self-governing and independent under its own constitution and conducts its own foreign policy without limitations. Micronesians must apply for visas and permits to work in the United States.
Economic		
Micronesia becomes part of the US economy, which means no tariff barriers, more income, eligibility for federal programmes, inflation adjusted, like any US state.	Micronesia can expect long-term US aid and rent for lands and services but no guarantees, and will be outside tariff and customs barriers.	Micronesia can request aid from the United States but ultimately must find its own sources of revenue. It will be outside tariff and customs barriers.
Military		
The United States has full defence authority, including the right to take land and involve Micronesians in military service and war.	The United States conducts defence, has the right to deny outside military activity in perpetuity and has base rights for 15 years (50 years in Palau), renewable. Land for bases cannot be seized.	Micronesia must defend itself. A mutual security treaty with the United States in exchange for base and denial rights is optional. Land cannot be seized.

Source: Adapted from *Annexe to report of UN observers to FSM plebiscite* in 1983, reproduced in Ranney and Penniman 1985, pp. 62–3.

Islands and Micronesian governments were obliged to grant the United States rights to existing bases for at least 15 years with the expectation that the period would be extended by mutual agreement. They also granted the United States the right to foreclose access to their territory by the military forces of any other country, popularly called the 'defense veto' or the 'right of strategic denial'.

In the Statement of Agreed Principles for Free Association done at Hilo, Hawaii in 1978, the Marshall Islands and Micronesian governments and the United States concurred on the broad terms of free association and for the next 4 years concentrated on specific provisions. The complexity of the issues involved was indicated by the length of each draft Compact of Free Association, over 200 pages, and the number and scope of titles, including Governmental Relations, Economic Relations, Security and Defense Relations, General Provisions, and Related Agreements covering telecommunications, marine sovereignty, law enforcement and extradition, federal programmes and services, property transfer, military operating rights and status of forces (Ranney and Penniman 1985, pp. 19–21). The Marshall Islands and Palau district governments each wanted specific assurances of limits on and payments for US military activities and bases in their territories, and insisted on separate talks with the United States. The district governments of Pohnpei, Truk and Yap, now joined by a new district government of Kosrae, coalesced into a third negotiating partner, which become Federated States of Micronesia on adoption by the four districts of the Micronesian federal constitution in 1979. Thereafter negotiations for free association proceeded on three parallel but distinct tracks.

In 1982 a separate Compact of Free Association was signed by each of the three governments, and in 1983 the compacts were submitted to their people in plebiscites under the supervision of United Nations Trusteeship Council observers. Voters were asked to choose yes or no to the question 'Do you approve of the Compact of Free Association and its Related Agreements?' The yes vote was 58 per cent in Marshall Islands, 79 per cent in Federated States of Micronesia and 62 per cent in Palau. The United Nations Trusteeship Council endorsed the results and in 1986 approved a US decision to terminate the trusteeships of Marshall Islands and Federated States of Micronesia. The State Department established an Office of Freely Associated States Affairs and an interagency committee to deal with the new entities. In 1990 the United Nations Security Council, which had final jurisdiction over the Trust Territory of the Pacific Islands, dissolved the trust, ending the last impediment to the recognition of Marshall Islands and Federated States of Micronesia as independent states (Williams 1991a p. 10). Only Palau remained under Trusteeship Council supervision.

Republic of the Marshall Islands

The Republic of the Marshall Islands Constitution was drafted by the district government and ratified by the electorate in 1979. It established a 33 member parliament called the Nitijela, which elects a president from among its members (Douglas and Douglas 1989, p. 326). The first president was Amata Kabua, who was re-elected

132 THE SOUTH PACIFIC FOREIGN AFFAIRS HANDBOOK

in 1984 and 1988 and has dominated government policy making ever since. There are no political parties or organised opposition movements, although there is some rivalry between the Kwajalein area where the US military base generates national income, and the Jaluit area where the government spends the money on developing the capital, Majuro, and between both of these built-up areas and the outer islands (Johnson 1988, p. 81).

When Marshall Islands achieved independence in free association with the United States in 1986, a high priority was securing diplomatic recognition and international organisation membership so as to diversify relations away from the United States. The new government soon established diplomatic relations with Federated States of Micronesia, Kiribati, Papua New Guinea, Fiji, Australia and New Zealand. In 1988 it refused to renew Japanese tuna-fishing licences or to admit Filipinos until the Japanese and Philippines governments recognised Marshall Islands as an independent state. The following year the government declined an offer of diplomatic links with the People's Republic of China, preferring to maintain an informal but cordial relationship with the Republic of China (Taiwan). In 1990 Marshall Islands and the United States set up embassies in each other's capital. Marshall Islands has no other diplomatic post abroad but relies on contacts made in travels by the president, the Minister of Foreign Affairs and the officers of the small Ministry of Foreign Affairs. The United States performs diplomatic and consular services on request. Marshall Islands joined the South Pacific Commission in 1983, the South Pacific Forum in 1986, and affiliated agencies of the forum including the Forum Fisheries Agency and the Pacific Forum Line in subsequent years. In 1990 it became a member of the Asian Development Bank (ADB) and in 1991 it took a seat in the United Nations General Assembly. It is also a signatory of the South Pacific Regional Trade and Economic Cooperation Agreement.

Marshall Islands revenue is still derived mainly from the United States. The Compact of Free Assocation provides for annual aid of US$30 million, annual rent for the Kwajalein missile-testing base of an estimated US$5.7 million, and project aid of US$80 million spread over a number of years (*Far East and Australasia* 1989, p. 765). Grants from the United States provided 62.4 per cent of budgeted revenue in 1984, and taxes and fees on the estimated 3000 US personnel at Kwajalein provided a significant portion of locally raised revenue (Douglas and Douglas 1989, p. 332). In addition the United States established a trust fund of US$150 million, the interest of which is to meet claims by Marshallese suffering from the effects of nuclear weapons tests in Bikini, Eniwetok, Rongelap and Utirik in 1946–58, and a total of US$62 million has been spent or is pledged to resettle the inhabitants and decontaminate the atolls over a period of years. Nevertheless, the volume of individual and government claims exceeds the funds promised by the United States, and Marshall Islands plaintiffs continue to press for more.

Frictions with the United States continue also over the relocation of Kwajalein residents to Ebeye Island to clear the atoll for missile splashdowns. Now 10 000 Marshallese are crowded into a 33 hectare islet with insufficient fresh water, poor sewerage and meagre public facilities, and workers have to commute to Kwajalein where US personnel live in comparative spaciousness. US aid programmes are addressing some of Ebeye's problems, but negotiations are time-consuming and irritating, and progress is slow. Land disputes may intensify as population pressure grows (Johnson 1986). Other issues on which Marshall Islands has been at odds with the United States were the South Pacific Nuclear Free Zone Treaty of 1986, the negotiations over the South Pacific Regional Fishing Treaty of 1987, the Johnston Atoll chemical-disposal controversy of 1990 and the claim to Wake Island.

An alternative source of revenue was royalties charged to Japanese tuna-fishing boats, but this was US$842 000 or only 2.8 per cent of government income in 1984, with limited prospects for increase. An aid programme has been established by Japan, which has funded a US$4.5 million dock at Uliga and a causeway to join Ebeye and Kwajalein. Australia has donated a US$12 million Pacific patrol boat and provided crew training and maintenance services for it, and New Zealand has made study and training awards (*Micronesian Investment Quarterly* 1990b, p. 3). Taiwan and South Korea are likely donors in future. A scheme introduced in 1989, to sell passports that would permit Asian businessmen entry into the United States for US$250 000 each, stalled for lack of customers. Negotiations with a US firm to sell garbage-dumping privileges in shallow atoll lagoons were halted after criticism by environmentalists, Nitijela opposition figures and neighbouring governments. Tourism promotion via Continental Air Micronesia and Airline of the Marshall Islands is under study, but distance, isolation and the lack of attractive facilities make this prospect dim. More promising are fees from the Ship Registry, which had sixteen ships totalling 3.6 million tons (3.7 million tonnes) under the Marshall Islands flag by 1990 (*Micronesian Investment Quarterly* 1990a, p. 3). Exports remain restricted to coconut products sold to Micronesian neighbours and the United States. The import bill for goods from the United States, Guam, Japan and Australia was more than ten times the export earnings in 1986.

Federated States of Micronesia

The locally drafted and ratified constitution of 1979 established Federated States of Micronesia (FSM) as a sovereign self-governing federation of four constituent states (Burdick 1988). Its federal legislature, the National Congress, elects a president, who until 1991 was John R. Haglelgam and thereafter Bailey Olter. There are no political parties and legislators tend to vote for the interests of their states. The Department of External Affairs advises the president, who sets the pace in foreign policy. The four state governments of Yap, Truk (officially Chuuk), Pohnpei and Kosrae also have limited powers to make external contacts, particularly to solicit trade, investment and tourism and to engage in limited-liability joint ventures.

Foreign policy was summed up by a FSM official as follows: 'we plan to concentrate on building strong relationships with our Pacific neighbours, pursuing every opportunity bilaterally and multilaterally to maximise our collective economic strength. Such strength is already apparent in the fisheries area and it can be developed in other areas as well' (Rubinstein 1988, p. 19). FSM signed the Law of the Sea Convention and joined the Nauru Group of fishing nations in 1982 and became an active member of the Forum Fisheries Agency the following year. Vigorous negotiations with the American Tunaboat Association and with Japanese, Taiwanese and South Korean fishing consortia followed. It joined the South Pacific Commission in 1983 and the South Pacific Forum and its affiliated agencies in 1987 and hosted the Twenty-first South Pacific Forum in 1991. FSM took especial interest in the South Pacific Regional Environmental Programme (SPREP) and in the implications for its atolls of the 'greenhouse effect' and of the disposal of nuclear and toxic waste in the South Pacific. It also joined the Economic and Social Commission for Asia and the Pacific (ESCAP), the United Nations Fund for Population Activities (UNFPA), the Food and Agriculture Organization (FAO), the International Labour Organization (ILO), the United Nations Educational, Scientific and Cultural Organization (UNESCO), the World Health Organization (WHO) and the International Civil Aviation Organization, and sought aid from ADB, the International Monetary Fund (IMF) and the United Nations Development Programme (UNDP). It participated in twenty other organisations specialising in topics ranging from arts, broadcasting and coconuts to shipping, tourism and women. In 1991 FSM was seated in the United Nations General Assembly.

Regarding bilateral relations, in 1990 President Haglelgam in his state-of-the-nation address noted that 'diplomatic recognition is an important ingredient of self-government and achieving it has not always been easy. It is much more difficult in our case because of the complex nature of our former political status and the refusal of some members of the international community to recognize the valid expression of self-determination of our people' (Federated States of Micronesia Government 1990a, p. 2). In the 5 years following the US Senate ratification of the Compact of Free Association in 1986, the FSM government established diplomatic relations with eighteen states including Marshall Islands, Vanuatu, Nauru, Papua New Guinea, Fiji, Tonga, Western Samoa, Israel, Australia, New Zealand, the Philippines and, in contrast to neighbouring Marshall Islands, the People's Republic of China. Full recognition by some European states was delayed until the United Nations Security Council terminated the trust in 1990. FSM has not sought relations with the Soviet Union because that country was thought to have delayed the security council decision to terminate the trust and because the Micronesians are strongly Catholic and suspicious of communism. The United States and Australia have ambassadors in Kolonia, and FSM has ambassadors in Washington, Tokyo and Suva and consuls in Guam and Honolulu, who deal with economic and consular matters. The Washington ambassador is accredited to the United Nations and several European states, and the Tokyo ambassador to several Asian states. The US Department of State provides additional diplomatic and consular services in its posts around the world and shares intelligence.

The primary source of income is the United States. From 1986 to 1991 FSM received US$60 million in grants annually (Rubinstein 1988, p. 18). Under the compact formula this was to reduce to US$56 million annually for the next 5 years and to US$40 million annually for the final 5 years to 2001. FSM also receives US cooperation in a variety of functions including weather reporting, air surveillance, satellite communications, and police and customs intelligence. Half of the federal programmes were to cease in 1986, but the following are to continue for the 15 year transition period: Farmers' Home Administration housing loans, Public Health Services block grants, National Park Service grants, Federal Emergency Management Agency disaster assistance, and Small Business Administration loans. FSM leaders have lobbied the US Congress to reinstate some of the discontinued federal programmes, with some success in the field of education, and it is likely that US aid and programmes will continue even beyond the 15 year transition period.

Other sources of income have been aid from: Japan for roads and fishing equipment, for example a US$4.5 million grant for fisheries development signed in 1989 and the Yap Harbour extension in 1990 (Federated States of Micronesia Government 1989, p. 5 and 1990c, p. 4); Australia in the form of two Pacific patrol boats and supporting training and maintenance services to police the fishing waters of the Exclusive Economic Zone (EEZ); and New Zealand in the form of air surveillance and education grants. The People's Republic of China has offered the development of power generators, canneries and light manufacturing facilities (Federated States of Micronesia Government 1987, p. 3). Earnings from fishing royalties totalled US$3.2 million in 1983. This compared well with aid receipts of US$1.2 million and earnings from copra exports, mainly to Japan, of US$1.3 million in that year (Rubinstein 1988, *passim*). There is some scope for further earnings from the export of timber, fish and seabed minerals, but these remain undeveloped. The United States, Australia and New Zealand have granted FSM products virtually unrestricted tariff-free access, but the economy is geared more to import substitution than to export production. FSM hopes to raise income from tourism by developing such attractions as the Truk lagoon in which 60 sunken Japanese warships lie.

The main foreign policy issue is whether to press the United States for more aid and protection, favoured by Truk state leaders, or to take a more independent stance, favoured by Pohnpei leaders. The US option still generates frictions over financial dependency, bureaucratic restrictions, trade and fishing disagreements, and nuclear and chemical weapons anxiety. The independence option could lead to a stance similar to that of Palau and Vanuatu and thus to debate over US ship visits, decline of income from the United States, and controversy over obligations to Japan, the Soviet Union, France or Taiwan—all countries with which FSM has had disagreements. FSM's strong stance against nuclear and chemical dumping has brought it into conflict with Japan and the United States, and its opposition to toxic waste disposal in nearby atolls has generated friction with neighbouring Marshall Islands. Separatist tendencies in Pohnpei and in outlying islands of Truk state, and divergent overseas economic contacts by the state governments, raise the possibilities of incoherence of foreign policy and, if disorder results, decline of attractiveness to investors and tourists and temptations to exploitation by swindlers, gangsters and drug traffickers.

Palau

The Palau district drafted and ratified its own constitution in 1979–81. Palau (officially Belau) became a self-governing republic with a popularly elected president and a bicameral legislature comprised of the House of Delegates and the Senate. The Palau Constitution in article II, section 3 and in article XIII, section 6 contains a unique clause:

> Harmful substances such as nuclear, chemical, gas, or biological weapons intended for use in warfare, nuclear power plants, and waste materials therefrom shall not be used, tested, or stored, or disposed of within the territorial jurisdiction of Belau without the express approval of not less than three-fourths of the votes cast in a referendum submitted on this specific purpose (Ranney and Penniman 1985, p. 28).

The voters approved the constitution in June 1979 by 92 per cent, but the results were invalidated by a court ruling (Boss 1987, p. 8; Clark 1987, p. 13). On the advice of the United States the district government removed the non-nuclear clauses and resubmitted the constitution to the voters in October 1979, but only 30 per cent approved. When the non-nuclear clauses were reinscribed, and the constitution was resubmitted in July 1980, 78 per cent of the voters approved it, and the world's first nuclear-free constitution came into effect on 1 January 1981.

Negotiations for free association proceeded parallel to those with Marshall Islands and Federated States of Micronesia, except that the United States requested a defence and base access period of 50 rather than 15 years because of Palau's strategic location near the Philippines and possession of a deepwater harbour at the capital, Koror. The United States secured 'contingency land-use rights' to four areas: a training area on the main island of Babeldoap; joint use of two airfields; and joint use of a portion of Koror Harbour. No bases were actually constructed, and to date there is no significant US military presence in spite of Palau's availability as an alternative to US military facilities in the Philippines. Palau agreed not to undertake foreign policies incompatible with the US defence responsibility and to allow the United States to foreclose any military activities of other states for 50 years. Palau was to receive a phased 15 year grant package worth approximately US$2.2 billion, adjusted upwards for inflation, similar to that of neighbouring Federated States of Micronesia. The Palau Compact of Association also contained section 314, which limited the routine deployment of nuclear weapons as follows:

> The government of the United States shall permit the presence of nuclear weapons in Palau only incident to transit and overflight, during a national emergency declared by the President of the United States, during a state of war declared by the Congress of the United States, in order to defend against an actual or impending armed attack on the United States or Palau, including a threat of such attack, or during a time of other military necessity as determined by the government of the United States (Ranney and Penniman 1985, p. 28).

The referendum on the compact was preceded by a lengthy period of political education by the government and also by considerably more controversy than in the neighbouring Micronesian states (Ranney and Penniman 1985; Quimby 1988, *passim*). Palauan opposition sprang from independence advocates, outlying district senators, women's and youth associations, and the churches, many of which had been active 4 years earlier in support of the nuclear-free constitution. The opposition was reinforced by funds, literature and campaigners from antinuclear groups based in Japan, Australia, Fiji, Honolulu and the mainland United States (Ranney and Penniman 1985, *passim*). In early 1983 the voters approved the Compact of Free Association by 62.1 per cent. A linked provision specifically to approve section 314 passed by 52.9 per cent. Neither achieved the 75 per cent approval required by the constitution, and the United States decided that the outcome was not satisfactory. The negotiators dropped section 314 from the compact and resubmitted it to the voters in 1984; 66.9 per cent approved it, but the United States did not accept the result because the required 75 per cent approval had not been achieved. While negotiations with Palau continued separately, President Reagan submitted the compacts with Marshall Islands and FSM to the US Senate, which ratified them in 1986.

To relieve voter anxiety over the nuclear question, a new section 314 was inserted into the draft Compact of Association, which stated that 'the United States shall not use, test, store, or dispose of nuclear, toxic, chemical, gas, or biological weapons intended for use in warfare' but at the same time asserted 'the right to operate nuclear capable or nuclear propelled vessels and aircraft within the jurisdiction of Palau without either confirming or denying the presence or absence of such weapons' (Boss 1987, p. 13). In February and December 1986, 72 per cent and 66 per cent respectively of voters approved the new compact. In August 1987 President Remeliik held two successive referenda to amend the constitution by dropping the non-nuclear clauses; 71 per cent and 73 per cent respectively approved, which was enough to amend ordinary clauses, but the courts held that 75 per cent was required to amend the entrenched non-nuclear clauses. In February 1990 a seventh referendum found 60 per cent approving the compact. Among those opposed, 50 per cent cited aversion to nuclear weapons, but the second most cited reason (35 per cent) was that the United States was not offering enough money (Gerston 1991, pp. 25–6). Even though the United Nations Security Council terminated the strategic trust in 1990, the US Senate indicated that it would not ratify the compact until the constitution was approved, and consequently Palau continued to be a dependency administered formally by the US Department of the Interior.

Not eligible for compact grants, Palau remained dependent on annual US budget appropriations. In 1985, for example, Palau received US$10.5 million in Department of the Interior budget support, US$2.07 million in federal grants, and US$3.7 million in project and programmes—a total of 68 per cent of budgeted revenue. Of US$7.5 million or 32 per cent raised locally, a portion of this was fees and taxation on salaries related to US federal and defence activities.

Palau has no significant export earnings. Income from remittances is thought to be substantial, but no figures are available. Tourism shows some promise; 16 695 visitors arrived in 1987 and 19 383 in 1989, mostly from Japan and mostly 'for pleasure' (South Pacific Commission 1989a, pp. 25–6; *Micronesian Investment Quarterly* 1990b, p.4). In 1990 three states and the Japanese construction firm COPROS entered a joint venture for airport and tourist facility development that could be worth US$150 million; it is to target Japanese vacationers who already come in large numbers to nearby Guam and Saipan (*Micronesian Investment Quarterly* 1990b; p. 4). Fishing royalties and exports are a further source of income that could be increased. Over 200 Japanese boats fish Palauan waters, paying an estimated US$500 000 in royalties annually, and a locally based firm Palau International Traders has begun airfreighting fresh fish weekly to Tokyo (*Micronesian Investment Quarterly* 1990d, p. 4). A scheme to mint commemorative coins earned US$1.3 million in royalties in 1989, and a new issue was planned with a Japanese company in 1990 (*Micronesian Investment Quarterly* 1990c p. 4). In 1991 Japan's reluctance to comply with Forum Fisheries Agency reporting standards delayed renewal of the annual fishing agreement and jeopardised Palau's earnings (*Pacific Islands Monthly* 1991e, p. 33).

Palau is self-governing, but in international relations and economic self-sufficiency it remains suspended between colonial status and independence (Smith and Pugh 1991). Until the US Senate approves the Compact of Free Association no other state will recognise Palau formally, and it remains ineligible for membership in most international organisations or for substantial international aid. Yet its government and non-government organisations have made numerous unofficial contacts abroad, and government statutes and policies already make provision for economic cooperation agreements. In 1983 Palau joined the South Pacific Commission, in 1986 it joined the Forum Fisheries Agency, and in 1991 it inquired about becoming an observer to the South Pacific Forum. These initiatives indicated the desire of the government to engage in full cooperation with other South Pacific states and regional organisations when permitted. The government establishment provides for a

Division of Foreign Affairs, which is to become the Ministry of Foreign Affairs on independence. Thus Palau is ready to make the transition to independence and take its place in the South Pacific community. It is an irony that the majority that passed the constitution in 1980 is thwarting the majority that wants independence under the compact in 1992.

10   Nauru

A single island of 21.3 square kilometres in the Micronesian cultural zone, Nauru is one of the world's smallest states. Its politics are democratic, and its foreign policy inclines clearly to the West in spite of its formal non-alignment and some disputes with former colonial powers. In economics it is simultaneously wealthy in phosphate export earnings and poor in prospects for onshore development. The 5000 Nauruans (and to a lesser extent the 3000 guest workers) look to their government for wise management of the country's assets to secure their autonomy, way of life and livelihood in an uncertain future.

Political evolution

The basis of traditional Nauruan social organisation was the twelve clans, led by chiefs, that inhabited the coastal fringe in semi-sovereign self-sufficiency. Land was owned by families within the clans. Contacts with Europeans began in the 1830s when whaling ships began to call regularly to barter for food and water (Craig and King 1981, pp. 202–3; Douglas and Douglas 1989, pp. 350–3). Beachcombers began to settle in 1837 and exacerbated clan feuds by introducing weapons. Peace was restored by German administrators who took control in 1888 and by missionaries who brought Protestantism, then Catholicism, and set up schools. The discovery of phosphate deposits in 1900 led to mining by the Anglo-German firm Pacific Phosphate Company, for which landowners were paid a small royalty (Viviani 1970, pp. 29 ff). Australia seized the colony from Germany in 1914 and, with Britain and New Zealand, secured a League of Nations mandate to administer it. The British Phosphate Commissioners, one appointed by each mandatory government, were authorised to run the mining industry and to direct exports to the three mandatory countries at the lowest possible price for the benefit of their farming industries. Australia, the principal administrator, set up an advisory Nauruan Council of Chiefs in 1922 and established a Royalty Trust Fund into which part of the Nauruan royalties were deposited.

After a destructive Japanese occupation in 1943–45, Australia, Britain and New Zealand secured United Nations agreement to a trusteeship that allowed prewar monopoly access to cheap phosphate to continue. The Long Term Community Investment Fund was set up in 1947, and prior savings and newly increased royalties were paid into it. However, the Nauru Council of Chiefs took note of United Nations Charter articles 73b and 76b on progress towards self-government and petitioned for an inspection visit, greater powers and more royalties (Macdonald 1988, p. 33ff). Prodded by the Third World members of the United Nations Trusteeship Council and later by New Zealand when it began setting up self-government in its own dependencies, Australia complied, albeit slowly. The Nauruan initiative, parallel to the petition by Western Samoan leaders, was an example of how local leaders could offset their powerlessness by appealing to international principles or, more crudely, playing the outside powers against one another.

The Nauru Local Government Council was set up in 1951. In 1956, led by its new chairman Hammer de Roburt, educated at Melbourne's Geelong College, it asserted Nauruan ownership of the phosphate and requested royalties linked to world prices (Macdonald 1988, p. 38). Royalties were increased, and pressure for political development eased until the United Nations Declaration on Decolonization in 1960 asserted that lack of economic or social development should not constitute barriers to independence. New Zealand complied and brought Western Samoa to independence in 1962. Britain, wishing to keep strategic bases in island dependencies, did not wish to move quickly, and Australia was adamantly opposed to independence. Manoeuvres by all the trustees to keep control of the phosphate, including Australian–Nauruan negotiations over possible resettlement of the population to an island in Queensland, achieved only delay and Nauruan irritation.

In 1964 de Roburt declared Nauru's intention to gain independence in 3 years, and the Nauru Local Government Council engaged Australian economic and academic consultants to document its claims to the phosphate. The three trustee governments offered a variety of alternatives including a protectorate similar to Tonga and free association similar to Cook Islands. But the Nauru council, with economic documentation in hand and confident of the political support of the United Nations Trusteeship Council and the newly formed Special Committee on Decolonization (Committee of Twenty-four), pressed for full ownership and sovereign independence. The United Nations General Assembly kept up the pressure with Resolution 2111 of 1965 reaffirming Nauru's inalienable right to self-government and independence. The trustees, under United Nations pressure and unable to agree on an alternative, were obliged to comply.

On 31 January 1968 Nauru became in independent republic within the Commonwealth. Its constitution established a parliament of eighteen popularly elected members who choose a president as head of state who is also the prime minister. The president in turn chooses four ministers to form a Cabinet ('Nauru' 1986a, 1986b). De Roburt served as president for most of the ensuing period, with Bernard Dowiyogo serving in 1976–78 and again in 1989–91. The Nauru Party proclaimed itself in 1976 and the Democratic Party in 1987, but these were little more than parliamentary caucuses contesting de Roburt's dominance of Nauru's politics, with little electoral or policy relevance (Crocombe 1988, p. 57; *Far East and Australasia* 1989, p. 771). A court system and a civil service, the largest employer besides the phosphate industry, were established. There is a small police force but no defence force.

Foreign affairs

Pre-independence frictions were forgiven, and de Roburt voiced the hope that relations with the three trustees would be 'friendly and warm' (Crocombe 1988, p. 52). Nauru opted to become a 'special member' of the Commonwealth, not represented at Commonwealth Heads of Government Meetings but contributing to the Commonwealth Secretariat, the Commonwealth Institute and the Commonwealth Fund for Technical Cooperation and receiving specialist advice on mining, civil aviation and treaty negotiation (Asia Pacific Research Unit 1982c, p. 4). It appointed a representative in London to maintain diplomatic links and posted consuls to Melbourne and Auckland.

Nauru also opened consulates in Tokyo, Suva and San Francisco and honorary consulates in Apia, Guam, Hong Kong, Honolulu, Nuku'alofa, Pago Pago, New Delhi and Saipan. The offices in London, Tokyo, Honolulu, Hong Kong, Pago Pago, Apia and Rarotonga were temporarily closed in 1989 as an economy measure when phosphate revenues fell. Nauru hosts an Australian High Commission and a Western Samoan Honorary Consulate. Resident diplomatic missions were exchanged in 1980 with the Republic of China (Taiwan), and in 1990 their missions were upgraded to full embassy status. The high commissioners of Britain, New Zealand and India in Suva were accredited to Nauru, as were the ambassadors of Japan, South Korea and the United States in Canberra and the ambassadors of Belgium and France in Wellington. Other states with which Nauru has formal relations include Germany, Switzerland, Turkey, the Soviet Union (since 1988) and the nearby South Pacific states. Diplomacy is conducted by the president, who is also the Minister of External Affairs, on visits abroad, and by officers of the Department of External Affairs, often in other capitals such as Suva, Canberra or London, or in the course of meetings of international organisations.

Nauru declined to join the United Nations General Assembly, which is curious given the political backing for independence it received from the United Nations Trusteeship Council and Special Committee on Decolonization (Committee of Twenty-four), but it is a member of the Economic and Social Commission for Asia and the Pacific (ESCAP), the World Health Organization (WHO), the International Telecommunication Union (ITU) and the Universal Postal Union (UPU). Nauru applied for membership of the Asian Development Bank (ADB) but was turned down because of its high income; but if revenues continue to decline, it may eventually be admitted as a borrower. It is active in South Pacific regional organisations including the South Pacific Commission and the South Pacific Forum and its affiliates, and hosted a forum meeting in 1976. It contributed generously to the forum's Natural Disaster Fund and to the University of the South Pacific and helped the Pacific Forum Line with a low interest loan of A$3.5 million in 1981 (Crocombe 1988, p. 54). It is the only island state to give aid to other island states. The employment of approximately 3000 I-Kiribati, Tuvaluans, Rabi Fijians and Filipinos in the mining industry is seen as a form of aid by way of remittances, particularly to the two neighbours whose phosphate on Banaba (Ocean) Island was exhausted in 1979. Nauru has been active in fisheries consortia and was the venue for the signing of the Nauru Agreement in 1982, which brought it together with four other Micronesian and two Melanesian states to form a bloc to bargain with distant fishing states (Doulman 1987c, p. 258); Teiwaki 1988b, p. 108).

Foreign policy has been guided by pragmatism, not ideology. Nauru was said to be 'a member of the Western bloc by accident rather than design', largely because of its investments, air links, sources of guest labourers and other business connections

(Crocombe 1988, pp. 52–3). It has inclined towards tolerant non-alignment, shown in its relations with such dissimilar partners as East and West Germany, the Soviet Union and the United States, and Taiwan and (informally) mainland China, but its Christian heritage has made its leaders wary of close connections with the communist states as shown by the preference for Taiwan. Only in 1988, after a decade of Soviet approaches, did the government agree to establish formal relations with the Soviet Union. Nauru's leaders avoid strong statements on affairs that do not directly affect their country's economic wellbeing, in contrast to Vanuatu's outspokenness. The government is comfortable with the consensus views expressed by the annual South Pacific Forum communiqués.

Economic relations

On independence the Nauru Phosphate Company took control of the mining land, bought the machinery of the British Phosphate Commissioners, and took charge of the export of phosphate, which was the mainstay of the economy. The main customers are Australia, New Zealand, Japan and South Korea; Indonesia, the Philippines and India also are buyers. Nauru imports food and consumer goods from Australia and Japan and refined fuels from Singapore. Trade statistics are not published, but figures derived from Australian and New Zealand statistics indicated a trade surplus of over 5 to 1 in 1986 (South Pacific Commission 1989a, p. 15).

Earnings not used for company and government operating expenses are lodged in a number of funds including the Long Term Investment Fund, the Development Fund, the Rehabilitation Fund, the Housing Fund and the Land Owners Cash Royalties Fund, all overseen by the Nauru Phosphate Royalty Trust. The funds are authorised by the Nauru Constitution, and guidelines for the trust's activities are set by Cabinet ('Nauru' 1986a, 1986b). The responsibility of the trust is to invest the monies of the funds so that interests and profits will support the governments and people after the exhaustion of the phosphate reserves, expected by the end of the century.

Initial investments were made in Melbourne, in the 52 storey, A$45 million Nauru House, from which the funds are managed. Subsequent investments of A$7 million were made in a real estate complex in Saipan in 1974 and of A$35 million in a phosphate-fertiliser joint venture with the government of the Philippines in 1981 (Asia Pacific Research Unit 1982c, p. 11). A similar venture with India was undertaken; smaller investments were made in hotels in Marshall Islands and Western Samoa, apartments in Guam, and buildings in Auckland, Hong Kong and Texas; and a large investment in a complex in Honolulu was made in 1985. One estimate put the value of the investments at A$2 billion, or nearly A$400 000 per Nauruan; but as the trust does not publish details, figures remain speculative (Crocombe 1988, p. 47).

Phosphate monies were also used to set up the Nauru Pacific Line, which owns several ships that ply South Pacific routes, and the Nauru Fishing Corporation to exploit the Exclusive Economic Zone (EEZ). Nauru initially invested also in Air Pacific, based in Fiji. However, that airline did not serve Nauru's transportation needs; so Air Nauru was set up, and four Boeing jetliners were purchased to link Nauru to Japan, Taiwan, Hong Kong, the Philippines, Australia, New Zealand and Fiji. Countries off the trunk routes—such as Niue, Cook Islands, Western and American Samoa, Guam, Federated States of Micronesia, Kiribati, Solomon Islands and New Caledonia—welcomed the additional services by Air Nauru.

Current issues

Many of Nauru's investments abroad have not performed to expectations, and some are losing money, although this cannot be confirmed in the absence of published figures. The Nauru Fishing Corporation has not generated significant exports of fish, and the Nauru Shipping Corporation has not realised its potential because Australian and New Zealand unions have prevented the recruitment of Nauru, Kiribati and Tuvalu seamen at Third World rates of pay by threatening strike actions. The issue precipitated a court action against the New Zealand maritime unions in which Nauru was awarded A$142 000 in damages in 1987 (Macdonald 1988, p. 64).

Air Nauru found few of its routes profitable because Qantas, Air New Zealand and Air Pacific monopolised their countries' landing rights on the more lucrative trunk routes. Air Nauru reportedly lost A$100 million in its first 10 years of operation and continues to consume the largest share of government expenditures besides salaries (Crocombe 1988, p. 63; Macdonald 1988, p. 66). In 1988 the New Zealand Ministry of Transport, which administers Nauru's civil aviation regulations, withdrew the airline's certificate because of safety concerns following a strike by and the sacking of the airline's Australian pilots. Air Nauru then terminated its contract with the New Zealand Ministry of Transport. This and other difficulties precipitated the cancellation of many routes and the sale of two aircraft. Criticism of investment policy by opposition parliamentarians led to a vote of no confidence in President de Roburt and his replacement by Kenas Aroi, then Bernard Dowiyogo, in 1989. The new government has exercised economy measures but has not altered the basic direction of investment policy.

In 1966 the government of Nauru appointed a commission of inquiry to document the damage done to the island by the British Phosphate Commissioners and the residual liability of the three former trustee governments to replace topsoil (Macdonald 1988, p. 67). A second commission conducted an inquiry in 1987 and confirmed that the cost of rehabilitating the landscape would be over A$200 million. In 1989 Nauru filed at the International Court of Justice a claim against Australia for A$72 million (Rose 1989, p. 20). Nauru claimed that the British Phosphate Commission had sold phosphate at below-market prices from 1919 to 1967, thus depriving Nauru of its share of royalties, and cited article 82 of its constitution, which states that the government of Nauru is not responsible for the rehabilitation of mined land, implying that responsibility lies with the former colonial powers ('Nauru' 1986a, 1986b). Australia—with agreement by Britain and New Zealand, which refused to accept International Court of Justice jurisdiction—argued that the government of Nauru accepted liabilities as well as assets when it paid US$21 million in return for the British Phosphate Commissioners' assets in 1967. The case is to be heard by the court in 1992 and a judgement reached by 1993 (Williams 1991b, p. 19). Meanwhile the rehabilitation and compensation issue, as well as shipping and civil aviation issues, continued to disturb relations between Nauru and the three former trustee governments, particularly New Zealand and Australia.

11 New Caledonia, French Polynesia, Wallis and Futuna

France's three possessions in the South Pacific are designated overseas territories. Constitutionally they are integral elements of the state of France. Yet each interacts with its neighbours in the economic, cultural and even diplomatic spheres, within limits set by metropolitan interests, and each enjoys a degree of self-government that is likely to grow in the future. Their relations with France and their neighbours are described below with a view to assessing the potential of each to become a significant player in the regional system.

New Caledonia as a territory of France

The third-largest South Pacific country in land area, New Caledonia was populated more than 1000 years ago by migrants from the island of New Guinea moving westwards and southwards along the Melanesian archipelago. It is composed of a main island (Grande Terre) and three main outliers known collectively as the Loyalty Islands. It was sighted by the explorers Bougainville, Cook (who named it after Scotland), d'Entrecasteaux and d'Urville in the later eighteenth century and visited by sandalwood buyers, beachcombers and runaways in the early nineteenth century (Craig and King 1982, p. 206). From about 1840 traders and missionaries from France established themselves, but misunderstandings led to friction and occasional massacres of Europeans by the Melanesians, called Kanaks.

France reacted to these, and to Anglo-French rivalry in the region, by annexing the main island in 1853 and the Loyalty Islands in 1864 (Douglas and Douglas 1989, p. 368). It used New Caledonia as a penal colony from 1864 to 1896. Kanaks revolted in 1878 against encroachments on their land and in 1917 against the imposition of a head tax and forced labour for those unable to pay it. Kanak hostility and indifferent land quality and rainfall discouraged settlers other than discharged prisoners (*bagnards*). These became petty ranchers (bush farmers or *broussards*) in the scrublands of the western coast. The discovery of nickel in 1863 and its exploitation paid for the colony's development and brought wage labour and eventually health care and education to many Kanaks. Occupation by US forces in 1942–45 brought further economic opportunities and new ideas, but neither dissolved ethnic divisions between Kanaks and *caldoches* (French settlers). Ethnic rivalry was complicated by the encouragement of Polynesian and Asian labour immigration, which eventually made the Kanaks a minority in their own country.

Political reforms after World War II transformed the colony into an overseas territory with an elected assembly. Kanaks obtained the right to vote in 1951, formed their first political party in 1953, acquired their first Kanak territorial minister in 1956, and won a majority in the territorial assembly in 1958 and in several subsequent elections (Uregei 1982). However, a referendum in 1958 saw a majority of voters (most of whom were non-Kanak) reject the independence option in favour of territorial autonomy within France. Kanak disturbances in protest, opposition to independence by local settler parties, and French assertion of strategic interests all led France to curtail local powers. Progress towards independence stalled throughout the 1960s and 1970s. Immigration from France and nearby countries during the nickel boom further diluted Kanak electoral strength.

The 1980s began with a resurgence of Kanak nationalism, led by former Catholic seminarian Jean-Marie Tjibaou. The newly elected socialist government of France, led by François Mitterrand, was ideologically more sympathetic to decolonisation than its predecessors. However, an inconclusive succession of plans, referenda, elections, boycotts, violent clashes, conferences and agreements punctuated the 1980s and frustrated the independence movement (Fraser 1987; *Far East and Australasia 1989* 1989; Robie 1989; Tanham 1990). After the bloody Ouvea kidnapping and rescue operation the situation stabilised on the basis of the Matignon Accords, signed in June 1988 by the Kanak leader Jean-Marie Tjibaou, the *caldoche* leader Jacques Lafleur and Prime Minister Michel Rocard, and endorsed by a French national referendum in November.

The Matignon Accords provided for elections in June 1989 of three autonomous province assemblies, each empowered to choose its own executive officers. The Northern and Loyalty provinces elected Kanak FLNKS (*Front de Libération nationale kanake socialiste*) majorities, and the Southern province around Noumea elected the *caldoche*-backed RPCR (*Rassemblement pour la Caledonie dans la République*) to power. A territorial congress was constituted of all the provincial assembly members. In 1989 it was composed of 19 Kanak FLNKS members, 27 *caldoche* RPCR members, and 7 minor party members who tended to support the RPCR rather than the FLNKS. Territorial executive powers were held by High Commissioner Bernard Grasset and Deputy High Commissioner Jacques Iekawe (a Kanak with a law degree from the University of Lyons), both appointed by the government of France.

The central feature of the Matignon Accords was a promise of a referendum on self-determination in 1998. The present electoral arithmetic does not favour the Kanaks, who made up only 45 per cent of the population in 1989 (*Far East and Australasia* 1989, p. 776). Europeans made up only 34 per cent, but past referenda indicated that their aversion to independence is supported also by the 12 per cent who are Polynesian immigrants from Wallis and Futuna and French Polynesia, the 3 per cent who are Indonesians and the 2 per cent who are Vietnamese. The Kanak leaders are counting on demographic and political trends in their favour including a higher birthrate, emigration by non-Kanaks, and conversion of marginal voters to the pro-independence cause as Kanak leadership becomes more responsible and attractive with experience.

The Europeans are counting on voters' economic self interest, mainly the realisation that without French subsidies, personnel and protection New Caledonia's economy, already shaken by volatile nickel prices, and the standard of living, dependent on French government support, will both decline rapidly if independence is chosen in 1998. They are also aware that the Polynesians and Asians will vote against independence for fear that they will be expelled by a Kanak government. Also, 20 per cent of Kanaks do not favour independence, and the 80 per cent who do, are led by a loose front, the FLNKS, of political parties of diverse inclinations, the more radical of which, FULK (*Front uni de Libération kanake*), boycotted the 1989 election. The assassination of Tjibaou in 1989 was an indirect consequence of this split.

A divided Kanak vote will perpetuate a pro-France majority in future elections and referenda. It is conceivable that the dynamics of the Single European Market after 1992 will bring more European investment and settlement, reinforcing the anti-independence sentiment among non-Kanaks just as it intensifies the pro-independence commitment of militant Kanaks, polarising the political spectrum. Among those not committed to either full independence or the status quo, optimists hope that a middle way such as free association with France on the Cook Islands model can be negotiated so as to have bicultural self-government but also keep French aid. Pessimists foresee a Kanak defeat at the polls and a renewed cycle of frustration, confrontation and violence, leading to either repression, partition or precipitate French withdrawal (Tanham 1990; Henningham 1989, 1990).

In the meantime the territorial and provincial governments depend on the government of France for a large portion of their revenues. In 1985 the territory budgeted for total current revenue of CPF (French Pacific francs) 29 765 million, of which CPF8631 million or 29 per cent was contributions and grants from the government of France (Douglas and Douglas 1989, p. 364). Of the 52 per cent of revenues from direct and indirect taxation, the bulk was income tax on French public- and private-sector salary and wage earners and duties on goods imported from France. Although indigenisation is official policy, in the 1980s the majority of civil servants and private executives and proprietors were metropolitan or locally recruited French residents. For most of the 1980s France kept up to 9500 military and police personnel in New Caledonia, including a marine regiment, five infantry units, an air transport and a helicopter squadron, and two frigates and four armed patrol boats. Spending by the French military in 1986 was estimated to be CPF5733 million, of which a portion accrued to the territorial government directly in rental and other fees and another portion indirectly through taxes on services rendered by the private sector (Henningham 1989, p. 51). More recently, of development funds budgeted for 1990, 1991 and 1992, 41 per cent is grants and credits from Paris, and a large proportion of the territorial contribution is derived from taxes and duties on French earnings and trade (New Caledonia Territorial Government 1990a, p. 3). Thus it may be estimated that 40–50 per cent of revenues, and a similar proportion of trained specialist personnel, are derived directly or indirectly from the connection with France, and that independence not on French terms could reduce revenues and the availability of expertise steeply.

New Caledonia as a regional player

As early as 1976 Kanak leaders took their appeal for independence to neighbouring governments who subsequently supported New Caledonian independence in the South Pacific Forum. Visits seeking support were made as far afield as Hong Kong, the Netherlands and Algeria, and appeals were made to the United Nations, the Organisation of African Unity and the World Council of Churches (Bates 1990, p. 58).

The objectives of the international campaign, led by Yann Celene Uregei, were as follows:

- to affirm in the eyes of the international community the wish of the Kanak people to establish themselves as a people;
- to obtain international recognition of the Kanak people's basic right to self-determination and independence;
- to denounce colonialism and French imperialism in the Pacific;
- to associate the Kanak people with all people struggling for liberation against any form of colonialism or imperialism;
- to force France to acknowledge the Kanak people's wishes and to submit to international opinion and thereby to proceed with decolonisation in order to establish peace in the Pacific (Uregei 1982, p. 128).

Kanak leaders adopted the model of the Vanuatu independence drive and formed close personal ties with Walter Lini and his counterparts such as Father John Momis in Papua New Guinea. In 1986 Vanuatu persuaded the Non Aligned Movement to endorse the Kanak cause and give the FLNKS (the main Kanak political association) observer status. Also, the South Pacific Forum gave its support to New Caledonian independence and asked Fiji to introduce a United Nations General Assembly Resolution to reinscribe New Caledonia on the list of non-self-governing territories maintained by the United Nations Trusteeship Council (France had unilaterally taken its territories off the list in 1947). The Fiji motion was supported by New Zealand and Australia, and in spite of strenuous French lobbying it passed by 89 to 24. Its passage subjected France's territory to inspection visits and obliged France to make annual reports of New Caledonia's progress to eventual independence in accordance with the United Nations Charter and the 1960 United Nations Declaration on Decolonization (Bates 1990, p. 87).

In 1986 the three Melanesian governments formed the Spearhead Group motivated largely by opposition to continued French colonialism; the FLNKS was a tacit fourth member (MacQueen 1990, p. 4). In 1990 and 1991 the South Pacific Forum deliberated on giving the FLNKS observer status but did not reach consensus because of Polynesian, Australian and New Zealand resistance based on the fact that the FLNKS was not a government. A breakaway Kanak party, FULK, led by Uregei, sent youth activists to train in Libya in 1984 and North Korea in 1989. Although these contacts were not endorsed by the FLNKS mainstream led by Tjibaou and had little educational value or domestic political effect, they obliged Australia and New

Zealand to take Kanak initiatives even more seriously (Hegarty 1987).

As outside interest in New Caledonia grew, France responded negatively, denying the international legitimacy or relevance of the independence movement generally and of the FLNKS specifically. However, in face of the widening acceptance of the Kanak leaders and their cause, and of growing anti-French sentiment in the South Pacific, France in 1986 adopted a flexible policy of consultations, economic cooperation and aid and encouraged its territorial governments to seek closer relations with their neighbours. This policy also offered the French budget the prospect of relief from the heavy subsidies by developing alternative sources of income for the territories.

The 1988 Law on Preparations for Self-determination of New Caledonia in 1998, which implemented the Matignon Accords, reserved the powers of external relations, defence, trade, investment and immigration to the French state but authorised economic and cultural exchanges with other Pacific states and territories and allowed the territorial government to approve private investments worth less than CPF60 million (New Caledonia Territorial Government 1988, pp. 1854, 1862). The French High Commissioner in 1990 listed as one of five principal achievements since 1988 the involvement of New Caledonia in the Pacific region. His Kanak deputy Jacques Iekawe was designated Deputy Commissioner for Cooperation and Economic Development, charged with improving relations with near neighbours, and a South Pacific Secretariat was set up to support the initiative (New Caledonia Territorial Government 1990b, p. 4 and 1990e, p. 9).

Manifestations of the new policy were visits to and by South Pacific leaders, contributions to and attendance (as observer or candidate member) at meetings of regional organisations, such as the South Pacific Applied Geoscience Commission (SOPAC) in November 1990, and offers to share scientific and educational expertise, facilities and data (*Les Nouvelles calédoniennes* 1990a, p. 10). New Caledonia has been a member of the South Pacific Commission since 1983, and it was hoped that participation, informal if not formal, could be achieved in other regional organisations (New Caledonia Territorial Government 1990d, pp. 10–11). An Australian parliamentary committee took a favourable view of the Matignon reforms and the new French policy by recommending that Australians establish regular exchanges with New Caledonia assembly members, business people, unionists, professionals and scholars of the new French University of the South Pacific to be established, and extend aid to education and that small-scale development projects be extended to Kanaks (Australia Government 1989c, pp. 11–13). In 1990 the foreign ministers of Australia and New Zealand and the Royal New Zealand Air Force Command and Staff College paid formal visits, and both governments extended scholarships to Melanesian students (*Les Nouvelles calédoniennes* 1990b, p. 6).

New Caledonia's trade is dominated but not monopolised by France, and some diversification is taking place. From 1984 to 1989 the proportion of mineral exports to France declined from 71.9 per cent to 43.4 per cent, with Japan, Germany, the United States, India, and others increasing their share correspondingly (Douglas and Douglas 1989, p. 363; Institute Territoriale 1990, p. 46). Nickel products make up 92.8 per cent of exports by value, but Japan and Australia also buy laterite. A small tuna and shrimp industry began exporting to Japan, Australia and Hong Kong in 1989. New Caledonia exports consumer goods to Vanuatu in return for beef. New Caledonia imports virtually all of its capital and consumer goods, but substantially and increasingly from Pacific region suppliers, as shown in Table 11.1. Imports of goods that compete with French and European Community products, such as wine, milk, flour and beer, are restricted by licence; non-European Community goods attract a tariff of up to 40 per cent; and all retailed items must have French language labelling. Australia and Japan have complained that this import restriction policy is discriminatory, illegal under the General Agreement on Tariffs and Trade (GATT), and contradictory to French policy of integrating its territories with regional neighbours. The Single European Market after 1992 may strengthen the bias against non-European Community imports and prove to be an ongoing irritant to Pacific neighbours.

Table 11.1 New Caledonia's trade partners, 1989

Country	Exports to (%)	Imports from (%)
France	36.4	44.0
Japan	28.4	5.3
European Community	8.6	6.0
United States	6.2	10.4
Australia	—[a]	9.1
New Zealand	—[a]	3.0
India	3.0	—[a]
Others	17.4	21.2
Total	100.0	100.0

[a] Included in Others.

Source: Far East and Australasia 1991 p. 781; New Caledonia Government 1990c, p. 6.

While the merchandise balance is often favourable, depending on demand and prices for nickel, trade in 'invisibles' is generally in deficit because of the repatriation of money not only by French firms and employees but also by Polynesian and Asian immigrant workers. The invisible deficit is offset by New Caledonia's second-largest industry: tourism. Tourism is estimated to generate 7.5 per cent of the gross domestic product (GDP), earn an equivalent to 20 per cent of merchandise earnings and employ 5 per cent of the labour force. Club Med and a number of other attractions drew over 80 000 tourists from Japan (33 per cent of all tourists), Australia (21 per cent), France (15 per cent) and New Zealand (10 per cent) in 1989 (New Caledonia 1990f). The tourist industry also attracts investment in hotels and transportation from France, Japan and Australia. New Caledonia is served by Air Caledonie, UTA, Air Nauru, Air New Zealand, Qantas and Polynesian Airlines. However, nickel mining and tourism are vulnerable to political disturbances. The Thio nickel mine was closed in 1985, and tourist arrivals fell by half as a result of Kanak demonstrations, barricades and shoot-outs with the police. Nickel and tourism have recovered to their 1984 levels, but continued growth depends on political stability.

New Caledonia or Kanaky?

The clash between Kanaks and *caldoches* is more than a local political dispute. Because of the interest taken by the Melanesian governments, the South Pacific Forum members, the United Nations, and outsiders such as Libya and North Korea, because of the implications for France's future role in the region, and because of economic, educational, scientific and cultural consequences for neighbouring peoples, the peaceful management of New Caledonia's political future is a matter of region-wide concern. New Caledonia as a territory of France will increasingly be an anomaly in a South Pacific of independent states, and probably a disruptive influence, a target for interference by outsiders with both idealistic and venal motives. An independent or freely associated New Caledonia is likely to undertake vigorous and extensive bilateral and multilateral diplomacy as Cook Islands, Marshall Islands and Federated States of Micronesia have done. A FLNKS government would doubtless pursue a non-aligned foreign policy similar to that of Vanuatu, with numerous Third World contacts, and would attempt to rename the country Kanaky. The claim to Matthew and Hunter islands, in dispute with Vanuatu, is likely to be settled amicably, although with some ambivalence (Day 1987, pp. 316–17; Prescott 1988). A RPCR government would try to retain the old name and close links with France and conservative Western governments, and with French backing would be reluctant to surrender Matthew and Hunter islands to Vanuatu. New Caledonia's foreign policy will reflect the uneasy balance of political power between France, the Kanaks and the *caldoches* for some years to come.

French Polynesia's relations with France

Settled by migrants from Samoa and Tonga, the Polynesians of the five archipelagos comprising French Polynesia were ruled by chiefs and nobles when European explorers came in the eighteenth century (Craig and King 1982, pp. 96–7). European sailors, traders and missionaries began settling as early as 1797. At that time the Pomare family chiefs and Papara family chiefs were on the point of civil war in Tahiti. European support helped the Pomare family to prevail, and Queen Pomare IV acceded to French protection in 1847. France transformed the protectorate into a colony in 1880 and gradually annexed the remainder of the islands by 1901.

World War II service in Europe and contact with US forces awoke the indigenous population to new possibilities. Tahitian nationalism emerged in 1947 with the establishment of a party and a newspaper calling for less French authority, more cultural freedom and Tahiti-anisation of the government service (Robie 1989, pp. 26–8; Danielsson 1982, p. 197). Its leader, Pouvanaa, became the first Polynesian elected to the French National Assembly in 1951, and his party captured a majority in the first Territorial Assembly election of 1953. Prodded by local advocates of autonomy, France in 1957 recast the colony as an overseas territory with limited powers of local self-government, in 1977 set up an executive responsible to the assembly, and in 1984 and 1990 devolved powers in regional external relations including commerce and cultural exchange.

The 41 member Territorial Assembly is elected every 5 years and chooses a territorial president from its members–Gaston Flosse as a result of the 1991 election. After the election of 1986 five main political parties held seats. The pro-French RPR (*Rassemblement pour la République*), which seeks greater autonomy within the French state, held 24 seats, but it split in 1987 and a new governing coalition was formed with Alexandre Leontieff as its head and president. The governing coalition of 29 members was united only by dislike of Gaston Flosse (president before 1987 and after 1991), by desire for the privileges of office and by personal connections; it included loyalists, autonomists and one 'independentist'. Its only coherent programme was the Leontieff Plan—a request to France for more development funds to prepare the territory for the eventual decline of the French military presence and the consequent reduction of economic subsidies (Henningham 1989, p. 21). The leading independence party was the *Front de Libération de la Polynesie* led by Oscar Temaru, Mayor of Faa'a, which held four seats in 1991; it was balanced by several other parties seeking varying degrees of autonomy in association with France and at least one party seeking closer ties with France. Final executive powers are held by a French-appointed high commissioner.

French Polynesia's economic dependency

French Polynesia's economy is distorted by the presence of the *Centre d'Expérimentation du Pacifique* and the *Commission d'Énergie Atomique*, which administer the nuclear testing sites at Mururoa and Fangataufa. The centre, in operation since 1965, is staffed by an estimated 2300 civilian and military scientists and supported by 5000 French military personnel (Bates 1990, p. 6). France directly spent CPF87.3 billion in the territory in 1986, of which 42.7 per cent was on the French military presence and 17.3 per cent was on the testing programme and a variety of French-sponsored projects, programmes and personnel. Of a total of CPF102.5 billion in budgeted public expenditures in 1990, 59 per cent was spent by French agencies, 41 per cent by the territorial government (Henningham 1989, p. 52; French Polynesian Territorial Government 1991a).

Regarding the territorial budget, over 20 per cent of territorial revenues (CPF72.1 billion in 1989) derived from development grants and loans from France (*Far East and Australasia* 1990, p. 773). The balance of revenue was raised by duties on imports, property and turnover taxes, and miscellaneous fees. The per capita GDP of French Polynesia is among the highest in the South Pacific, along with that of Northern Marianas and Nauru, and exceeds that of New Zealand. However, prices are correspondingly high because import restrictions and tariffs discourage goods from sources other than France or European Community countries. Income is maldistributed in favour of government employees who tend to be French or of mixed ancestry (called *demis*), and service sector proprietors who tend to be Chinese. Polynesians tend to do lower-paid or subsistence work or be unemployed, particularly those living on the outer islands. Migration to Tahiti in search of French-generated economic opportunity has led to shantytowns, unemployment, criminal activity and occasional riots, mostly recently in 1987 and 1991.

French Polynesia's export earning potential is limited. The major export in 1990 was black pearls (82 per cent of export earnings), followed by coconut oil (4 per cent) and small amounts of vanilla, fruit and handicrafts, the balance being made up of re-exports

(French Polynesia Territorial Government 1991a). France took 50 per cent of exports and the United States 19 per cent. Imports—from France (52 per cent in 1987), European Community countries (12 per cent), the United States (10 per cent) and New Zealand (5 per cent)—exceeded exports by a factor of 20 to 1 in 1990, leaving the territory deeply dependent on French subsidies. Tourism is an alternative earner; 139 705 people visited the territory in 1989, and some 9000 jobs were related to the tourist industry. Tourists in 1987 came from the United States (40 per cent), France (15 per cent), Australia (6 per cent), New Zealand (3 per cent), Japan (3 per cent) and a variety of Pacific countries (South Pacific Commission 1989a, p. 25). Luxury hotel investments have been made recently by Japanese firms such as EIE, JIN and Taiyo. The territory is linked to tourist sources by Air France, UTA, Qantas, Air New Zealand, Minerva Airlines, LAN Chile and Hawaiian Airlines. Some revenue is earned by licensing fishing rights to Japanese and Korean boats, and potential exists for exploitation of fish, timber and phosphate resources by the territory. Nevertheless, volatile prices, distance from markets, and a dearth of capital and skilled labour restrain the development of all these alternative sources of income.

French Polynesia in the South Pacific

As in New Caledonia, France has encouraged the government of French Polynesia to seek contacts and partners in the South Pacific. France in 1984 granted the government of French Polynesia the power to negotiate regional agreements in the economic and cultural sectors ('French Polynesia' 1986, pp. 21–22). In 1986 Gaston Flosse, a *demi*, then President of the territorial government, was appointed Secretary of State for the South Pacific and provided with a fund for aid to the region. Flosse cultivated sympathetic island leaders, including the prime ministers of Cook Islands, Western Samoa and Fiji and the King of Tonga, and negotiated hurricane relief and development grants to their countries (Bates 1990, pp. 97–102). He encouraged the King of Tonga's idea of a Polynesian Economic and Cultural Community of which French Polynesia would be a member. French Polynesia took an increasingly active role in the South Pacific Commission and spoke up against driftnet fishing practices by Japan and Taiwan.

France's President Mitterrand during his address to the Territorial Assembly in 1990 suggested that the territorial government's powers to negotiate and sign agreements with regional neighbours, clarified by French statute in April, 1990, were 'equivalent to those of many so-called independent countries' (French Polynesia Territorial Government 1990, p. 75). The following year Flosse concluded his inaugural address with hopes for the 'greater good of the Polynesian people, whose destiny is parallel to that of the people of France', this phrase replacing the originally drafted phrase 'within the bosom of the French nation' (French Polynesia Territorial Government 1991b, p. 17). Flosse then created a new post of Special Advisor for Foreign Affairs and filled it with a former territorial cabinet minister.

Foreign policy issues in future are likely to include demands to end nuclear testing and work towards independence—demands that will receive support from the Polynesian Protestant churches and the governments and peace groups of the region. However, in 1986 parties committed to these policies gained only 20 per cent of the vote, because those parties cannot work together on other issues, and because their members are suffering from 'fatigue and futility' after 25 years without success (Henningham 1989, p. 20; *New Zealand Herald* 25 January 1991). Too many of the leaders of all the ethnic groups find their economic future linked to continued French presence and see few alternatives to the status quo.

Likely to spark new controversy is the impact of France becoming part of the Single European Market after 1992, which will open French Polynesia to unrestricted trade, investment and migration from Europe. This would be to the advantage of the entrepreneurs, and to the disadvantage of the ordinary Polynesians. Clashes have been seen already in the protest of 200 Polynesians against sale of an atoll near Bora Bora to Japanese investors in 1990 and a tax revolt blockade of Papeete roads and the defeat by referendum of a Japanese luxury golf course project on Moorea in 1991 (*New Zealand Herald* 10 May 1990, 8 July 1991). Further confrontations between urban elites and ordinary citizens could have a profound effect on French Polynesia's relations with France, regional neighbours, and potential economic partners.

Wallis and Futuna

This pair of islands and several uninhabited outliers were formerly a colony of Tonga. The country's Polynesian inhabitants were converted to Catholicism beginning in 1837, and their principal king petitioned France for protection in 1842, which was granted in 1887 (Douglas and Douglas 1989, p. 627; *Far East and Australasia* 1990, p. 784). In 1959 the Wallisians voted to become an overseas territory of France. A resident French Administrator is head of the territory but shares powers with three Polynesian kings and an elected territorial assembly.

The government's budget is underwritten almost entirely by grants, subsidies and services from France and by import duties on goods imported from France. There are few resources save fishing waters and virtually no exports save trochus shells. Tourism has little potential because of remoteness. More Wallisians live abroad than at home, most of them in New Caledonia, and remittances are a significant contribution to the economy (Rensch 1982, p. 11). The principal airline connection is with New Caledonia, and New Caledonian currency is used.

There is no sentiment for independence, only for more autonomy and more development funds from France. The local leaders' greatest foreign-policy concerns are the possibilities of the withdrawal of France from the region and the expulsion of Wallisians by a nationalistic government of New Caledonia in future, as already happened in Vanuatu in 1980 (Henningham 1989, p. 26). Wallis and Futuna, comparable to Tokelau and Pitcairn in its minuteness, isolation and dependency, does not play a significant role in the affairs of the South Pacific region, and its political status is not likely to be an international issue.

12   Papua New Guinea

Papua New Guinea is by far the largest and most populous of the island countries. It is also the oldest, with settlement beginning as early as 30 000 years ago. Its minerals, silviculture and maritime endowments make it a sought-after partner by resource-scarce Japan. However, the underdevelopment of its infrastructure and governmental authority retard full realisation of its potential, and the majority of its citizens remain near subsistence. Papua New Guinea is a natural leader of the South Pacific, but its relatively late independence and urbanisation and its location off trunk air routes have relegated it to a secondary role to Fiji as a venue for international organisation meetings and headquarters. It is also troubled by security problems, both internal and external—the result of its fragmented human and physical geography and its proximity to giant Indonesia. Forging a consensus on identity and easing away from the pervasive influence of Australia so as to play an independent international role and speed economic development are premier objectives of Papua New Guinea's leaders.

Political evolution

Melanesian socio-political fragmentation arose out of the crosscutting migrational patterns and variegated geography of the archipelago and was reinforced by the evolution of up to 700 separate languages. Authority remained dispersed in villages and clans, and contact between valleys, plateaus, coastal fringes and islands was minimal. The Portuguese explorer Jorge de Meneses in 1526 was the first European to land on the island of New Guinea, but he and subsequent Spanish, Dutch, British, French, Germany and American explorers left no mark on the people during the next three centuries (Douglas and Douglas 1989, pp. 466–70; Craig and King 1981, pp. 220–4).

In the mid 1800s contacts were made with copra, pearl and *bêche-de-mer* traders, missionaries and blackbirders. The end of the Franco-Prussian War precipitated a search for new colonies, and in 1884 the British annexed Papua in the south and Germany annexed New Guinea in the north. Blackbirding was halted, Western law was imposed, and in subsequent decades trading posts, towns, plantations and mines were established on land appropriated by the colonial governments and by favoured companies from tribal custom users. The coastal inhabitants enjoyed some wage-labour opportunities and health and education improvements, but the people of the interior remained unaffected. New Guinea was seized from Germany by Australian in 1914, was awarded to Australia as a C class mandate by the League of Nations in 1920, was lost to Japan in 1942–44, and was joined administratively with Papua in 1946. Australia administered the combined Territory of Papua and New Guinea under United Nations trusteeship until 1975.

Colonial decision-making and administration were monopolised by Australian and British expatriates until as late as the 1960s. A few local persons were engaged in the lower ranks of the colonial service and a handful were co-opted onto the legislative councils, but the vast majority remained in villages untouched by government or, at best, in towns, where some were employed by or served on municipal councils. The retarded progress towards self-government attracted criticism by a United Nations visiting mission in 1962 (Premdas 1975). Australia responded by establishing the House of Assembly in 1964, with 44 out of 64 members elected by indigenes.

This experience led to the formation of the first political party, the Pangu Pati (from *Pa*pua *N*ew *Gu*inea party) in 1967, which adopted a nationalist and pro-independence posture (Pokawin 1982, pp. 41–6; Craig and King 1981, pp. 231–3). In response, European planters helped form the United Party in 1970 to urge continued Australian tutelage until local people could be trained for the public service and the economy developed sufficiently for the country to be viable. Around these two parties clustered others, some with programmes, some representing localities, some grouped around strong personalities. The conservative United Party won a plurality in the election of 1972, but the Pangu Pati led by Michael Somare was able to command a majority by attracting minor party and independent members into a coalition.

Somare formed the territory's first indigenous government, led the country to independence on 16 September 1975 and became Papua New Guinea's first prime minister. Papua New Guinea became a parliamentary democracy within the Commonwealth with titular allegiance to the Queen represented by a locally chosen governor general. A court system administered British law as modified by Australian, national and custom elements. To forestall Bougainville and Papua Besena secessionist movements, and to protect diverse regional interests, nineteen elected provincial governments were set up in 1976 as an intermediate tier between the municipal and national governments.

Somare led his party to another electoral victory in 1977. In 1979 his coalition partner, the People's Progressive Party, representing islands interests, deserted the coalition, and its leader, Julius Chan, formed a new government. However, Somare and the Pangu Pati won the 1982 election and returned to power. The Pangu Pati split in 1985, and defectors backed Paias Wingti for the prime minister-ship. Wingti's government lasted until 1987. Then Pangu Pati's Rabbie Namaliu, a former Minister of Foreign Affairs, became compromise prime minister at the head of a six-party coalition, with Somare as his Minister of Foreign Affairs.

Foreign policy

The alternation, fracturing and regrouping of parties did not drasti-cally affect the substance (as contrasted to the rhetoric) of foreign policy. The Pangu Pati presented itself as nationalist and democratic socialist, comparable to Vanuatu's Vanuaaku Pati. The United Party took a pro-Australia and free enterprise stance. The People's Pro-gressive Party, which shared the United Party's commitment to economic growth policies, spoke for the centre right of the ideo-logical spectrum. However, these formal ideologies were crosscut by *wantok* (linguistic) loyalties, economic interests, religious affili-ations and 'big man' (influential personality) obligations, and re-flected the regional differences between Papuans, highlanders, northerners and islanders. The parties lacked mass bases and stable organisations and funding, and their leaders operated pragmatically, as power brokers as much as policy makers (Jennings 1990, pp. 269–70); Tanham 1990, pp. 6–8, 15–16).

The parties, the interest groups—such as unions, professional groups, women's committees, clan associations and churches—and the media all lacked the depth of experience, structure, education or motivation to debate foreign policy and clarify alternatives. A partial exception was the students' association of the University of

Papua New Guinea in Port Moresby, but it was dogmatically critical of Australia, Indonesia, and their own government's alleged weakness and mistakes. Nevertheless, the mainstream parties, groups and media reached consensus on a few fundamentals: all shared a wish to replace Australians by indigenous civil servants and experts, to gain greater economic autonomy from Australia, to achieve harmony with neighbouring Indonesia, to project Papua New Guinea as an influential player in the South Pacific, and to secure international resources that would assist in rapid economic development. They differed only on priority between these goals and on the best means and pace to achieve them.

An early indication of the thrust of foreign policy was given by Michael Somare, then chief minister, in 1974 and is quoted here at length because it foreshadows much that was to occur:

> Papua New Guinea must adopt a universalist stance. While we are interested in the ideological and security questions which face the world, our country will not neglect its commitment to her people by involving itself in international squabbling on these issues. It will not be our aim to seek any form of ideological or military grouping with the big powers. Papua New Guinea supports a zone of true peace and neutrality in the oceans which lie to either side of her—the Pacific and the Indian. We wish them to be kept free of the arms race in which the big powers compete for military prestige. We believe in the principles of the charter of the UN and will co-operate with all efforts to promote peace, security, and international justice (Somare 1974, p. 5).

Somare asserted that his government wanted a foreign policy that was 'home grown and not one with large sections borrowed from others' and so 'we are willing to take our time about developing such a policy, and not jump in too quickly to form alliances, or take sides in world issues' (Somare 1974, p. 14). He urged close relations with Australia and the Commonwealth, South Pacific neighbours and regional organisations, and Southeast and East Asian states, particularly Indonesia and Japan, but not at the expense of an independent national viewpoint and integrity. The Papua New Guinea Constitution of 1975 reflected this caution in its call for 'wise assessment of foreign ideas and values so that these will be subordinated to the goals of national sovereignty and self-reliance' and to 'the integrity of the Nation and the People' ('Papua New Guinea' 1985, p. 28 and 1986, p. 100).

Implicit in this and other goals of the constitution, most of which focus on internal objectives and ideals, was the need to establish an independent identity, not only in the eyes of the international community but also as 'a tool of nation-building to establish a consciousness of Papua New Guinea amongst our own people'

(Olewale 1974, p. 70). It was hoped that building consensus and pride in foreign policy might ameliorate the regional, socio-economic and political divisions that threatened to jeopardise effective domestic governance. The successive slogans summing up foreign policy were 'friends to all, enemy to none' at independence, 'selective, constructive engagement' during the early 1980s, and 'independent commitment to international cooperation' adopted by the Wingti government in 1987 (Saffu 1988, p. 249).

Diplomacy

Four years prior to independence the development of a foreign service began with the recruitment of Papua New Guineans into the International Affairs Branch of the Department of the Administrator. The Department of Foreign Relations and Trade was set up in 1973. It was headed by the minister with the assistance of the secretary and five assistant secretaries for political affairs, customs, international trade, migration, and protocol and consular affairs, and a staff that eventually grew to 175, largest in the South Pacific. Its terms of reference were:

- to maintain friendly relations with neighbouring states;
- to formulate and implement overseas trade policies;
- to encourage overseas assistance;
- to protect Papua New Guinea's interests and nationals overseas;
- to provide hospitality for visitors from abroad;
- to control the entry of visitors and immigrants;
- to collect customs and excise revenues; and
- to guard against the unlawful entry or export of restricted goods (Papua New Guinea Government 1975, p. 127).

Prior to independence ministers and officials had attended meetings of international and regional organisations including the United Nations General Assembly, the Economic and Social Commission for Asia and the Pacific (ESCAP), the Food and Agriculture Organization (FAO), the South Pacific Commission, the South Pacific Forum, and the Law of the Sea Conference. On independence Papua New Guinea became a full member of these and others and became particularly active in the South Pacific Commission and the affiliated agencies of the South Pacific Forum. It became a member of the Commonwealth and worked with the Commonwealth Secretariat, the Commonwealth Foundation and the Commonwealth Fund for Technical Cooperation. It joined the African, Caribbean and Pacific (ACP) Group and signed the Lome Convention making it eligible for STABEX (export price stabilisation) payments. It received aid and technical assistance from other bodies including the United Nations Development Programme (UNDP), the United Nations Fund for Population Activities (UNFPA), the Asian Development Bank (ADB), the International Monetary Fund (IMF) and the European Development Fund (EDF). By 1988 Papua New Guinea was a member of 127 intergovernmental organisations, including the Non Aligned Movement from 1988, well ahead of Fiji's 113 memberships and approaching the 168 memberships of New Zealand (Union of International Associations 1988, table 4).

Papua New Guinea's overseas diplomatic missions were established first in Canberra and Sydney before independence, and then in 1975 in Wellington, Suva, Jakarta, Tokyo, Washington and New York. The high commission in Suva facilitated contact with South Pacific states and organisations, and the New York post was a mission to the United Nations where the ambassador liaised with counterparts from around the world. By 1980 new posts had opened in Brussels, facilitating contact with the European Community states, and in London and Manila. By 1986 posts were operating also in Kuala Lumpur and Bonn, and in 1990 a 'representative office' was opened in Taipei. Posts opened in Singapore and Honiara had to be closed as a temporary economy measure. Australia provided liaison and consular services in countries in which Papua New Guinea was not represented.

In Port Moresby the governments of Australia, Britain, Indonesia, Japan, New Zealand, the Philippines and the United States established resident diplomatic posts. In 1990 Port Moresby became the first South Pacific capital to host a Soviet diplomatic post. By 1991 Papua New Guinea had formal diplomatic links with 64 countries including fourteen Western European states, six Eastern European states, fourteen Asian states, and a dozen from African, the Middle East and South America. Relations with contrasting partners—such as the United States and the Soviet Union, North and South Korea, Israel and Iraq, West and East Germany (until 1990), and India and Pakistan—and growing quasi-official links with the Republic of China (Taiwan) alongside formal relations with the People's Republic of China since 1976, all embodied the policy of non-alignment (Papua New Guinea 1980, pp. 55–6 and 1986, pp. 48–9).

Foreign policy focus

Papua New Guinea's foreign policy has three principal focal points: Australia, Indonesia and the neighbouring Melanesian states. Frictions with Australia were inherent in the post-colonial relationship as nationalist leaders resisted 'paternalism' and hastened to replace

Australian officers and experts with local, often inexperienced personnel but continued to rely on Australian financial and other assistance, which it sometimes misused, in Australian eyes. Establishing a 'one-to-one relationship', a relationship of equals, has been a major goal of the government. A step in this direction was taken in the Joint Statement on a Long Term Defence Arrangement in 1977 wherein the two governments pledged to consult 'on matters affecting their common security' and to engage in joint training, exercises and logistics and in technical cooperation. However, in 1980, when Papua New Guinea prepared to dispatch troops to assist Vanuatu's government to quell a secessionist movement, Australia delayed a week before giving approval for the participation of twenty Australians, invoking the 1977 Consultative Procedures on the Use of Australian Loan Personnel in Politically Sensitive Areas (Maketu 1988, p. 12). Australia was thought to have discouraged defence force actions at the Indonesian border, in the highlands, in the Port Vila riots and in Bougainville in the 1980s. These perceived constraints remain a source of irritation, stimulating calls to dispense with Australian secondments entirely so as to nullify the consultative procedures and attain complete sovereignty in the use of armed force.

In 1979–85 a treaty was negotiated demarcating the controversial Torres Strait boundary. However, the continued movement of Torres Strait islanders into Australia raised criticism among Queensland nationalists of poaching and illegal immigration and reawakened bitterness among Papuans about disagreements over boundaries, migrations and citizenship rights going back to 1879 (Griffin 1974, pp. 6–11). In 1980 Papua New Guinea signed the South Pacific Regional Trade and Economic Cooperation Agreement and in 1987 renegotiated the Papua New Guinea–Australia Trade and Commercial Relations Agreement. It hoped to gain access to Australia's market, but found that non-tariff barriers and lack of consumer demand prevented redress of the trade balance, which persistently remained in Australia's favour.

In 1987, at the instigation of Prime Minister Wingti, the two countries drafted and signed an omnibus Declaration of Principles Guiding Relations between Papua New Guinea and Australia, covering all aspects of the relationship (Australia Government 1987c, pp. 615–16). Other agreements were negotiated on specialised matters including aid and economic cooperation and are discussed below. Together, these instruments asserted Papua New Guinea's sovereign equality and, in the face of continuing disagreements and criticisms, contributed to smoother government-to-government relations.

Papua New Guinea's second foreign policy concern is Indonesia.

The two countries share a poorly demarcated land boundary 800 kilometres long that has arbitrarily divided highland clans since 1828. To moderate tensions generated by movements of the Free Papua Movement rebels, the governments of Papua New Guinea and Indonesia signed a border agreement in 1979 and established a Joint Border Committee to supervise demarcation and discuss and report on alleged violations (Tanham 1990, pp. 20–5). In 1983 Papua New Guinea complained about the routing of an Indonesian north–south road through portions of Papua New Guinea territory. In 1984, Indonesian counterinsurgency operations sent 11 000 West Papuans fleeing across the border, placing financial and political burdens on the provincial and central governments.

Papua New Guinea complained in the United Nations General Assembly, and the United Nations High Commission for Refugees was invited to assist and mediate. However, Indonesia would not take responsibility, students at the University of Papua New Guinea agitated for a firm stance against Indonesia, and the Papua New Guinea Cabinet divided on whether the West Papuans were political refugees or just economic migrants. The new Wingti government criticised the outgoing Somare government for inaction, resettled 8000 refugees away from the border, deported rebel leaders to the Netherlands, and negotiated a Treaty of Mutual Respect, Friendship and Cooperation with Indonesia in 1986. As relations warmed, Papua New Guinea, sponsored by Indonesia, became an observer at meetings of the Association of Southeast Asian Nations (ASEAN), participated in several subsidiary committees, acceded to ASEAN's Treaty of Amity and Cooperation in 1987 and for a time explored the possibility of membership in ASEAN (Saffu 1988, p. 250).

In 1988 a series of Indonesian military incursions in pursuit of West Papuan guerillas threatened Papua New Guinea's territorial integrity again (Hegarty 1990, p. 185). Only skilful personal diplomacy by Foreign Minister Somare kept the dispute from escalating and preserved the government's credibility in the face of criticism by nationalistic students in Port Moresby. By 1991 the relationship returned to harmony. Nevertheless, the possibility of future Indonesian military violation of Papua New Guinea's sovereignty dominates the strategic thinking not only of the defence force but also of neighbouring Australia, which is reluctant to antagonise its large neighbour but is obligated to assist Papua New Guinea.

The third foreign policy concern is the Melanesian neighbourhood. In 1980, at the request of Vanuatu's Prime Minister Walter Lini, the government of Papua New Guinea sent 400 troops of the Kumul Force to Espiritu Santo to quell a secessionist movement (Wolfers 1981, pp. 280–2). The operation was a success, and a defence treaty and an agreement to train members of the Vanuatu Mobile Force were signed subsequently. This linkage, added to the attractiveness of Papua New Guinea's 'Melanesian socialism' to the Vanuaaku Pati, crystallised a sympathetic relationship, in which Solomon Islands was later included. However, a proposal by Prime Minister Julius Chan and Foreign Minister Noel Levi to set up a permanent South Pacific peacekeeping force was not backed by the South Pacific Forum and was discouraged by Australia and New Zealand; all felt that the costs and complications would be excessive, the influence wielded by Papua New Guinea unpredictable and their own room for manoeuvre reduced (Fry 1990).

In 1986 Prime Minister Wingti resurrected an idea that had been broached by Solomon Islands Prime Minister Mamaloni 5 years before: a Melanesian grouping to protect and promote mutual Melanesian interests, including opposition to Japanese waste dumping, French nuclear testing, French colonialism and great power intrusions in the region (MacQueen 1990). This initiative became the third thrust of Wingti's foreign policy, the first being a distancing from Australia and a second a rapprochement with Indonesia. The Melanesian Spearhead Group came formally into existence with the signing by Papua New Guinea, Solomon Islands and Vanuatu of its Agreed Principles of Cooperation at Port Vila on 14 March 1988. Fiji was invited to join but declined. It is expected that an independent Kanak government will eventually join. The group has held annual meetings, but has confined itself to the promotion of cultural and economic relations and avoided taking a radical political stance or precipitating any splits in existing organisations such as the South Pacific Forum. Bougainville's secession raised suspicions that local leaders appealed to nearby Solomon Islanders for assistance and used Solomon Islands territory as a base. This and the boundary dispute over Pocklington Reef, could put the Papua New Guinea–Solomon Islands relationship at risk (Prescott 1988, p. 17).

Defence

Motivated by Indonesian independence, then the takeover of West New Guinea, Australia set up the Papua New Guinea Defence Force in 1950 and upgraded it in 1963 (Maketu 1988, pp. 1–2). At present the Defence Force consists of three infantry battalions, a squadron of four patrol boats and two landing craft, an air transport squadron of six aircraft and four helicopters, and support units including medical, engineers, logistics, signals and military police, for a projected total of 5000 personnel. Australian officers and advisors have been reduced from 465 in 1975 to less than 90 in 1990, but considerable assistance is still received through the Defence Cooperation Programme, including four patrol boats under the Pacific Patrol Boat Project, three Nomad aircraft and four Iroquois helicopters. Australia also provided mapping, intelligence, air surveillance and long range transport and, in 1988/89, gave 350 personnel specialist training. Training and exercise opportunities have also been received through the New Zealand Defence Mutual Assistance Programme, the United States International Military Education and Training Program, and exchanges with Britain's Ghurka Rifles based in Hong Kong.

The functions of the Defence Force as specified in the constitution are:

- to defend Papua New Guinea and its territory;
- to assist in the fulfilment of international obligations;
- to assist civilian authorities in civil disaster, the restoration of public order or declared national emergency; and
- to perform tasks of a civil nature to participate in national development and improvement ('Papua New Guinea' 1985, p. 138 and 1986, p. 185).

Two threat scenarios have been sketched by a former Secretary of Defence (Maketu 1988, pp. 5–6). The first is conflict at the western border either with Free Papua Movement rebels using Papua New Guinea as a base for cross-border operations, or with the Indonesian armed forces in hot pursuit or pre-emptive strike or occupation, or all simultaneously. Libyan assistance to the rebels, reported in the late 1980s, and Australian political and media sensitivity, heightened by Indonesian military operations in East Timor and elsewhere, could escalate the tension and internationalise the conflict. The solution lies in military control of the border region to keep rebels out and to convince Indonesia not to intervene. However, this is difficult at a time when the defence budget has been reduced. It is also politically controversial in Port Moresby, where sympathy for the West Papuans is high and for Indonesia low.

The second scenario is the breakdown of domestic law and order as a result of highland tribal feuding, urban rioting or rascal gang violence, or secession, in which cases the Defence Force is tasked to back up the police. In 1989–90 secession became a reality after militant landowners engaged in guerilla attacks on Bougainville Copper Limited facilities at Panguna. A state of emergency was declared, Defence Force units were sent, and Francis Ona of the Bougainville Revolutionary Army issued a declaration of independence on 17 May 1990 (Polomka 1990). New Zealand offered its tanker HMNZS *Endeavour* as a venue for negotiations between the rebels and the government in September 1990. The government of Solomon Islands hosted further talks in January 1991, and a fragile peace was restored. Defence Force units were removed, but not without criticism of their heavyhandedness and unpreparedness for intervention in political controversies.

The Defence Force has been used to advance Papua New Guinea's foreign relations, as in assistance to Vanuatu and the reinforcement of encouragement to Kanak nationalists, and in civil actions such as crowd control and disaster relief. Political involvement was seen in 1988 when People's Action Party leader and former Defence Force Commander Ted Diro, backed by several highlander officers, manoeuvred for reinstatement; all were sacked. In 1988 and 1989 servicemen refused to carry out orders and demonstrated openly to back pay claims (Hegarty 1989b, pp. 182, 186; Tanham 1990, p. 14). The Bougainville theatre commander was sacked in 1991 for exceeding his authority and using Australian-donated transport helicopters as gunships. The possibility of a military takeover—or at least of more overt military involvement in government decision making, provoked by a combination of low pay, poor political leadership and the breakdown of law and order—is guardedly discussed. Such a contingency would damage Papua New Guinea's diplomatic, aid and trade relations with Australia and other democracies, and it might raise tensions with Indonesia if the intervention took on a nationalistic character. But it would be accepted with little reaction by the South Pacific Forum states, as the Fiji precedent has shown. Its more serious effect might be to fracture the fragile political consensus and to precipitate secessions and civil strife, which would drive investors out and draw Indonesia in.

Economic relations

In 1974 Somare, noting Papua New Guinea's attractiveness in a resource-hungry world, stressed that his government would manage trade, aid and investment to keep control of resources for the benefit of the people (Somare 1974, p. 6). Economic independence became a major theme, expressed in the Eight Aims and promulgated by the government in 1974. The following excerpts summarise the economic objectives:

- a more self-reliant economy, less dependent for its needs on imported goods and services and better able to meet the needs of its people through local production;
- a rapid increase in the proportion of the economy under the control of Papua New Guinea individuals and groups; and

172   THE SOUTH PACIFIC FOREIGN AFFAIRS HANDBOOK

- an increasing capacity for meeting government spending needs from locally raised revenue (Papua New Guinea Government 1974, p. x).

These objectives were formalised in the constitution, which called for government control of the economy, use of local skills and resources, and the gearing of foreign capital to internal social and economic policies. The third principal goal, National Sovereignty and Self-Reliance, concluded as follows:

> We accordingly call for the constant recognition of our sovereignty, which must not be undermined by dependence on foreign assistance of any sort, and in particular for no investment, military or foreign-aid agreement or understanding to be entered into that imperils our self-reliance and self-respect or that may lead to substantial dependence upon or influence by any country, investor, lender, or donor ('Papua New Guinea' 1985, p. 28 and 1986, p. 100).

The reality was extensive penetration by foreign plantations, mining operations and commercial enterprises and unavoidable dependence by the government on Australian budgetary support and capital aid. Nevertheless, the country's natural resources, particularly minerals, provided a strong export earings base and a source of government revenue to finance development. In 1970 the country earned by exports only one-third of the value of its imports. Subsequently infrastructural improvements and overseas demand lifted exports until a merchandise trade surplus was achieved in 1978 and 1979 and from 1985 to 1988, with only a slight deficit in 1989 (*Pacific Economic Bulletin* 1990b, p. 60). The composition of exports diversified in the 1970s and 1980s as copper and gold deposits in Panguna, Ok Tedi and Porgera were opened up, as shown in Table 12.1. Gas reserves were confirmed, and petroleum deposits at Kutubu showed promise, leading to the expectation of petrochemical export earnings by the mid 1990s. During the past two decades

Table 12.1 Papua New Guinea's exports, 1970 and 1989 (%)

Commodity	1970	1989
Coffee and cocoa	38.1	16.8
Copra and palm oil	21.1	6.4
Marine products	1.0	0.7
Gold	0.9	28.9
Copper	0.0	31.4
Logs	0.0	8.3
Re-exports	23.6	4.4
Total	100.0	100.0

Source: Pacific Economic Bulletin 1990b, p. 61.

Table 12.2 Papua New Guinea's trade partners, 1970 and 1988 (%)

Exports to	1970	1988
Australia	44.1	6.6
Britain	16.5	5.1
United States	11.9	2.7
Japan	9.2	39.4
Germany	8.0	21.2
Other Europe	4.6	4.3
Other Asia	—[a]	8.4
Others	10.3	12.3
Total	100.0	100.0

Imports from	1970	1988
Australia	53.6	45.0
Japan	12.4	17.8
United States	10.6	9.0
Britain	5.8	2.8
Germany	1.8	2.3
Other Asia	2.5	11.4
Other Europe	—[a]	1.4
Others	12.1	10.3
Total	100.0	100.0

[a] Included in Others.

Source: *Pacific Economic Bulletin* 1990b, p. 61; Papua New Guinea Government 1990b, p. S40.

Papua New Guinea diversified its trade from Australia to focus more on partners in Asia and Europe, as Table 12.2 shows.

Papua New Guinea's abundant resources have attracted massive foreign private investments and facilitated government borrowing. These financial flows have been directed to the mining sector, particularly Bougainville and Ok Tedi copper, with visible returns. These flows have also raised the level of indebtedness borne by the economy. From 1979 to 1987 debt rose from 26.5 per cent of gross domestic product (GDP) to 68.3 per cent, and debt service as a percentage of export earnings rose from 12.2 per cent to 19.8 per cent. Initially the bulk of borrowing was by the government from international agencies at concessionary rates. But pressure for more rapid investment raised private and government commercial-rate debt to more than half of the aggregate national debt in 1982–86, and the debt service ratio rose to a peak of 29.9 per cent in 1985 (Browne 1989, p. 106; Papua New Guinea Government 1990b, p. S28). Repayments eased the burden by the end of the 1980s, but the government in 1988 still depended on overseas borrowing for

Table 12.3 Papua New Guinea's creditors, 1990

Creditor	US$million
Japan	485.8
Australia	99.0
Britain	33.7
Germany	27.7
United States	9.7
Switzerland	8.2
Kuwait	7.7
France	1.6
International Development Association	376.8
Asian Development Bank	310.9
European Community	101.3
European Investment Bank	46.7
International Fund for Agricultural Development	10.5
Organisation of Petroleum Exporting Countries	4.0
Others	93.8
Total	1 894.6

Note: Figures are aggregates of loans, suppliers credits and bonds.

Source: World Bank 1991a, p. 174.

13 per cent of its revenue, and Papua New Guinea remained the South Pacific's most indebted country (Australia Government 1989a, pp. 12, 52).

Debt service is projected to rise to over 30 per cent of export earnings in the 1990s (World Bank 1991a, p. 43). Papua New Guinea's creditors in 1987 are listed in Table 12.3 showing their diversity and relative importance.

Aid remains an essential component of government revenue. In 1974, 1976, 1981 and 1985 Australia entered into multiyear aid commitments that underwrote approximately 30 per cent of the Papua New Guinea budget. In 1989 a Treaty of Development Cooperation ended Australia's participation in the budgetary process and signalled a reduction of budgetary assistance to around 10 per cent of Papua New Guinea's budget. The treaty reaffirmed Australia's long-term aid commitment as partial compensation for the advantages Australia received from its investments in, and favourable trade balance with, Papua New Guinea (Australia Government 1989d, pp. 6–11). Other bilateral and multilateral donors have contributed increasing amounts, and together they have moderated Australia's predominance to less than half of the total, with this trend expected to continue (see Table 12.4). Also, rising revenues derived from domestic and trade taxes and overseas borrowing have reduced dependence on aid from 32.6 per cent of government revenues in 1982 to 18.3 per cent in 1989 (Australia Government

Table 12.4 Papua New Guinea's aid donors and receipts, 1987

Donor	A$ 000	%
Australia	296 740	59.2
Japan	39 424	7.9
Britain	4 778	1.0
Germany	2 881	0.6
New Zealand	419	0.1
European Community	79 638	15.9
Asian Development Bank	23 216	4.6
United Nations Development Programme	4 544	0.9
Others	49 185	9.0
Total	500 825	100.0

Source: South Pacific Commission 1989a, p. 14.

1989a, p. 52; Papua New Guinea Government 1990a, p. 6). On a per capita basis Papua New Guinea has one of the lowest rates of aid in the South Pacific (see Table 2.9).

Tourism is not a major factor in the external economy. Visitor arrivals, the bulk from Australia to engage in business or aid work, are only one-fifth of the number of visitors to Fiji annually, and they take out more in salaries than they spend locally. Tourism brings benefits to only a thin stratum of the urban economy. Emigration also is small relative to the population, and remittances are correspondingly a minor element in external earnings. Fishing access fees are paid by Japan, South Korea and Taiwan in accordance with bilateral treaties. In 1984 fishing fees totalled US$4.2 million, equivalent to 0.6 per cent of total government revenues (Doulman 1986, p. 9). Since 1987 the United States has paid a formula fee under the terms of the United States–South Pacific Regional Fisheries Treaty estimated to be over US$6 million annually. In the current account the balance of invisibles (that is, services) is typically in deficit, in contrast to the balance of merchandise trade and the capital accounts, which are often in surplus (Browne 1989, p. 103).

Economic policy issues

The government's declaratory policies from 1972 have been protectionist, and the acceptance of foreign aid and investment was conditional at best. The National Investment Development Authority (NIDA) reserved for local enterprise all small-scale activities such as land transport, coastal fisheries, smallholder coffee growing and alluvial gold mining, and encouraged local participation in foreign ventures. Yet the policy of indigenising the public service and reducing dependence on Australian aid entailed heavy borrowing and private investment to stimulate export earnings to finance development, with attendant Australian private-sector penetration.

The dilemma gave rise to three schools of thought in the mid 1970s. The 'nationalist' view, held by influential figures in the Constitutional Planning Committee, and supporters of John Momis's Melanesian Alliance and the radical wing of the Pangu Pati, was reflected in the ideals stated in the Eight Aims and the constitution. It was frankly protectionist and implied considerable government intervention for social purposes. Its opposite was the 'production maximising' school, which emphasised a liberal use of foreign financial and technical resources to stimulate economic growth; indigenisation and rural development were seen as secondary to the generation of jobs in the modern and urban sectors. This view was supported by the expatriates, the private sector and the public servants in the ministries for Industries and Agriculture, and was advanced by the United Party, the People's Progressive Party and Prime Minister Julius Chan.

The intermediate 'benefits maximisation' school tried to rationalise dependence on foreign expertise and finance by focusing on their long term benefits, optimistic that local officials and enterprises would mature and gradually take over foreign activities as the economy matured. This view was held by the ministries of Finance and Planning and by the mainstream of the Pangu Pati led by Prime Minister Somare. Economic policy has been the outcome of fluctuating tensions and alliances between these three schools, with a tendency towards pragmatic compromise (Daniel and Sims 1986, pp. 19–21).

Accordingly, after independence the protectionist ideals did not prevent government hospitality to foreign expertise and enterprise. The National Planning Office stated in 1978 that 'the government has established a framework of economic policy which provides for stable growth and insulates the economy from shocks. An economic environment which allows the investor to plan ahead with reasonable confidence is probably the most effective investment incentive of all' (Daniel and Sims 1986, p. 14). The 1980 budget formalised a number of tax and financial incentives to enhance the investment climate, including write-offs for depreciation, training, decentralisation and exporting, provisions of infrastructure, and loans for new ventures, import duty relief and tariff margins (Daniel and Sims 1986, pp. 107–14). A Foreign Enterprise Registration Board was set up to speed approvals of foreign applications, and in the late 1980s public enterprises including the national airline, bank, investment

corporation and housing commission were privatised. The government replaced NIDA by an Investment Promotion Authority in 1991,
liberalised investment regulations and streamlined their administration, and made access to land more secure (World Bank 1991a, p.
89).

This movement away from the 'nationalist' view towards the
'production maximising' view was rationalised by the 'benefits
maximising' argument and reflected the dominance of urban elite
political leaders. The shift has generated opposition from leaders of
outlying areas and adherents of traditional and socialist views. The
environmental lobby has also decried the shift of policy as unre-
strained mining and logging have caused not only ecological despoliation but also the economic dislocation of thousands of rural
dwellers, many of whom swell the numbers of unemployed in the
towns. The debate between the economic policy schools is expected
to continue through the 1990s and to produce varied political
alliances and further policy alterations.

13 Solomon Islands

Solomon Islands is the second-largest, and third most populous, Pacific island country. Its evolution through colonialism to independence in 1978 was slow but non-violent. It is now a parliamentary democracy cooperating with the West, the Commonwealth and its South Pacific neighbours, although with occasional rhetorical turbulence. Moderately well endowed with arable land, deposits of bauxite, phosphates and gold, and abundant seas, Solomon Islands nevertheless remains a poor country in need of foreign assistance to develop. Promoting economic cooperation is the major objective of the government's foreign policy.

Political evolution

First seen by the Spanish explorer Mendana in 1568, and visited by Dutch, French, British and American explorers, whalers and sandalwood cutters during the following three centuries, Solomon Islanders experienced no regular contact with Europeans until Anglican missionaries, and blackbirders, established themselves in about 1870 (Craig and King 1981, pp. 264–7; Douglas and Douglas 1989, pp. 515–19). Solomons culture was 3000 years old, but socio-political organisation remained dispersed among islands and villages; and unlike Polynesian culture with its chiefly hierarchies, each clan group spoke a different language and their 'big men' had to be approached separately. To end blackbirding and to protect its position in the rivalry with Germany and France, Britain brought the islands under its protection in 1899 and administered them from Fiji without significant Solomon Islander participation until the Japanese occupation and Allied liberation in 1942–43.

Early nationalism was manifested by the Marching Rule—a movement of defiance of colonial taxes and regulations led by local chiefs of Malaita Island in the 1940s. This, and the worldwide trend towards decolonisation, led the British to establish local government councils in 1952, a Legislative Council in 1960, and a constitution providing for elections in 1970. Solomon Islanders gained internal self-government in 1976 and achieved independence on 7 July 1978. A local governor general was chosen to represent the Queen as the titular head of state. The chief minister, Peter Kenilorea, elected from Malaita Island with the United Party, became prime minister. His executive council became the Cabinet, numbering fifteen ministers, and the Legislative Assembly became the national parliament of 38 elected members. Below the national government a tier of eight elected provincial councils was established to respond to local island interests (Saemala 1982, pp. 64–81).

Since independence the Solomon Islands government has conducted regular free elections, and power has passed to new leaders constitutionally. However, the political culture has remained fragmented, institutions have remained undeveloped, and leadership changes have been unpredictable. Political parties were slow to achieve organisation, discipline or mass base and remained expressions of provincial interests and dominant personalities in the Honiara political arena. Governments tended to be coalitions, and cabinets were reshuffled between elections as members changed parties or were co-opted (Larmour 1983b, *passim*). In 1981 Kenilorea lost the support of his coalition partners and was replaced by Solomon Mamaloni leading a coalition of the People's Alliance Party and other opposition members. Kenilorea's United Party won the election of 1984, but a scandal over misused French aid funds obliged Kenilorea to step aside for Ezekiel Alebua in 1986.

Mamaloni and the People's Alliance Party formed a one-party government after the election of 1989. However, the following year he reshuffled his Cabinet to bring in the United Party's Sir Baddeley Devesi as deputy prime minister and Kenilorea as Minister of Foreign Affairs and to co-opt Liberal Party deputy leader George Luialamo as Minister for Agriculture and Lands. More significant than its party composition was the fact that the new Cabinet contained four ministers from Malaita, three from Guadalcanal, three from Western Province, and one from each of the four smaller provinces and Honiara. Mamaloni proclaimed it 'a government of national unity and political reconciliation' while critics predicted the end of responsible party government and its replacement by an oligarchy of island leaders dividing the spoils of office (Angiki 1990a, pp. 10–11; Keith-Reid 1990a, pp. 18–23).

Diplomacy

On independence Solomon Islands adopted a low key policy of non-alignment within the framework of international cooperation. The Secretary for Foreign Affairs in 1980 stated to parliament, 'we would work to influence the international community to ensure the Solomons can prosper in security and peace, keep intact its national identity in an interdependent world, and contribute towards the general benefit of mankind the best way we can' (Sitai 1983, p. 227).

The principles adopted to guide Solomon Islands foreign policy were:

- to support the United Nations and the Commonwealth and encourage peace, stability and security;
- to oppose nuclear testing, storage and dumping in the Pacific and prohibit visits by nuclear weapons carrying vessels;
- to oppose colonialism and neocolonialism and promote independence of Pacific peoples;
- to safeguard sovereignty and uphold non-interference;
- to establish diplomatic relations only with honest, friendly, and stable countries likely to bring benefits;
- to welcome foreign aid for national development only if it is given free of obligations (Solomon Islands Government 1989, pp. 6–7).

Solomon Islands committed itself to international morality and the right of self-determination and condemned apartheid and 'the cold assessment of self-interest in world power politics'. However, it also signalled that it would participate constructively in the United Nations, the Commonwealth and South Pacific regional organisations, and would maintain relations with traditional friends.

One of the principal objectives of the National Development Plan 1985–89 was entitled Promotion of International Cooperation and World Peace (Solomon Islands Government 1985, p. 19 and 1988a, p. 42). The means chosen was to participate in international and regional organisations and to engage in bilateral diplomacy. In 1978 Solomon Islands became the thirty-seventh member of the Commonwealth, began attending Commonwealth Heads of Government Meetings, and received advice and assistance from the Commonwealth Secretariat and Commonwealth Fund for Technical Cooperation. The government took immediate steps to join the United Nations. Prime Minister Kenilorea in his first address to the United

Nations General Assembly said, 'we want to contribute and participate, as well as receive, in this world body of nations. We cannot
offer arms and ammunition. But we have good common sense and
believe in our ability to give in some small way, for peace and
harmony in this our wonderful world' (Sitai 1983, p. 227).

Solomon Islands subsequently set up a small diplomatic post
accredited to the United Nations and began participating in general
assembly sessions and in affiliated bodies—such as the United
Nations Educational, Scientific and Cultural Organization (UNE-
SCO), the United Nations Development Programme (UNDP), the
United Nations Industrial Development Organization (UNIDO), the
Food and Agriculture Organization (FAO), the International Labour
Organisation (ILO) and the World Health Organization (WHO)—to
the extent possible with limited funds and personnel. Links with
Britain led Solomon Islands to accredit an ambassador to the Com-
mission of the European Communities and, after joining the African,
Caribbean and Pacific (ACP) Group of states, to sign the Lome
Convention in 1979, thereby becoming eligible for aid and STABEX
(export price stabilisation) payments. Within a year of independence
Solomon Islands had joined the South Pacific Commission and the
South Pacific Forum and all its affiliated bodies. Solomon Islands
was a founder member of the Forum Fisheries Agency and hosts its
secretariat in Honiara. It is now a member of 23 international and
regional organisations.

The objectives of bilateral diplomacy were to signal independence,
enhance goodwill, provide information and facilitate economic cooperation. Early relations were established with the United States,
the leading states of Europe and the North Pacific—such as Britain,
France, Germany, Belgium, Sweden, Norway, Canada, Japan and
South Korea—and South Pacific neighbours including Papua New
Guinea, Australia and New Zealand. Subsequent relations were set
up with most other South Pacific states, some Southeast Asian states
including Malaysia, Indonesia and Singapore, and India, bringing
the total to 33 (Solomon Islands Government 1989, p. 16).

Feelers by the Soviet Union, Cuba, Libya, the Palestine Liberation
Organization (PLO) and the Non Aligned Movement to establish
relations have been welcomed by the small opposition Labour Party,
but successive governments have avoided relations with radical
states and movements. Solomon Islands has a complicated relationship with China. Since 1982 it has recognised the Republic of China
(Taiwan), which maintains an embassy in Honiara and has provided
substantial aid for hospitals. But the Guadalcanal Province government has links with mainland China's Guangdong Province, and
mainland China has provided aid for the Solomons fishing industry

(Biddick 1989, p. 807). This dual link is comparable to Vanuatu or Fiji with the positions of the two Chinese governments reversed.

The government of Solomon Islands set up a Ministry of Foreign Affairs and Trade Relations in 1981 (Sitai 1983, pp. 232–4). Its role was to advise on foreign policy matters, administer diplomatic affairs, and promote aid and trade. High cost and the scarcity of trained personnel imposed a working ceiling of less than 20 ministry officials, less than half those provided for in the 1989 organisation chart. Solomon Islands opened three overseas posts: embassies at the United Nations in New York and at the European Community headquarters in Brussels and a consular office in Brisbane. International contacts were effected by the Secretary for Foreign Affairs who was appointed roving ambassador by the government, by the two ambassadors abroad who were accredited to other organisations and states, and by ministers and officials travelling abroad or meeting their counterparts when they visit Honiara. The concepts of 'home base' from which 'roving envoys' worked was advanced as an economical way to keep up international ties (Solomon Islands Government 1989, p. 8). The diplomatic missions of Britain, Japan, Australia, New Zealand, China (Taiwan), Papua New Guinea and the Commission of the European Communities and the German honorary consul located in Honiara also provide contacts and information to the government. Additional contacts are made via cross-accredited diplomats visiting from Port Moresby and Canberra. In the first years of independence much diplomatic advice and assistance were rendered by the British Foreign Office, and at present Australia and New Zealand assist by sharing information.

Economic relations

'Aid and trade are the mainsprings of our country's foreign relations', wrote a former foreign affairs officer soon after independence (Sitai 1983, p. 235). The search for peace was emphasised because it would forestall the diversion of development resources into an armed forces establishment. Security was to have an economic and political rather than military focus (Saemala 1989, pp. 50–3). 'Economic considerations will be central in determining increased representation in the outside world' (Solomon Islands Government 1988a, p. 49 and 1987, p. 91). Trade relations were diversified so as to avoid post-colonial dependence on Britain or any other single partner. Japan has been the most important market since 1970 and took 39.0 per cent of exports in 1989 (see Table 13.1). Britain was second, taking 23.6 per cent, followed by Australia and the Asian states. Imports came mainly from Australia (36.1 per cent), Japan

Table 13.1 Solomon Islands trade partners, 1990 (%)

Country	Exports to	Imports from
Japan	39.0	18.7
Britain	23.6	1.6
Australia	4.4	36.1
New Zealand	—ᵃ	9.7
Netherlands	1.7	—ᵃ
Singapore	—ᵃ	10.3
Asian states	14.1	12.2
Others	17.4	27.3
Total	100.0	100.0

ᵃIncluded in Others.

Source: Solomon Islands Government 1991, pp. 52–3.

(18.7 per cent), Singapore, New Zealand and Asia. These trade partnerships parallel Solomon Islands' diplomatic links.

The Solomons production base has remained narrow, concentrated on primary produce for export. The fishing industry has predominated, employing up to 10 per cent of the workforce and generating a quarter of the gross domestic product (GDP). Fishing industry leaders were Solomon Taiyo Limited, a joint venture with Japan, and the government's National Fisheries Development Limited (sold in 1990 to BC Packers, a Canadian food conglomerate) (Hughes 1987, p. 203). In 1990 fish fell to 29.9 per cent of export earnings from 47 per cent in 1988. Timber rose from 24.1 per cent to 34.1 per cent. Copra accounted for 7.5 per cent, palm oil for 10.9 per cent and cocoa for 6.7 per cent of export earnings (Solomon Islands Government 1991, p. 18). Some value was added by the processing of fish into canned fish and timber into sawn timber and veneer, but it remained low. Export earnings covered only 74 per cent of the import bill in 1990, leaving a deficit of SI$62.7 million.

Remittances contributed only SI$2.8 million and fishing zone royalties earned an estimated SI$2 million in 1989 (*Pacific Economic Bulletin* 1990c, pp. 63–4). Tourism, still undeveloped in contrast to other South Pacific countries, and hampered by the distance of the islands from international trunk routes, has contributed a relatively insignificant proportion of external earnings. In 1990 the government asked the South Pacific Tourism Council to prepare a draft tourism plan and received a US$125 000 grant to stimulate tourism (*Trade News* 1990a, p. 11). The biggest contributions to the balance of payments remain aid, long term borrowing and private investment.

About 95 per cent of the government's development budget, or about one-third of total government expenditures, is financed externally, that is, by bilateral grants and concessionary loans by international agencies. In 1980 Britain provided over 70 per cent of aid, but this proportion declined to 13.8 per cent by 1986 as other bilateral donors picked up 33.3 per cent of the burden and multilateral donors picked up 52.9 per cent (Solomon Islands Government 1988b, p. 3). Japan, Australia and the European Community countries were the major donors, together providing 64.2 per cent of public development funds in 1988 (see Table 13.2). Japanese aid has tended to concentrate on fishing infrastructure, Australia has focused on agriculture and education, Britain has provided personnel expertise and capital for pipelines and other infrastructure, and the European Community has funded economic infrastructure, rural development and human resources (Solomon Islands Government 1988b, pp. 10-11).

Borrowing has increased steadily since independence and remains necessary to economic stability. Government borrowing comprises about two-thirds of the total, private sector borrowing about one-third. Total overseas debt as a proportion of GDP rose from 21.4 per cent in 1980 to over 100 per cent in 1990. This trend would normally erode creditworthiness and necessitate drastic government economies. However, Solomon Islands' status as a developing country made it eligible to borrow from international finance agencies at concessionary low-interest rates. Consequently, the debt service ratio to export earnings of goods and services remained manageable for most of the 1980s, at 7.2 per cent in 1987 (2.4 per cent for the government, 4.1 per cent for private borrowers), and overseas reserves were sufficient to cover 6 months of imports (Browne 1989, pp. 132–3). However, by 1990 debt service approached 10 per cent and reserves shrank to the equivalent of one month's imports (Solomon Islands Government 1991, pp. 20–2).

Investment by overseas enterprises was officially encouraged by the 1979 Investment Guidelines, the 1986 Industrial Development Policy, and the amalgamation of the Foreign Investment Division with the Ministry of Trade, Commerce and Industry in 1987 to streamline approvals and administration. Tax and repatriation privileges were offered, as the possibilities of moving from primary processing to light manufacturing for export were explored (Solomon Islands Government 1988c, p. 25; South Pacific Forum 1987, pp. 190–8). The Mamaloni government was successful in soliciting investments in timber processing, hotels and bottling of beverages. In 1990 government borrowing and private foreign investment totalled SI$83.1 million. This, added to SI$102.7 million received as aid and other transfers, was enough to make up for the trade and services deficits (Solomon Islands Government 1991, p. 19). Nevertheless, rising imports and debts and sluggish exports raised

Table 13.2 Solomon Islands sources of development finance, 1988 estimates

Source	Finance (SI$000)	%
Grants		
Japan	10 410	14.5
Australia	8 819	12.2
New Zealand	1 833	2.5
Britain	1 140	1.6
Canada	461	0.6
United States	200	0.3
European Community (incl. STABEX)[a]	15 558	21.6
European Development Fund	10 895	15.1
Asian Development Bank	850	1.2
World Health Organization	669	0.9
United Nations Fund for Population Activities	232	0.3
Others	940	1.8
Total grants	52 244	72.6
Concessionary loans		
Asian Development Bank	7 352	10.2
International Development Association	5 814	8.1
Organization of Petroleum Exporting Countries	800	1.1
International Fund for Agricultural Development	778	1.1
Britain	589	0.8
Total concessionary loans	15 333	21.3
Commercial loans	4 400	6.1
Total development finance	71 977	100.0

[a] Export price stabilisation grants.

Source: Solomon Islands Government 1988b, p. 4.

the risk of inflation and will require further borrowing and direct investment in future to maintain the momentum of development that underpins political stability (*Pacific Economic Bulletin* 1990c, p. 63).

Foreign policy issues

International issues are 'basically the concern of the Honiara elite' (Roughan 1988, p. 13). Discussion of public issues by churches, women's associations, non-governmental organisations, unions and the media is increasing as education, urbanisation and national self-consciousness spread. But foreign affairs remains a minor concern. Of the political parties, only the Labour Party led by Joses Tuhanuku has a distinctive foreign-policy platform. It was sponsored by the Council of Trade Unions, one of whose constituents in the late 1970s affiliated with the Soviet-funded World Federation of Trade Unions in order to combat 'the evils of colonialism, imperialism, exploitation, poverty, inequality, and racism' (Roughan 1988, p. 11). The Labour Party advocated opening diplomatic relations with communist and fundamentalist Muslim countries, supported the aspirations of radical PLO, Aboriginal and Maori leaders and proposed the nationalisation of overseas enterprises and curbs on future foreign investment (Jennings 1990, p. 19). It won only two parliamentary seats in the 1989 election, and its policies are contrary to those of the mainstream of Solomon Islands political elites, but it serves to illustrate one end of the possible spectrum of foreign policy.

Prime Minister Mamaloni has shown an inclination occasionally to veer towards that end of the spectrum. In 1981, when first elected, he asserted that his government 'will not allow a sovereign Solomon Islands to become a puppet of other countries, Australian and New Zealand, or even Russia and the United States of America' (Larmour 1983a, p. 274). Mamaloni subsequently indulged in rhetoric hostile to international organisations, aid agencies, overseas companies, foreign (especially Australian) journalists and expatriate officials, and asserted that aid and foreign capital should come under closer government control and that expatriates should be phased out in favour of Solomons officers. Complaining that aid from traditional donors had 'too many strings', he proposed sending delegations to Asian countries and to the Soviet Union and Eastern Europe to seek new aid and markets.

Regarding French nuclear testing, Mamaloni adopted a critical posture parallel to that of neighbouring Vanuatu; likewise he supported the Kanak independence movement in New Caledonia. He regarded the South Pacific Commission as dominated by former colonial powers, particularly France, and advocated that it be absorbed by or subordinated to the South Pacific Forum. To reinforce his independent views Mamaloni upgraded the police into the paramilitary Police Field Force, now numbering 100, and proposed a Melanesian Alliance—a joint defence and security arrangement with Vanuatu and Papua New Guinea (Hegarty 1983, p. 129; Larmour 1983a, pp. 273–7).

Mamaloni's government also refused to admit US nuclear-powered warships into Solomon Islands waters and disputed US claims of freedom to fish for migratory tuna inside the Solomons Exclusive Economic Zone (EEZ) of 200 miles (332 kilometres). In 1984 Solomon Islands arrested, prosecuted and confiscated the US seiner *Jeanette Diana* for poaching. The US government retaliated by declaring an embargo on Solomons exports, interrupting exports of fish to canneries in American Samoa and Puerto Rico (Kengalu 1988). The embargo was lifted in 1985 when the Solomons government sold the *Jeanette Diana* back to its owners. The event had a constructive outcome: it stimulated the United States to conclude the United States–South Pacific Regional Fisheries Treaty of 1987 with the mediation of the Forum Fisheries Agency. But in 1991 a US offer to fund a new Parliament building stalled over disagreements over design and land tenure, causing further frustration of good relations.

Nevertheless, many of Mamaloni's more radical policies, including his stated desire to break ties with the Crown, declare Solomon Islands a republic and leave the Commonwealth, have yet to be reflected in action. His 1981 and 1989 governments, and the intervening governments of Kenilorea and Alebua, have eschewed relations with radical partners and cultivated relations with anticommunist Taiwan and Indonesia, and with Britain, Europe and the United States. Cooperation with Australia and New Zealand has flourished and extended to the military sphere, signalled by grants of three Australian patrol boats and advisory, training and maritime surveillance assistance. The value of the South Pacific Commission as a complement to the South Pacific Forum was tacitly acknowledged.

France's South Pacific role was accepted after the Matignon Accords of 1988 offered the possibility of New Caledonian independence in 1998. The Melanesian Spearhead Group superficially recalled the Melanesian Alliance idea, but it differs significantly, has no military element and has not attracted Mamaloni's enthusiasm because Papua New Guinea is likely to dominate it. In economic policy Mamaloni has maintained his predecessors' drives to attract foreign investment, has negotiated new loans from Arab and Southeast Asian countries, and has undertaken an extensive deregulation and privatisation programme designed to make the Solomons a more attractive venue for business (Angiki 1990b, pp. 12–13); South Pacific Forum 1987, pp. 190–8).

Solomon Islands policy appears erratic when viewed at the level of rhetoric, but this belies the moderate substance of actual relations and programmes. The present course of foreign policy is conditioned by an historical affinity for the Crown, gratitude to the United States for liberation from Japan, the influence of many officials' schooling and training in Australia and New Zealand, and socio-political pluralism and individual materialism. The radical alternatives in diplomatic and economic policy appear to have little appeal as long as there is no immediate security threat and steady progress is made in economic development.

But rivalries between the provinces and the centre, awareness of the growing gap between subsistence villagers and government officers, and increasing political consciousness and mobilisation will doubtless intensify the turbulence of the political process of which the 1991 public service strike may be a foretaste. Political disturbances could well have adverse consequences for the attraction of foreign capital, the efficacy of development assistance, and the ability of the government to fund and staff the institutions of diplomacy and trade promotion. Any government reaction in an authoritarian manner as in Fiji would further exacerbate the situation and damage Solomon Islands' international standing. On the positive side, a solid precedent of toleration in domestic politics and moderation and cooperation in foreign affairs has been set by the Kenilorea, Alebua and Mamaloni governments. This will be a baseline against which the progress or retrogression of future governments may be assessed.

14 Tonga

Tonga's civilisation stretches back to the Lapita culture period more than 3000 years ago. Tonga's monarchy was founded in 950 AD (Craig and King 1981, p. 289; Douglas and Douglas 1989, p. 552). In the thirteenth century Tonga is thought to have been the centre of a Polynesian complex of kinship and trade that included the Samoan and Fijian islands at various times. Following a period of civil wars Taufa'ahau, King George Tupou I, converted to Christianity (English Methodism) in 1831, brought Tonga under unified rule (1852), promulgated a Code of Law (1862) and a British style constitution (1875), and negotiated treaties with France (1855), Germany (1876), Britain (1887) and the United States (1888).

Imperial rivalries, domestic disorder and, according to some versions, a request by King Tupou II led Britain in 1901 to establish a protectorate and to take responsibility for foreign policy and defence. But the monarchy ruled without interruption domestically (Ritterbush and Patolo 1988, p. 16). Queen Salote reigned from 1918 to 1965 and earned wide respect for her education and health reforms. Her skilful diplomacy prepared the way for the return of Tonga to full independence in 1970. Her son, King Taufa'ahau Tupou IV, has carried on the reform tradition and done much to consolidate Tonga's secure place in South Pacific and world affairs.

Political system

Tonga is unique in the South Pacific not only as an authoritarian system in a region of democracies but also as an apparent pillar of stability in a region of post-colonial change. The Tongan Constitution was drafted on the British model in 1875 and has continued in force through the colonial period to the present, making it one of the world's oldest. It establishes the authority of the king, the Cabinet of twelve ministers appointed by the king, and the Privy Council, composed of the king plus ministers, which also acts as the final court of appeal (Afeaki 1983, pp. 62–71).

The Legislative Assembly, which passes laws and approves the annual budget, consists of the king's Cabinet ministers (about twelve), nine noble assemblymen elected by the hereditary 33 nobles of Tonga, and nine commoners elected by the people. The king chooses the speaker of the assembly from among the nine nobles and opens and closes the annual assembly sessions. Because the nobles tend to work with the ministers (who are picked by the king and are predominantly nobles), and because the commoners are not organised in a stable caucus, the combination of king, Cabinet and assembly nobles dominates government decision making. Opposition by the assembly commoners is limited to asking questions, requesting inquiries, making statements and, as happened in October 1988, walking out of an assembly session.

Given that there are no political parties in Tonga, and that most print and all broadcast media are government-controlled, formal political opposition is unknown. However, in the 1980s church leaders such as Reverend Amanaki Havea (Free Wesleyan Methodist) and Bishop Patelisio Finau (Catholic) used pulpits and petitions to speak out against government abuses.

In the mid 1980s a commoner teacher 'Akilisi Pohiva used a radio programme, then started a newssheet called *Kele'a* (meaning the conch shell trumpet used to call villagers to meetings), to question ministers' salary and expenditure excesses; he was summarily fired from the public service. Pohiva took the government to court for wrongful dismissal, was elected to the assembly in 1987, led the walkout of 1988, and now leads an informal opposition movement with growing backing from church leaders, public servants and educated non-noble Tongans (Keith-Reid 1990b, pp. 16–21). He and others are demanding an end to ministerial privileges and secrecy, an increase of commoner assembly seats, and stronger powers and pay for civil servants. Recent government foreign policies exposed by Pohiva and the *Kele'a* group include hasty plans to purchase a Boeing to start an international airline, environmentally risky schemes to import toxic refuse from the United States, and the indiscriminate sale of passports to Hong Kong Chinese with the proceeds unaccounted for; in each case the policy has been shelved or modified (*Pacific Islands Monthly* 1990b, p. 38).

Foreign journalists, academics and officials have speculated that Tonga's political stability may be threatened by either a populist uprising or a noble–military backlash if the present tensions degenerate into class confrontation. These extremes are unlikely. Tongan socio-political conservatism has deep historical roots in the monarchy and is reinforced by Christian church organisation and doctrine. Emigration relieves pressure on the scarce arable land and removes many potential challengers from the political scene, and remittances ease the economic hardships of those who remain. King Taufa'ahau Tupou IV is remembered as a genuine reformer with the people's interests at heart in his younger days, and his family are still regarded as benign leaders even though they tolerate corruption. The Tongan Defence Services number about 200, with only 49 in the Land Force and 37 in the Royal Guards (Douglas and Douglas 1989, p. 540). They are thought to be loyal to the king, disinclined to factional manoeuvring with the nobles, and insufficiently well equipped to accomplish political intervention on a national scale.

Civil servants agree with the government's ministers that Tonga's real problems stem basically from the country's weak international economic position and only secondarily from the constitutional structure, and they appreciate that political turmoil risks a reduction of the aid and loans on which their livelihoods depend. They, and the opposition figures, are asking only for incremental changes. Crown Prince Tupouto'a has hinted that he will favour constitutional liberalisation when the monarchy passes to him from his father the king, who celebrated his 70th birthday in 1988. Optimists hope that popular pressure will stimulate orderly reform from above and Tonga, following British precedent, can evolve into a democracy stabilised by a respected monarch and a responsible nobility by the early twenty-first century. This evolution would be welcome to Tonga's diplomatic and economic partners and would go far to restore Tonga's leadership role in Polynesian affairs.

Foreign affairs

Tongans first encountered Europeans when the Dutch explorers Schouten and Le Maire in 1616 and Tasman in 1643 made brief stops. James Cook visited and made maps in 1773, 1775 and 1777 (Douglas and Douglas 1989, p. 552). Sustained experience with Western culture began with John Thomas's Wesleyan mission in 1826, which led to widespread Christianisation, study of English and adoption of British political practices by the end of the century. Another British Wesleyan missionary, Shirley Baker, drafted the constitution and served King George Tupou I as premier and

Minister of External Affairs. The king responded to the threat of European imperialism by negotiating with France, Britain, Germany and the United States treaties that recognised Tonga's status as an independent state, and finally by acceding to British protection in 1901. Britain subsequently conducted external affairs in accordance with Tongan wishes. In 1970 the two governments dissolved the protectorate by mutual agreement, and Tonga emerged with political integrity intact—the island state least disrupted by colonialism.

Tonga immediately joined the Commonwealth, appointed its first diplomat as high commissioner to Britain, and took steps to solicit loans and aid from international agencies. As a small country Tonga restricts itself to only one full-scale diplomatic mission (staffed by four officers) in London, a consulate in San Francisco, and small trade offices in Australia and New Zealand. However, it cultivates a wide circle of diplomatic contacts by means of the cross-accreditation of the high commissioner in London to twelve other countries and the European Community, the appointment of honorary consuls in other capitals, and the hosting of foreign missions and recognition of local honorary consuls in Nuku'alofa. Table 14.1 lists the major bilateral links.

Tonga is not a member of the United Nations General Assembly, mainly because of the cost and manpower demands of membership, but the Minister of Foreign Affairs can turn to his British, Australian and New Zealand counterparts for advice on matters of mutual interest. It is a member of the Economic and Social Commission for Asia and the Pacific (ESCAP), the International Telecommunication Union (ITU), the Universal Postal Union (UPU) and the World Health Organization (WHO), and it contributes to the United Nations's Children's Fund (UNICEF), the United Nations Conference on Trade and Development (UNCTAD), the International Committee of the Red Cross, the International Convention on Elimination of Racial Discrimination, the International Criminal Police Organisation, and the African, Caribbean and Pacific Secretariat. It signals its commitment to the Commonwealth by contributions to regional get-togethers of the Commonwealth Heads of Government Meetings, the Commonwealth Secretariat, the Commonwealth Fund for Technical Cooperation, the Commonwealth Foundation, the Commonwealth Institute, the Commonwealth Youth Programme, the Commonwealth Legal Advisory Service and the Commonwealth Magistrates' Association (Tonga Government 1987a). Tonga also participates in international development, aid and finance organisations, principally the Asian Development Bank (ADB), the United Nations Development Programme (UNDP), the United Nations Industrial Development Organization (UNIDO) and

Table 14.1 Tonga's bilateral diplomatic links

Tongan missions abroad
Australia (Sydney), trade office
Britain (London), high commission (also accredited to Belgium, Denmark, European Community, France, Germany, Italy, Luxembourg, the Netherlands, the Soviet Union, Spain, Sweden, Switzerland and the United States)
New Zealand (Auckland), government agent
United States (San Francisco), consulate general

Honorary consuls for Tonga abroad
Australia (Sydney)
Germany (Bergheim)
Italy (Milan)
Japan (Tokyo)
Switzerland (Zurich)
(France, Nauru and Korea under consideration)

Foreign missions in Nuku'alofa
Australia, high commission
Britain, high commission
Commission of the European Communities
New Zealand, high commission
Republic of China (Taiwan), embassy

Honorary consuls in Nuku'alofa

France	Nauru
Germany	Spain
Korea	Sweden

Other diplomatic partners by cross-accreditation

Chile	India
Malaysia	Israel

Source: Tonga Government 1989, app. I, II; Tonga Government 1987c, *passim.*

the United Nations Fund for Population Activities (UNFPA) (Tonga Government 1987c).

Tonga keeps in touch with South Pacific neighbours through regular participation in the South Pacific Forum since 1971, the South Pacific Commission since 1983, and a variety of specialised regional agencies, including the Conference of South Pacific Chiefs of Police, the South Pacific Judicial Conference, the Pacific Islands Law Officers' Meeting, the University of the South Pacific, the South Pacific Board for Educational Assessment, the Pacific Forum Line, the South Pacific Regional Meeting on Telecommunications, the South Pacific Shipping Council, the South Pacific Regional Civil Aviation Council, the South Pacific Forum Fisheries Agency, the Pacific Islands Tourism Development Council, the Pacific Islands Conference, the South Pacific Labour Ministers' Conference, the South Pacific Applied Geoscience Commission (SOPAC) and the Tourism Council of the South Pacific (Haas 1989, *passim*). Participation in the South Pacific Regional Environmental Programme (SPREP) is under consideration.

Important state-to-state visits and some negotiations are frequently conducted in person by King Taufa'ahau Topou IV, or by Crown Prince Tupouto'a as Minister of Foreign Affairs and Defence. Routine diplomacy is conducted by the secretary or deputy secretary/protocol officer or one of the nine other officers of the Ministry of Foreign Affairs and Defence or by the seven diplomats stationed abroad. This ministry also administers the Tongan Defence Services of approximately 200 men and manages the links with Australia's Defence Cooperation Programme and the New Zealand Defence Mutual Assistance Programme. Tonga receives specialist instructors and training and exercise opportunities, air and maritime surveillance intelligence, and, more recently, three Australian Pacific patrol boats with Royal New Zealand Navy personnel training backup (MacKinnon 1990, pp. 59–60). These programmes provide trade and technical training in electrical work, carpentry, motor repair and computer work applicable to civilian economic-development objectives and these are welcomed as much as the military-related activities (Tonga 1987c). Tonga also conducts exercises with the US Army and attends the annual Pacific Armies Management seminars in Honolulu.

Economic relations

A long term and officially emphasised objective of the kingdom is to 'develop harmonious relations and mutual cooperation in economic, social and related spheres with all nations and international organisations' (Tonga Government 1987b, p. 1). This reflects Tonga's expanding horizon of international contacts in the post-protectorate period. In spite of Britain's historical and continuing diplomatic importance to Tonga, Britain's once substantial shares of exports, imports and aid have shrunk markedly relative to the shares of new partners in the decades from 1970 to 1990. The most important trading partner is now New Zealand, which took 35 per cent of exports and provided 30 per cent of imports in 1989/90, followed by Australia, Japan and the United States (see Table 14.2). If American Samoa and Hawaii were included, the US share of trade would rival Japan's. Fiji and Singapore have become significant new suppliers.

The drive to increase production for export has motivated much of Tongan development planning and expenditure for infrastructural and transportation improvement, for example the upgrading of Queen Salote wharf and Fa'amotu International Airport. The Indus-

Table 14.2 Tonga's direction of trade, 1975 and 1989/90 (%)

Destination of exports	1975	1989/90
New Zealand	20	35.0
Britain	10	—[a]
Australia	3	22.4
Japan	—[a]	16.6
United States	0	13.3
Others	67	12.9
Total	100	100.0

Source of imports	1975	1989/90
New Zealand	35	30.2
Australia	26	23.4
Britain	11	—[a]
United States	6	12.0
Japan	5	6.9
Others	17	27.6
Total	100	100.0

[a] Included in Others.

Source: Tonga Government 1987b, p. 23; Tonga Government 1990, pp. S29, S23.

trial Development Incentives Act 1978 provides tax and tariff concessions for export-oriented enterprises, and the Tonga Development Bank provides loans and advisory services (Asia Pacific Research unit 1982e, p. 14; South Pacific Forum 1987, pp. 226–30). Tonga can offer foreign investors in joint ventures tariff-free entry into New Zealand, Australian and European markets under the South Pacific Regional Trade and Economic Cooperation Agreement and Lome Agreement, reduced tariff entry into the US market under the Generalised System of Preferences, and assistance under the New Zealand Pacific Islands Development Scheme and Australian Joint Venture Scheme.

However, isolation, transportation uncertainties, undeveloped infrastructure, narrow supplier and consumer bases and lack of skilled labour hold back industrial development, and the economy remains dominated by primary agricultural production. Consequently export earnings play a relatively minor role in Tonga's economic survival. Principal earnings have traditionally come from the export of coconut products (60 per cent in 1984/85), bananas and vanilla. However, falling commodity prices undercut incentives to reinvest, and their proportion of the total has fallen to less than 20 per cent in 1989/90, replaced by fish (12 per cent), light manufactures such as knitwear (19 per cent) and a surge of squash exports to Japan (17 per cent) (Tonga Government 1990, p. S27).

Export earnings covered only one-seventh of the value of imports in 1989/90 (Tonga Government 1990, pp. S29, S33). To meet rising public expectations and to finance raw materials and machinery for production, the government of Tonga is obliged to balance its current account by means of concessionary borrowing, aid, remittances and earnings from services, mainly tourism. Although Britain remained significant after Tonga's independence as a source of development finance, British loans comprising 14.2 per cent of total loans in 1980–85 were only fifth in importance, overshadowed by larger loans from Germany, the ADB, WHO and the UNDP (Tonga Government 1987b, pp. 23, 60–2). In the later 1980s the European Investment Bank (EIB) became an important source of funds. Overall borrowing has been moderate, and at concessionary rates; so debt service has not been a serious drain on the development budget.

Tonga's bilateral aid relationships during the 1980s found Australia emerging as the most significant donor, followed by Japan and New Zealand; France and Taiwan also became significant donors for the first time (see Table 14.3).

With an estimated one-quarter of all Tongans living abroad,

Table 14.3 Tonga's aid sources, 1980–1985 and 1988/89 (%)

Source	1980–85	1988/89
Bilateral		
Australia	35.7	21.3
Japan	22.7	18.0
New Zealand	17.2	18.8
Germany	1.5	3.4
France	0.5	12.0
Taiwan	0.0	1.4
Others	1.2	3.7
Total bilateral	78.9	78.6
Multilateral		
United Nations Development Programme, Food and Agriculture Organization, World Health Organization	12.8	4.4
European Community	6.1	10.9
Commonwealth Fund for Technical Cooperation and others	2.2	5.7
Total multilateral	21.1	21.0
Total	100.0	100.0

Source: Tonga Government 1987b, p. 61; South Pacific Commission 1987a, p. 14; World Bank 1991b, vol. II, p. 167.

mainly in New Zealand, remittances have reached the equivalent of 30 per cent of the gross domestic product (GDP) in recent years (Browne 1989, p. 137). Tourism earnings too are dependent on New Zealand, from which 24 per cent of arrivals by air came in 1988/89, followed by arrivals from the United States (22 per cent), Australia (14 per cent), other Pacific countries (12 per cent), and Europeans and others (29 per cent) (Tonga Government 1990, p. S30). The importance of tourism is recognised in the Tourist Act 1976 and in objectives, targets and allocations set out in the Fifth Development Plan 1986–90. Tourism earned T$14.5 million in 1987/88 according to one study, supplementing aid receipts of T$20 million and remittances of T$36 million, and providing a multiplier effect on local income, government revenues and employment (Milne 1990, pp. 26–7).

Investment has been sluggish, and overseas private borrowing has been unnecessary until recently. The government of Tonga has been able to borrow sufficient funds from international agencies at concessionary rates to meet private sector needs by relending through the Bank of Tonga and the Tonga Development Bank; so the relative significance of private borrowing is small. A growing source of earnings was interest from the Tonga Trust Account held mainly in British banks, which has been swollen by proceeds from sales of Protected Persons Passports. This and the other four major components of external economic relations are set out in Table 14.4.

Foreign policy issues

Tonga has been perceived as slightly eccentric in foreign policy. In the 1970s the king visited the Soviet Union and in 1976 held talks with Soviet officials over the possibility of establishing a Soviet fishing base in return for upgrading Tonga's international airport.

Table 14.4 Tonga's balance of payments, 1988/89

Item	T$ million (*pa'anga*)
Merchandise trade	-50.3
(Exports)	(+10.3)
(Imports)	(-60.6)
Aid	+12.3
Remittances	+30.5
Tourism and services	+1.9
Investments, private capital, other	+4.2
Balance	-1.4

Source: Tonga Government 1990, p. S26.

During a period of Western anxiety about Soviet military initiatives in the Pacific, these talks precipitated concern in Washington and an upsurge of countervailing aid from Australia and New Zealand. However, the king declined the Soviet offer, not because the West made a better bid, but because he judged the Soviets difficult to deal with. He consistently refused to let Soviet research ships visit.

Tonga is one of four island countries hosting an embassy of the Republic of China (Taiwan)—a vigorous anticommunist government—while neighbouring Western Samoa and Fiji recognise only the People's Republic of China. Yet Tonga has not hesitated to arrest two Taiwanese fishing boats for poaching in its Exclusive Economic Zone (EEZ). In the least militarised region in the world Tonga is the only South Pacific country allied formally to the United States. The 1888 Treaty of Amity, Commerce and Navigation with the United States was publicly reaffirmed by the king in 1988.

Tonga is a faithful member of the South Pacific Forum, but has refused to sign the Treaty of Rarotonga establishing a South Pacific Nuclear Free Zone and has welcomed nuclear-powered ships. The king accepted an invitation to visit Mururoa and is muted in his condemnation of French nuclear testing and US chemical-weapons disposal at Johnston Atoll. In 1988 the king proposed to extend the Polynesian Heritage Trust precedent to form a Polynesian Economic and Cultural Community that would encompass not only the independent island states but also Hawaii, American Samoa and French Polynesia. This has been interpreted variously as a counterbalance to Melanesian and Fijian predominance in the South Pacific Forum, as a bid to restore Tonga's traditional prominence enjoyed under Queen Salote, and as a way to attract French aid in return for easing French Polynesia's integration with its neighbours.

Relations with Fiji have been troubled by Tonga's claim to Minerva Reefs. Following a private American group's attempt to proclaim a Republic of Minerva, the king in 1972 reaffirmed Tonga's claim, supervised the erection of markers on the two low-lying reefs, and secured from the South Pacific Forum an acknowledgement of Tonga's historic association with and special interest in the Minerva Reefs. However, the reefs lie within Fiji's EEZ as conventionally defined; and if Tonga claimed an EEZ around them, the claim would conflict with not only Fiji's but also Tokelau's EEZ (Prescott 1988, p. 19).

Recurrent controversies have arisen over proposals by US firms to export toxic waste to Tonga for incineration or landfill (*Pacific Islands Monthly* 1990, p. 38). There is a growing market for rubbish disposal services with potential for foreign exchange earnings, and a member of the royal family has been reported to have interests in the scheme. There is some public concern about the proposal, based not only on grounds of irreversible environmental despoliation but also suspicion that corrupt transactions may take place. A second but equally unorthodox scheme involving massive oil-storage tanks to hold surplus Libyan oil was postponed when the embargo of Iraqi oil in 1990 absorbed Libya's production and Libya lost interest in the South Pacific generally.

Another controversial initiative was the sale of passports to Chinese and other Asians seeking alternative countries of residence. Called Tongan Protected Persons Passports, they were conceived as a revenue-generating scheme, and 426 were reported sold at up to US$20 000 each. In 1990 a number of emigrating Chinese found that few countries would honour them. Several dozen arrived in Tonga and found that they were unwelcome there as well. Tongan opposition leaders queried why the proceeds, rumoured to be up to US$20 million, were kept in a San Francisco bank and not budgeted as government income (Fraser 1990, p. 4). The scheme was revamped, and a constitutional amendment was passed in 1991 to legalise the passports, which were to be sold for US$50 000. The government reported that US$12 million was held in the Bank of America and US$4.7 million in the Bank of Tonga, but critics continued to press for a fuller accounting and to dispute both the constitutionality and propriety of the scheme (Robie 1991, pp. 12–15; *Islands Business Pacific* 1991b, pp. 24–5; Gittings 1991, pp. 10–17).

Emigration to New Zealand and to a lesser extent Australia was both an opportunity and a problem. It acted as a safety valve and generated educational improvements and remittances, but returnees were less inclined to accept the restrictions of the traditional system. New Zealand and Australian journalists were sometimes blunt in their criticism of the monarchy and the nobility, and this encouraged disrespect among educated commoners. New Zealand's and Australia's periodic campaigns to restrict immigration and expel overstayers, most recently in 1991, were perceived by Tongans as ungenerous and insensitive, even racist, and generated friction between the governments.

In light of its circumstances, and making allowances for individual malfeasance and impulsiveness, Tonga's recent initiatives may be seen as rational moves to widen the room for manoeuvre and broaden the resource base of a small island state. The foreign policy elites have seen Britain then New Zealand decline in ability to look after Tonga, and may regard Australia's new vigorous South Pacific policy of 'constructive commitment', or the Melanesian Spearhead caucusing, as bids for dominance of the South Pacific at Tonga's expense. In that light, opening relations with newly wealthy countries of East Asia, tapping into the aid flows that the Japanese, the

Chinese, the European Community and the French seem prepared to direct to the South Pacific, and maintaining cordial relations with the United States while at the same time assessing proposals from the Soviet Union, Libya and private sector entrepreneurs, all are means whereby Tonga can gain information and experience and avoid dependence on any one source of diplomatic support, aid, loans, remittances or markets.

The conclusion is that the government of Tonga has moved within the consensus of the Western community and of the South Pacific Forum for three decades since 1970. It has succeeded in remaining politically stable and economically solvent during a period of post-colonial and Cold War turbulence and a worsening international-trade environment. It has kept its old friends and made new ones. No coherent alternative to present external-policy goals has been advanced by any Tongan politician or popular spokesperson, only calls for accountability in administration, suggesting widespread acceptance of the king's approach to world affairs. It is against this background that Tonga's foreign policies may be judged.

15 Vanuatu

Emerging from exploitation, division and violence, Vanuatu has adopted the most radically independent posture of any island state. It is strictly nuclear-free and outspokenly anti-colonial. Until 1988 it was the only South Pacific member of the Non Aligned Movement, and was a diplomatic partner of Libya, Cuba, North Korea and Vietnam. Yet is it also a member of the Commonwealth, and its relations with its South Pacific neighbours and the Western powers (save France) are harmonious. Its economic policies are orthodox, and considerable income is earned by selling tax haven services to international capitalist enterprises.

The seemingly contradictory nature of its policies is more rhetorical than real—a manifestation of idiosyncratic leadership of Prime Minister Father Walter Lini, who led the country to independence. Behind the headlines Vanuatu ministers and diplomats may be seen to have drawn on their unique political experiences to weave a network of precedents and contacts that steady the nation's standing in the region as it pursues self-reliance and development.

Nationalism and politics

Insensitivity, injustice and violence by unscrupulous European sandalwood buyers and blackbirders left a scar on the political memory (Douglas and Douglas 1989, pp. 607–12; Craig and King 1981, pp. 315–18). The suspicion so generated hampered Protestant evangelical and teaching activity and led to occasional massacres. The

201

Table 15.1 Vanuatu's political evolution

4000 BC Settlement began, probably from Papua New Guinea through the Solomons. Demographic and cultural patterns were dispersed in villages, and over 100 separate languages evolved.

1606 Spanish explorer Quiros was the first European to sight Vanuatu. He gave Espiritu Santo its name.

1768 French explorer Bougainville sailed through the northern islands.

1774 British explorer Cook charted parts of the archipelago and gave it the name New Hebrides.

1825–65 Sandalwood was discovered, and European traders began to exploit it, often unscrupulously, generating local hostility.

1847 Blackbirding began and continued until banned by Britain in 1872. The xenophobic element of Vanuatu nationalism is traced back to this experience.

1885 After four decades of effort, Anglican and Presbyterian missions were established in most islands. Marist missions opened soon afterwards, and religious rivalry reinforced political rivalry.

1887 International manoeuvrings in the region led Britain and France to set up a Joint Naval Commission to protect their citizens and forestall annexation bids by either party or Germany.

1906 Britain and France decided to establish a jointly ruled colony—a condominium. Each commissioner looked after his own nationals and headed a separate structure that administered and taught its own language to Melanesians.

1920–30 Permissive French policy allowed the importation of Vietnamese labourers which drove British plantations out of business, leaving the French predominant in the plantation sector in the northern islands.

1940 The Jon Frum cargo cult began, seen now as an early expression of nationalism.

1968 The Na-Griamel movement, led by Jimmy Stevens, began demanding the return of customary lands from colonial owners and in 1971 petitioned the United Nations for an act of free choice on independence.

1971 The first political party, the New Hebrides National Party, was established with support from the anglophone community. Its leader, Anglican minister Father Walter Lini, announced in 1974 his intention to seek independence. A rival francophone party was established in response.

1975 The National Party won the majority of seats in the colonial Representative Assembly, but little power was devolved because of French reluctance.

1977 Lini changed his party's name to Vanuaaku ('our land') Pati, called his country Vanuatu ('the land remains'), boycotted the assembly elections, and declared a People's Provisional Government in opposition to the condominium-dominated one.

1979 The Vanuaaku Pati won the assembly elections, and Lini was named chief minister.

1980 Jimmy Stevens and other leaders on Espiritu Santo and Tanna attempted to secede. The French and British commissioners could not restore authority. Papua New Guinea sent troops to assist Lini's government to restore its authority.

Independence was declared on 30 July. Vanuatu became a parliamentary democracy within the Commonwealth.

1983, 1987 The Vanuaaku Pati won general elections, and Lini remained prime minister.

1988 Francophone leader Barak Sope and his followers were expelled from parliament for allegedly fomenting riots in Port Vila. Sope formed the rival Melanesian Progressive Party, was reinstated by the court of appeal, then resigned. President Sokomanu dissolved parliament, dismissed Lini, and appointed Sope interim prime minister. Lini's government, backed by the police and recognised by Australia, New Zealand and Papua New Guinea, arrested Sope and Sokomanu and charged them with treason.

1989 Sope's and Sokomanu's convictions were overturned on appeal, but some of their followers defected to the Vanuaaku Pati and Lini's authority was restored.

1990 Lini questioned the appropriateness of the Westminster constitutional system and proposed introducing traditional elements.

1991 The Vanuaaku Pati lost its majority in the December general election. The francophone Union of Moderate Parties formed a government and Maxime Carlot became prime minister.

Source: Far East and Australasia 1990 1990, pp. 817–18.

anti-Western streak that characterises Vanuatu nationalism is said to have originated with these experiences (see Table 15.1).

Colonialism by the British–French condominium in 1906 brought order, but subsequent alienation of the best land to foreign plantation owners brought little economic benefit to the people, who remained in their villages. US occupation of the New Hebrides during World War II brought jobs and temporary prosperity but also engendered unreal expectations of wealth to come, which were disappointed. The condominium administration was divided, paralysed and irresponsible. Education was retarded by low standards and English–French divisions, and political self-consciousness was slow to develop because of linguistic diversity and settlement dispersion. Nationalism was manifested by the Jon Frum cargo cult and the Na-Griamel land-return movement, proto-political forms puzzling to Westerners.

Political parties did not form until 1971. Then, an Anglican minister who had been educated in New Zealand, Father Walter Lini, set up the predecessor to the current ruling Vanuaaku Pati, and *colons* (colonists) with French encouragement set up countervailing parties (Plant 1977, pp. 15–34); *Far East and Australasia 1990*, pp. 817–18). Once declared, Lini's party attracted a growing following and moved steadily towards its goal of independence, employing unorthodox tactics such as boycotts when necessary to prod the British and French to devolve power. Within 9 years the

Vanuaaku Pati had brought Vanuatu to independence against considerable resistance by the French and opposition by French-supported political parties. However, political loyalties were still dispersed among the 'big men', clans and villages, divided between islands and regional centres and split into anglophone and francophone camps.

The first task of the new government was to overcome a secessionist movement sparked by the Na-Griamel and surreptitiously backed by French officials and *colons* and US land speculators (Robie 1989, pp. 76–80). The second was to surmount a challenge by a francophone faction of the Vanuaaku Pati, led by Barak Sope, in 1988. After a turbulent series of events—including alleged Libyan meddling, riots in Port Vila, an appeal for foreign military assistance, the dismissal of Lini by President Sokomanu, arrest of the president and Sope by Lini, the appeal court reversal of Lini's actions, and defections to the Vanuaaku Pati—Lini regained control by the end of 1989 (Steeves 1989, pp. 141–74). However, the events led Lini to question whether the Westminster system of parliamentary democracy was appropriate to Vanuatu's traditions and social structure, citing the Fijian precedent, and parliament convened a constitutional review committee in 1990 (*Pacific Islands Profile* 1990, p. 19).

In mid-1991 the Vanuaaku Pati replaced Lini with former foreign minister Donald Kalpokas. Kalpokas pledged to restore government stability and promote foreign investment. The Vanuaaku Pati lost the December 1991 general election and the Union of Moderate Parties formed a government led by Maxime Carlot as prime minister. The potential for political disruption remained in the factionalism of the government and opposition parties, the uncertainties of constitutional revision, the ambivalence of southern and outer island leaders and 'big men' in the villages towards the government, the disparity of income between the subsistence villagers and government employees, and the disappointment of expectations of prosperity among migrants to the towns (Ross 1990, pp. 95–115; Jennings 1990, p. 273).

Foreign policy

The legacy of exploitation, penetration, bifurcated colonialism, fissures in language and religious groups, and foreign-supported conspiracies has produced a radical foreign outlook among Vanuaaku Pati leaders. Their ideological base is Melanesian socialism, and their objective is a Melanesian renaissance (Premdas and Howard 1989, pp. 73–95). Melanesian socialism has its roots not in Marxism but in Melanesian community sharing practices reinforced by Christian values such as mutuality, compassion, caring for one another and their obverse, the subordination of materialism, individualism and self-interest. It was developed in the early 1970s by Papua New Guinea nationalists such as Father John Momis and Bernard Naro-kobi. Its inspiration stemmed from Julius Nyerere's African social-ism expressed in the Arusha Declaration. Vanuatu nationalists used it as a radical challenge to Britain's colonial authority. Their contacts with their Papua New Guinea and Tanzanian counterparts led them easily to a doctrine of non-alignment. The Melanesian renaissance was to be an ideological alternative to Western ideologies—an assertion of 'our God-given right to develop in our own way and in accordance with our own values and expectations, casting away many of the inherited attitudes that at present bolster practices that are alien to the Melanesian mind' (Lini 1983, p. 8)

The foreign policy implications of Melanesian socialism and renaissance were listed in a 1975 statement issued by the New Hebrides National Party as follows:

- Non-allegiance: The party does not want to be regarded as allied with any other country.
- National freedom: The party pledges support for all freedom move-ments striving towards self-determination and national liberation.
- Non-nuclearism: The party condemns any form of nuclear activities and supports the move by other Pacific countries to declare the Pacific a nuclear-free zone.
- Pacific community: The party believes in a need for a Pacific commu-nity to bind ties amicably for better communication, understanding and trade relationships.
- Economic policy: The party aims to promote and develop a self-reliant economy.
- Foreign aid: Aid does not bind or align the New Hebrides to the donor government or country.
- Foreign investment: Such investment will be encouraged only where it introduces new sectors of employment, expertise and overall benefits to the New Hebrides, and where New Hebridean participation is included.
- Tourism: Tourism will be continued but not encouraged (Plant 1977, p. 41).

Thus the principles of non-alignment, liberation, anti-nuclearism, regional self-consciousness, economic self-reliance and political autonomy were clear 5 years before independence. They were reit-erated by Minister of Foreign Affairs Sela Molisa in 1984 when he pledged Vanuatu's 'support for the principles of self-determination, independence and denuclearisation, especially in the South Pacific region, recognition of the existence of states, respect for human rights, territorial integrity and sovereignty, support for socio-economic advancement in the Third World, and commitment and support to the charter of the United Nations' (Premdas and Howard 1989, p. 130).

In 1989 the following official foreign-policy objectives were stated:

- to safeguard the integrity of the Republic of Vanuatu as a sovereign and independent state;
- to maintain Vanuatu's non-aligned foreign-policy stand and beliefs;
- to expand socio-economic ties, cooperation, friendship and international understanding with other countries;
- to develop and foster diplomatic relations with foreign states;
- to represent government views at regional and international gatherings and forums;
- to become party to international treaties and conventions that promote peace, stability, equality and development;
- to support inalienable rights of colonised countries and peoples to self-determination and independence;
- to support genuine denuclearisation and disarmament initiatives;
- to encourage peaceful initiatives towards the elimination of all forms of racism and human rights violations; and
- to oppose military interventionism and expansionism (Vanuatu Government 1989a, chs 3.05, 3.22).

Diplomacy

In pursuit of these goals Vanuatu has been cosmopolitan in its diplomatic contacts but selective in its relations with its partners (see Table 15.2). By 1989, to reinforce its newly achieved sovereignty and to balance its links with varied ideological and geographical blocs of states, Vanuatu had arranged diplomatic relations with 67 countries and joined 29 international organisations (Vurobaravu 1989, pp. 3, 6; Vanuatu Government 1989a, tables 3.01, 3.02). The United States was fifty-seventh in the queue, reflecting a deliberate distancing from the Western superpower camp (Hamnett and Kiste 1988, p. 52).

In spite of France's role as a major aid donor, the French Ambassador has been expelled twice, once in 1981, a second time in 1987, for allegedly financing the opposition parties, and in 1984 the visit of the French Minister for Aid was cancelled because France had not paid damages arising out of the secessionist movements in 1980. Substantial exports of beef to New Caledonia have not deterred Vanuatu from pressing its claim to Matthew and Hunter islands, which France claims as part of New Caledonia.

Table 15.2 Evolution of Vanuatu's foreign relations

1980 The Republic of Vanuatu was proclaimed on 30 July. It became a member of the Commonwealth. It signed a defence agreement with Papua New Guinea and received military assistance against secessionists. It began to establish diplomatic contacts with other states, including Third World and communist states.

1981 Vanuatu expelled the French Ambassador and joined the Non Aligned Movement, the United Nations General Assembly, the South Pacific Forum and subsequently all the forum affiliated organisations.

1982 Vanuatu laid claim to Matthew and Hunter islands, claimed also by France as part of New Caledonia. It established links with China.

1983 Vanuatu established diplomatic contact with Cuba and invited Cuban agricultural advisors to visit in 1984. In the South Pacific Forum Vanuatu lobbied for a communiqué supporting self-determination for New Caledonia. Vanuatu joined the South Pacific Commission. A separate Ministry of Foreign Affairs and Trade was set up.

1984 Vanuatu established diplomatic contact with Vietnam and announced support for the New Caledonian Independence Front's call for independence from France.

1986 Vanuatu established diplomatic contacts with the Soviet Union and Libya and entered into negotiations with Papua New Guinea and Solomon Islands to form the Melanesian Spearhead Group, which announced its Agreed Principles of Cooperation in March 1988.

1987 Vanuatu expelled the French ambassador and signed a 1 year agreement permitting Soviet fishing in its Exclusive Economic Zone (EEZ).

1988 The first diplomatic mission abroad was set up in New York, accredited to the United Nations and the United States. Prime Minister Lini requested military equipment and diplomatic backing from Australia and New Zealand to quell riots and a domestic political challenge.

1989 Diplomatic relations were established with the Palestine Liberation Organization (PLO). A fisheries treaty was signed with the Republic of China (Taiwan).

1990 Vanuatu hosted the Twenty-first South Pacific Forum.

Source: *The Far East and Australasia 1990* 1990, pp. 817–18; Premdas and Howard 1989, pp. 130–6.

Diplomatic relations were established with distant radical regimes such as Vietnam, North Korea (and South Korea), Cuba, Nicaragua, East Germany (and West Germany) and the Palestine Liberation Organization (PLO). When talks began with Libya in 1987 about setting up a diplomatic mission in Port Vila, and with the Soviet Union over a 1 year fishing agreement, Australian officials and media expressed anxiety. Prime Minister Lini responded by accusing Australia of trying to isolate and destabilise his government. Vanuatu also denounced Indonesia for suppression of the independence movement of East Timor and military encroachments on the border with Papua New Guinea.

Recognition of Beijing as China's sole government attracted a resident Chinese chargé d'affaires to Port Vila, the only non-Western mission, and substantial project and loan aid, most visibly Vanuatu's new parliament building. Nevertheless, Vanuatu has pursued economic relations with wealthier Taiwan; in 1989 the two countries signed a fishing treaty and discussed opening a Taiwan trade office in Port Vila in spite of objections from Beijing. Vanuatu's commitment to good relations with South Pacific neighbours was shown by its hosting the Twenty-first South Pacific Forum at Port Vila, but the government has not signed the forum-sponsored South Pacific Nuclear Free Zone Treaty because it is not strict enough, and is a member of the Melanesian Spearhead Group, which runs the risk of dividing Melanesian from Polynesian members (Mac-Queen 1990).

In practice Vanuatu's relations are concentrated on a few important partners. These include the two former colonial powers Britain and France, and neighbouring Australia and New Zealand, each of which maintains a high commission or embassy in Port Vila. The People's Republic of China maintains a chargé d'affaires. Vanuatu also is the venue for the Pacific Operations Centre of the Economic and Social Commission for Asia and the Pacific (ESCAP), a delegation of the Commission of the European Communities, and a branch of the Asian Development Bank (ADB).

Except for the mission in New York established in 1988, Vanuatu has no posts overseas because of the cost and scarcity of trained personnel. In 1983 the government designated the Secretary of Foreign Affairs, then Barak Sope, as roving ambassador, accredited him to a number of countries, and conducted relations through him backed by the newly established Ministry of Foreign Affairs. In 1988 the new ambassador to the United Nations took over the secretary's accreditations and became the roving ambassador; there he could make contact with the representatives of all the members of the United Nations General Assembly. Vanuatu also depends on direct contacts by ministers and officials travelling abroad and with foreign representatives visiting Port Vila. The Minister of Foreign Affairs is supported by the secretary, three deputy secretaries, four assistant secretaries in charge of divisions for Political Affairs, Protocol and Consular Affairs, Economic Cooperation, and Administration, and eleven other officers plus clerical and building staff. They are assisted by temporary expatriate staff; for example, a British officer was seconded to the ministry in 1991 to set up a treaty register.

Economic relations

Vanuatu's approach to economic policy reflects the idealism of its foreign policy, but it is tempered by pragmatism. High principles of independence, social justice and cultural integrity coexist with the orthodox goals of raising growth and productivity by means of overseas investment in the private sector and earnings from exports, tourism and services. Vanuatu's declared national-development objectives are as follows:

* to increase economic self-reliance based on the productive utilisation of natural resources;
* to promote new domestic and foreign investment in tourism and the processing of primary produce;
* to expand the private sector's contribution for the benefit of the whole country;
* to promote both the smallholder and the large commercial plantation agricultural subsectors;
* to accelerate human resource development for increased ni-Vanuatu participation in and control of the economy;
* to ensure that Vanuatu's unique environmental and cultural heritage is not damaged; and
* to ensure a stable political environment based on parliamentary democracy (Vanuatu 1988, pp. 51–2 and 1989a, chs 2.02, 2.16).

Resources are mainly agricultural, and export earnings in 1989 were dominated by copra (29.3 per cent), beef (10.2 per cent), timber (8.0 per cent) and cocoa (6.8 per cent) (Vanuatu Government 1990, p. 4). Re-exports of petroleum and fish products constituted 37.0 per cent of total export earnings, reflecting the underdeveloped nature of the domestic export base. The principal markets for domestic exports were the Netherlands and Belgium, which took cocoa and copra for processing, and Japan and New Caledonia, which took beef. Principal suppliers of imports of machinery, chemicals, fuels and manufactures were Australia, New Zealand, Japan and Fiji (see Table 15.3).

In 1989 the import bill exceeded export earnings by V$7882 million to V$2563 million or over 300 per cent, necessitating dependence on other sources of external finance to make up the V$5320 million trade deficit. The most important was aid, which totalled V$2305 million in 1989, equivalent to between 15 and 20 per cent of gross domestic product (GDP). Aid is the source of about half of government revenues and underwrites over 90 per cent of the development budget (Browne 1989, p. 161; Australia Government 1990a, p. 4; Vanuatu Government 1989b, p. 81). Britain and

Table 15.3 Vanuatu's trade partners, 1989 (%)

Country	Exports to	Imports from
Netherlands	28.6	—a
Japan	18.5	11.6
Belgium	16.7	—a
Australia	10.1	39.1
France	9.6	5.4
New Caledonia	7.7	3.0
New Zealand	—a	13.0
Fiji	—a	9.3
Hong Kong	—a	3.7
Others	8.8	14.8
Total	100.0	100.0

a Included in Others.

Source: Vanuatu Government 1990, pp. 6, 7.

Table 15.4 Vanuatu's aid donors, 1983 and 1987 (%)

Donor	1983	1987
Britain	33.1	15.1
France	30.5	16.5
Australia	21.9	17.8
New Zealand	3.0	3.1
Japan	1.1	11.0
United Nations Development Programme	1.9	1.2
Asian Development Bank	1.5	2.7
International Development Association	0.0	1.6
World Food Programme	0.0	0.8
European Community (incl. STABEX)a	3.7	28.2
Others	3.7	2.4
Total	100.0	100.0

a Export price stabilisation grants

Source: Australia Government 1990a, table 12.

France, initially the major donors, have been joined by Japan and European Community sources and overtaken by Australia, which emerged in 1987 as the largest bilateral donor (see Table 15.4).

Grant aid and concessionary loans have made government borrowing overseas less urgent, and the public overseas debt and debt service ratio have remained manageable, being 6.8 per cent of GDP and 2.9 per cent of export earnings respectively in 1987 (Brown 1989, p. 178). Nevertheless, borrowing, mostly private sector, totalled V\$1200 million in 1989, equivalent to 74 per cent of export earnings. Private transfers brought in the equivalent of about 30 per cent of export earnings; these included remittances by ni-Vanuatu (natives of Vanuatu) abroad (about one-third) and expenditures by expatriates working in Vanuatu (about two-thirds). The 1 year fishing treaty with the Soviet Union brought in the equivalent of 10 per cent of export earnings in 1987 but was not renewed when the government doubled the royalty.

In spite of Vanuatu's ideology of Melanesian socialism, the government is pragmatic about earnings from international capital movements. The government maintained the Finance Centre established by the British in 1971. By imposing no taxes and promising confidentiality it has attracted over 1500 registered companies, which pay registration fees equivalent to 10 per cent of export earnings. The finance sector in its entirety, including other fees, secondary taxes and contributions to service sector employment, is thought to contribute 12 per cent of Vanuatu's GDP. A US Senate report in 1990 accused sixteen tax havens including Vanuatu of becoming money-laundering centres for proceeds from international drugs trafficking; the government rejected the charge and took steps to reform its laws and oversight procedures (Browne 1989, p. 162; Mangnall 1990b, pp. 26–7; *Pacific Islands Monthly* 1990a, pp. 35–6).

Further earnings are generated by the Vanuatu Ship Registry, established in 1982 and managed by a trust in New York. Turmoil in Panama and Liberia swelled the registry from 375 to 560 in 1989/90, resulting in earnings equivalent to 10 per cent of exports (*New Zealand Herald* 24 August 1990; *Pacific Islands Monthly* 1990a, p. 35). Investments of a more conventional sort are encouraged by tax concessions provided that they use local raw materials, employ local people and generate export earnings. Some occupations are reserved for Vanuatu citizens (South Pacific Forum 1987, pp. 258–64).

Earnings from tourism emerged as the largest contributor to the current account in 1989, exceeding aid income by 9 per cent and export earnings by 56 per cent, and contributing about 15 per cent of the GDP (Vanuatu Government 1989b, pp. 81, 85). On independence the government was ambivalent about tourism, more radical members viewing it as degrading. However, its potential was soon appreciated, and a policy was developed that included linking Air Vanuatu with Ansett for direct flights to Australia, setting up the National Tourism Office, opening a tourist liaison office in Sydney to manage a tourism promotion campaign, acquiring jet aircraft for Air Vanuatu and improving Port Vila's Bauerfield International Airport. Official policy is 'to promote Vanuatu's image as a high class tourist destination, attracting visitors from the upper income groups' but 'with explicit attention given to the conservation of vulnerable aspects of the environment and cultural heritage' (Vanuatu Government 1989a, ch. 17.02). Visitor arrivals have risen from about 20 000 in the early 1980s to 31 047 in 1989. The bulk, 45 per cent, were Australian, 14 per cent French (most resident in New Caledonia), 9 per cent New Zealander and 7 per cent British (many resident in Australia, Fiji and other island countries). Japanese visitors were only 3 per cent but were forecast to increase, particularly with Japanese capital flowing into the Iririki Island hotel and other tourist ventures.

Foreign policy issues

Foreign policy alternatives are only partly clarified by the political party debate. The Union of Moderate Parties with support from local French interests has decried the Vanuaaku Pati's radical declarations, impulsive diplomatic initiatives and touchiness towards the French and has advocated closer relations, especially economic relations, with France. It is sceptical of what it calls 'Australian neo-colonialism'. however, it does not disagree with the substance of the government's pragmatic economic policy. Barak Sope, in spite of his leadership of the Melanesian Progressive Party, is a former associate of Lini, a former roving ambassador and an architect of the radical foreign policy. Although he criticised the government during the 1991 election campaign, he did not put forward a significantly different foreign-policy platform. The party rivalries tend to be regional, religious and personal and to concentrate on issues of who has access to government powers and privileges as much as on principle and ideology. Parliamentary foreign policy debate is episodic and of secondary importance to most elected members and party elites.

Public debate is almost unknown. The academic community—Port Vila has a branch of the University of the South Pacific—remains tiny and moderated by expatriates. Journalists are few and preoccupied with domestic events, and church and union leaders have only sporadically come forward in public affairs. The domestic private sector is focused on petty local production, trade and services, and the expatriate private sector is concerned with international business infrastructure such as telecommunications and air links, and with keeping government restrictions and fees to a minimum. Neither participates in public debate on issues but rather lobbies the political leaders or government ministers directly. Civil servants are the most numerous salaried elite of the country. However, the

Ministry of Foreign Affairs and Trade numbers little over a dozen officers who are burdened with day-to-day diplomacy and administration and have little time and few resources for long term planning or policy brainstorming. Ultimately foreign policy has been made by a handful of ministers, principally by the prime minister, Walter Lini.

Personalistic politics, which is permitted by undeveloped institutions, results in abrupt, seemingly arbitrary, decisions. This illustrated by the example of immigration. Recalling the importation of Asian labour by the French colonial administration, which led to the alienation of ni-Vanuatu lands, the government has pursued an indigenisation policy and does not encourage immigration. A 10 year residence period is mandatory, and administrative inertia can prolong the period. Expatriates have been deported on several occasions since independence. Under law no reason need be stated. The government hints that deportees are often persons suspected of crime in which prosecution would be difficult, and no controversy results.

However, in 1990 deportation orders were served on six French, Australian and New Zealand businessmen. The reason was rumoured to be their business contacts with Barak Sope and their competition with interests owned by local businessman Dinh Van Thanh, an advisor to Lini. The decision, made by the prime minister ostensibly to signal that foreign interference would not be tolerated, was criticised as arbitrary, unfair to longtime residents and detrimental to the credibility of Vanuatu as a home for foreign capital (Lini 1990, p. 17). This episode illustrated a fundamental tension between the sovereignty of Vanuatu and the need to adopt Western legal and administrative standards to attract investment, aid and expertise from abroad or, to put it another way, the tension between the needs of the ni-Vanuatu and the interests of the expatriates.

Vanuatu has carried several other unresolved foreign policy questions into the 1990s. The first is when the government will sign the South Pacific Nuclear Free Zone Treaty, thus contributing to a South Pacific united front against the nuclear powers instead of remaining aloof. The second is whether the Melanesian Spearhead Group will become a focal point of Vanuatu's regional cooperation rather than just a supplement, and whether that will divide the South Pacific Forum. The third is the related question of how much confidence the government has in the South Pacific Forum Secretariat, in light of Lini's criticism of its growing bureaucracy and of its director until 1991, Henry Naisali, over his handling of the Johnston Atoll chemical-disposal controversy with the United States. The fourth question is how disputes with France over independence period interference and boundary claims, and disagreements over nuclear testing and the decolonisation of New Caledonia, can be resolved sufficiently for a French Ambassador to be invited to Port Vila again, and whether, in the absence of settlement, France will continue its substantial aid programme. The fifth relates to growing Australian prominence in trade, aid, tourism and investment, to the alleged narrowing of Vanuatu's room for economic manoeuvre vis-à-vis its large neighbour, and to how export and aid receipts can be raised and diversified—perhaps to Japan and the Asian Newly Industrialising Countries (NICs) including Taiwan. The sixth is whether in the face of challenges by outsiders, secessionists and political rivals the government may upgrade the Vanuatu Mobile Force, now a police force, into an armed force, tempting military solutions to political problems.

The new Kalpokas and Carlot governments moved cautiously in 1991 and 1992 to resolve these issues. Kalpokas revoked deportation orders, reaffirmed expatriates' citizenship rights, and otherwise reassured foreign investors. The leaders of the Union of Moderate Parties, who dominated the government in 1992, advocated closer relations with the United States, Australia, France, and the European Community. They proposed the sale of freehold land to foreigners and other liberalisation measures to encourage overseas investors. A shift from idealistic independence to pragmatic interdependence in rhetoric as well as in policy seemed likely to bring Vanuatu more in harmony with its extraregional partners.

But Prime Minister Carlot governed in coalition with the National United Party, a breakaway party led by former prime minister Walter Lini. Lini declined to serve in the government but five of his former associates joined the new cabinet. The idealism of the Vanuaaku Pati's Melanesian socialism remained alive not only among the opposition but also among some ministers. New policies compromising independence and extending liberalisation had to be made cautiously to preserve the fragile political consensus and maintain the coalition government's slim majority.

Nevertheless leaders of all political parties were increasingly aware, after a decade of independence, that Vanuatu survived politically and prospered economically thanks in part to support by regional and international systems. The many international links that Vanuatu had forged to bolster its sovereignty and to finance development also restrained its actions by imposing obligations in return for granting resources. Balancing independence with cooperation, development with obligations, and indigenous rights with expatriate interests was increasingly the objective of Vanuatu's more thoughtful foreign policy leaders of the 1990s.

16 Western Samoa

Since becoming the first Pacific island country to achieve independence, in 1962, Western Samoa has played an active role in regional and international affairs. Its modern political heritage is Anglo-New Zealand, its orientation is pro-West, and its style is moderate. Its foreign policy outlook and initiatives are the product also of deep historical roots and cultural integrity that transcend the institutions and connections bequeathed by the colonial period.

Political heritage

The Samoans were introduced to European languages, learning and religion by French explorers, American seamen and traders, British and New Zealand missionaries, and German company agents, and adapted these new elements to their traditional ways (Davidson 1967). Imperial naval rivalry between Britain, Germany and the United States complicated the endemic feuds between leading Samoan clans, who sought assistance and protection from one or another of the outside powers (Meleisea 1987, appendix 3). The preferred outside power was Britain, whose constitutional monarchy was admired, but the order imposed by Germany and the United States when they divided the islands in 1899 was not unwelcome. New Zealand took over in Western Samoa from Germany in 1914 and, in spite of a poor start marred by epidemic, violence and mistrust, introduced physical and administrative improvements and tutored Samoan leaders in the art of modern self-government (Boyd 1969, 1987). The Samoans were quick learners but selective, and retained strong elements of *fa'a Samoa* (Samoan traditional culture) in their constitution and political life. The 1961 plebiscite on self-government was a curiosity inasmuch as the entire adult population voted to disenfranchise itself in favour of an electorate comprised of 4594 *matai* or titled chiefs. Western Samoa's head of state is a paramount chief elected by the Legislative Assembly. The Queen is recognised only as head of the Commonwealth, of which Western Samoa is a member.

Rather than enhancing modernisation, Samoa's hierarchical relationships were thought to distort and corrupt the administration of investment, loans and development aid. Communal ownership was thought to deny land use for individual entrepreneurship and production for export (Yusuf and Peters, 1985). Thus a new generation of urbanised Samoans, many returned from higher education abroad, has begun pressing for reforms (Meleisea and Schloeffel 1983, pp. 105–12; Maiava 1988, p. 5). In the plebiscite of 1990 a slim majority opted for universal adult suffrage, but a majority of Samoans either voted against it or did not register or vote, indicating the strength of tradition. The 1991 election returned the Human Rights Protection Party for a fourth term of office, but it and the opposition Samoa National Development Party remained oriented as much to personalities as to programmes, and the present system of a *fono* (parliament) led by a prime minister and Cabinet of traditional influentials is likely to persist. Reforms may be made to address the concerns of teachers, civil servants and professionals in Apia, and the suggestions by outsiders such as investors, aid administrators and international agency advisors will be taken seriously, but these will be adapted to *fa'a Samoa*, and change will be evolutionary rather than revolutionary.

Bilateral relations

Current foreign orientations are consistent with Western Samoa's colonial links and experiences (see Table 16.1). Western Samoan leaders respected Britain's international influence, stable political system and apparent wealth and consequently joined the Commonwealth in 1972.

The German connection is reflected more in the economic sphere: in the volume of exports sold to Germany, at 23.2 per cent the highest proportion of any South Pacific country (see Table 16.2), and in the generosity of aid received from Germany (see Table 16.3). Germany is important also as a leading member of the European Community, which is a significant trade partner and a source of loans, European Development Fund (EDF) aid, and export price stabilisation (STABEX) grants in accordance with the Lome Convention.

Table 16.1 Evolution of Western Samoa's foreign affairs

1000 BC The Samoan islands were settled by voyagers from Fiji and Tonga, and may have been the source of further Polynesian migrations to French Polynesia and New Zealand. The islands were frequently divided by clan rivalries and wars with Tonga.

1768, 1787 French explorers Bougainville, then La Perouse, were the first Europeans to visit Samoa.

1800 European beachcombers began to settle.

1835 Methodist and London Missionary Society workers arrived and in the following decades established churches and schools, introduced English and Western knowledge, and composed a Samoan dictionary.

1838 Apia chiefs signed a commercial agreement with Britain. Trade grew with the European powers, the United States, New Zealand and Australia.

1848 The first resident British Consul was accepted by local chiefs.

1853 Samoans accepted the first United States commercial agent.

1860 A consul from Hamburg was appointed, foreshadowing German trading and later imperial interests.

1868–99 The Malietoa, Tamasese, Mata'afa and Laupepa families engaged in sporadic wars complicated by rivalry between British, German and US forces.

1884 Malietoa, Tamasese and 45 other chiefs petitioned Britain to annex Samoa to bring peace and end international manipulations.

1889 Britain, Germany and the United States in the Berlin Treaty assumed joint responsibility to manage Samoan external affairs.

1899 The three powers, which had taken control of the Apia municipal treasury in 1893, disarmed the warring families and apportioned Western Samoa to Germany and Tutuila (American Samoa) to the United States. Britain was compensated by gaining from Germany islands for its Solomon Islands colony.

1914 New Zealand forces seized Western Samoa from the German administrators.

1918 Massive casualties from influenza introduced from Auckland induced scepticism of colonialism but also stimulated New Zealand to improve the administration of public health and preventive medicine.

1920 The New Zealand parliament passed the Samoa Act establishing an Anglo-New Zealand system of law and administration. The League of Nations confirmed Western Samoa as a New Zealand mandate.

1921 Annual income from seized German plantations—the Reparation Estates—was retained as a subsidy for local improvements and further aid and technical assistance was provided by the New Zealand Department of Native Affairs (later the Department of Island Territories).

1926 Nationalism began with the *mau* (opinion or testimony) movement. Eleven Samoan leaders were shot by New Zealand troops during a demonstration in 1929, and others were banished.

1936 New Zealand's first Labour government legalised the *mau*, encouraged Samoans into public service, and accelerated improvements in health and education.

1942–45 US troops used Western Samoa as a rear base. The traditional economy was disrupted by abundant cash and goods.

1944, 1946 Samoan chiefs petitioned New Zealand, then the United Nations, for self-government. With New Zealand's approval Western Samoa was brought under the United Nations Trusteeship Council.

1947 The New Zealand parliament passed the Samoa Amendment Act implementing United Nations Trusteeship Council recommendations on preparing trusts for eventual self-government. The first Samoan Legislative Assembly was convened the following year.

1949–60 Under High Commissioner Sir Guy Powles institutions were created, powers were devolved, and Samoan leaders were educated and urged to prepare for self-government.

1957 The Reparation Estates were transferred to Samoan ownership. Samoan members of the Executive Council were designated ministers, and Western Samoa became virtually self-governing.

1960 The Constitution of Western Samoa was drafted and adopted.

1962 In accordance with a United Nations supervised plebiscite Western Samoa became independent with its own chiefly head of state. It signed a treaty of friendship with New Zealand, which offered its diplomatic network to assist international contacts.

1965 Western Samoa became the first Pacific island state to join the South Pacific Commission.

1971 Western Samoa became a founder member of the South Pacific Forum.

1972 Western Samoa became a member of the Commonwealth.

1976 Western Samoa became a member of the United Nations General Assembly, opened its first diplomatic mission abroad, in Wellington, and accepted an embassy from the People's Republic of China.

1977 A diplomatic mission was opened in New York, accredited to the United Nations, the United States and Canada.

1980 The South Pacific Regional Trade and Economic Cooperation Agreement gave Western Samoa free access to Australian and New Zealand markets.

1983–85 Overseas indebtedness became critical, requiring economic reforms under International Monetary Fund (IMF) guidance.

1985 A high commission was set up in Brussels to deal with the European Community, Britain, Germany, Belgium, France, Italy and Switzerland.

1989 An embassy was opened in Washington, and the United States opened a one-person consulate in Apia. A mission was opened in Canberra to complement Australia's office in Apia.

Source: Craig and King 1981, *passim*; Douglas and Douglas 1989, pp. 646–51; Meleisea and Meleisea 1987, appendix 3.

The US connection is significant not only because of the US presence in neighbouring American Samoa since 1899 but also because of trade and diplomatic relations for over a century, benign occupation during World War II, and leadership in the containment of communist expansion during the Cold War. The United States is a major source of investment, airline connections (to Honolulu by Hawaiian Airlines), visitors (46 per cent of the total in 1987, counting Samoans from American Samoa), and remittances by emigrant Samoans working in Hawaii and the West Coast. It is also an influential member of international agencies on which Western Samoa depends for capital and aid (Western Samoa Government 1988, p. 117).

In the 1980s Australia became an important partner. The two countries have worked together diplomatically in the South Pacific Commission, the South Pacific Forum and the United Nations for nearly two decades. In 1987 Australia took 20 per cent of Western Samoa's exports and provided 18 per cent of imports, 33 per cent of project aid and 9 per cent of tourists (Western Samoa Government 1988, pp. 117, 212, 129). Western Samoa benefits from Australian maritime surveillance and defence mutual assistance (civil aid) and received a fisheries patrol boat as part of the Australian Pacific patrol boat project. Japan, distant and with no historical ties, is nonetheless accepted now as a 'Western' partner and has become a growing source of imports and tourists and the leading aid donor. When funds permit, the Western Samoan government hopes to open a diplomatic mission in Tokyo.

New Zealand remains the country towards which Western Samoa is most directly oriented. Gradual improvements were effected during the mandate and trust periods of 1920–62, and since then New Zealand has remained sympathetic and engaged in spite of occasional frictions between the two governments. The Treaty of Friendship of 1962 enjoined New Zealand 'to consider sympathetically requests for technical, administrative and other assistance' and to provide diplomatic and consular services abroad if asked. Accord-

Table 16.2 Western Samoa's trade partners, 1989 (%)

Country	Exports to	Imports[a]
New Zealand	34.5	41.2
West Germany	23.2	3.5
United States	18.5[b]	5.6
Australia	8.7	18.0
Japan	0.4	12.8
Others	14.7	18.9
Total	100.0	100.0

Note: a 1987, b of which, half to American Samoa.

Source: Western Samoa Government 1989, pp. 41–2; World Bank 1991b, vol. II, pp. 245–6.

Table 16.3 Western Samoa's aid donors and receipts, 1989

Donor	S$ million	%
Japan	4.5	28.1
Australia	3.7	23.1
New Zealand	2.2	13.8
West Germany	1.2	7.5
European Community (incl. STABEX)[a]	2.1	13.1
United Nations Development Programme	0.8	5.0
European Development Fund	0.4	2.5
Others	1.3	8.1
Total	16.0	100.0

[a] Export price stabilisation grants.

Source: Western Samoa Government 1989, p. 48; World Bank 1991b, p. 247.

ingly, in the 1960s and 1970s New Zealand assisted in diplomacy and defence, seconded experts, gave aid and granted free trade access. It extends immigration privileges second only to those extended to Australia, Cook Islands and Niue (Hoadley 1989, p. 113). Over 50 000 Samoans live in New Zealand, more than anywhere else except in their home islands (Bedford 1991, p. 155) and their remittances constitute an essential component of the Samoan economy. Western Samoa opened its first overseas diplomatic post in New Zealand in 1976. In 1987 New Zealand took 37 per cent of Western Samoa's exports and provided 41 per cent of imports, 19 per cent of project aid and 28 per cent of overseas visitors (Western Samoa Government 1988, pp. 117, 121, 129). Western Samoa also benefits from the New Zealand Defence Mutual Assistance Programme.

At present Western Samoa conducts diplomatic relations with over 30 countries, including the South Pacific Forum fifteen, the four northern Pacific powers (United States, Canada, Japan and China), and the European Community twelve, particularly those with present or historical ties with the South Pacific. Early diplomatic and aid relations with the People's Republic of China led Samoan Prime Ministers Tupuola Efi in 1980 and Tofilau Eti Alesana in 1990 to visit Beijing, resulting in a low interest loan that enabled the building of the Apia sports complex and the completion of three water-supply and agricultural projects (Biddick 1989, p. 805). However, neither the Chinese connection nor intermittent talks with Soviet diplomats over possible fishing agreements nor former Prime Minister Tupuola Efi's non-aligned rhetoric in the 1970s has shifted Western Samoa from its fundamentally pro-Western orientation.

Diplomatic contacts and foreign policy generally are administered by the Ministry of Foreign Affairs in Apia, comprised of the minister, the secretary and his deputy, and divisional officers responsible for (1) the South Pacific (including Australia and New Zealand), (2) the Americas, (3) Asia and (4) Europe. They are assisted by two functional divisions specialising in (5) politics, policy and protocol and (6) economics (trade, aid, investment) and working in close coordination with the Ministry of Economic Development and the Treasury. The missions in New Zealand, the United States and Brussels are used to deal with a large number of counterparts; so opening costly missions in each partner country is unnecessary. Frequent ministerial and official travel also serves the function of diplomatic contact.

Multilateral relations

Western Samoa's participation in multilateral organisations arises not only out of national pride but also out of necessity. Global organisations such as the United Nations provide venues where Samoa's political leaders and officials can meet their counterparts from around the world without the cost of maintaining embassies or undertaking extensive travel. The specialised agencies are repositories of ideas and expertise that Western Samoa can tap instead of maintaining costly education and research establishments of its own. The lending and aid agencies are sources of technical assistance, grants, concessionary loans and other benefits without which the government of Western Samoa could not sustain its operations and carry out its development programme, and their multilateral backing reassures bilateral lenders and donors (see Table 16.4). The regional organisations are also political forums where a small state such as Western Samoa can be heard and project its influence to larger states as part of a collective endeavour.

Economic relations

External economic relations are driven by the needs of economic development, defined as the improvement of the quality of life of all Samoans (Western Samoa Government 1987, p. 24). This entails increasing production in the fisheries, forestry, agricultural and industrial sectors, and raising the volume and value of exports of goods and services so as to pay for necessary imports. External policies thus concentrate on attracting capital by means of government borrowing, official aid, private investment, tourism and remittances, and on facilitating exports by means of transportation and

Table 16.4 Western Samoa's multilateral participation

Universal organisations
Food and Agriculture Organization
United Nations Educational, Scientific and Cultural Organization
United Nations General Assembly
World Health Organization

Regional organisations (general)
Economic and Social Commission for Asia and the Pacific
Pacific Islands Conference
South Pacific Commission
South Pacific Forum (and Forum Secretariat)

Regional organisations (specialised)
Conference of South Pacific Police Chiefs
Pacific Forum Line
Pacific Islands Law Officers Meeting
Pacific Islands Tourism Development Council
South Pacific Applied Geoscience Commission
South Pacific Board for Educational Assessment
South Pacific Forum Fisheries Agency
South Pacific Judicial Conference
South Pacific Labour Ministers Conference
South Pacific Regional Civil Aviation Council
South Pacific Regional Environment Programme
South Pacific Regional Meeting on Telecommunications
South Pacific Regional Shipping Council
South Pacific Regional Trade and Economic Cooperation Agreement
Tourism Council of the South Pacific
University of the South Pacific

Multilateral aid agencies
Commission of the European Communities
European Development Fund
United Nations Childrens Emergency Fund
United Nations Development Programme
United Nations Fund for Population Activities

Multilateral lending agencies
Asian Development Bank
International Development Association
International Monetary Fund
International Fund for Agricultural Development
Organisation of Petroleum Exporting Countries

Source: Haas 1989, *passim*; Western Samoa Government 1988, pp. 121–2.

market-opening initiatives. For example, the Enterprises Incentive
Act 1965 and the Industrial Free Zone Act 1974 offer tax holidays,
duty exemptions and profit repatriation (Western Samoa Government n.d.).

Western Samoa participates in New Zealand's Pacific Islands
Industrial Development Scheme, Australia's Joint Venture Scheme,
the European Community's Centre for Development of Industry, and

special studies by the United Nations Industrial Development Organization (UNIDO) (United Nations 1986, pp. 126–44). Its exporters benefit from the South Pacific Regional Trade and Economic Cooperation Agreement, the Lome Convention and the Generalised System of Preferences. The government encourages private banks from Australia, New Zealand and Hawaii, and its Development Bank of Western Samoa manages and disburses the government's loan and aid receipts in a generally responsible manner. The Visitors Bureau Act 1984 and modernisation of Faleolo International Airport to take jumbo jets signalled the initiation of a positive tourist promotion policy by Prime Minister Tofilau Eti after two decades of ambivalence by his predecessors. Corresponding shipping and telecommunications upgrading was undertaken to keep the country in touch with the world.

The policies have not been uniformly successful. Fishing resources were underexploited, agricultural production and exports stagnated, and industry remained rudimentary. Monopoly producer boards discouraged initiative and constrained exports. In 1984 the country exported goods—lightly processed coconut products, foodstuffs and timber—worth only one-third of the value of imported goods (Western Samoa Government 1988, p. 131). To meet rising expectations after independence the government borrowed overseas. Rising oil prices and falling export revenues pushed Western Samoa's debt level from 21 per cent of gross domestic product (GDP) in 1975 up to 80 per cent a decade later. By 1984 the debt service burden had grown to over 18 per cent of the value of all export, tourism and remittance income (Browne 1989, p. 205). Seventy per cent of this debt was owed to the multilateral lending agencies listed in Table 16.4, the bulk of it to the Asian Development Bank (ADB), and the balance to Germany, China, New Zealand, Nauru and Saudi Arabia.

On advice from the International Monetary Fund (IMF) the government curbed spending, raised bank interest rates and privatised some enterprises. Exports rose marginally, boosted by recovering commodity prices, and the government rescheduled its debts and accomplished some repayments, easing the interest burden to 12.5 per cent of export earnings by 1987 (Browne 1989, p. 205). Imports, however, continued to grow, reaching six times the value of exports by 1989.

Nevertheless, the overall external balance of payments became positive and foreign reserves increased because loans, investments, remittances, aid and earnings from tourism increased. As shown in Table 16.5, remittances were the largest contributor to the balance of payments, equivalent to over three times the earnings from trade.

Table 16.5 Western Samoa's balance of payments, 1989

Item	US$ million
Merchandise trade	−62.6
(Exports)	(+12.9)
(Imports)	(−75.5)
Travel and tourism	+18.4
Investments	+2.4
Remittances	+38.2
Project and cash aid	+15.2
Loan aid	+5.3
Balance	+16.9

Source: World Bank, 1991b, p. 242.

In the 1980s remittances were equivalent to about half of the government budget.

Thus the reforms of 1983–86 did not make Western Samoa more productive, only more 'donorworthy'. This economic dependency has generated rhetorical concern among political leaders and criticism from younger intellectuals. However, public servants who administer, and are indirectly paid by, funds from overseas are generally supportive of present arrangements. No feasible alternative to current government policy is offered by any opposition party or leader. Thus Western Samoa is likely to remain vulnerable to characterisation as a 'MIRAB economy', based on migration, remittances, aid and bureaucracy, for the foreseeable future (Watters 1987, pp. 32–54).

Foreign policy issues

Western Samoa's international policies are not as controversial as those of Vanuatu or neighbouring island states such Fiji, Tonga and Cook Islands. The government has taken a moderate position on a variety of issues—such as China's and the Soviet Union's presence in the region, sanctions against South Africa and France, and Third World versus First World debates—and is content to move within the broad consensus established by annual South Pacific Forum discussions and the deliberations of the United Nations General Assembly and the Commonwealth Heads of Government Meetings.

In the early 1980s Western Samoa did not support proposals for the absorption of the South Pacific Commission by the supposedly more independent and authoritative South Pacific Forum, viewing each regional organisation as useful in its particular sphere of activity. When Cook Islands, Tonga and French Polynesia mooted extending the Polynesian Heritage Trust to form a Polynesian Economic and Cultural Community as a counterpart to the Melanesian Spearhead Group, Western Samoa remained noncommittal (Maiava 1988, p. 16). Prime Minister Tofilau Eti Alesana was not among those leaders who openly criticised the Fiji coups in 1987 or US chemical-agent disposal plans on Johnston Atoll in 1990, and he seemed comfortable with Australia's and New Zealand's leading roles in South Pacific affairs and with Japanese investors' growing ownership of Samoan tourist assets such as the Tusitala Hotel. Perhaps the reward for international moderation was the outpouring of aid from numerous countries and international agencies in response to the devastation caused by Cyclones Ofa and Val in 1990 and 1991. With no defence pacts or official enemies, and with a benign image, Western Samoa can attract aid, business and tourism from all quarters.

The immigration relationship with New Zealand was the most emotional issue of the 1980s. The number of Samoans living in New Zealand is estimated to be approaching 60 000, in the United States 50 000 and in Australia 3000—a total living abroad greater than any other Pacific island group (Bedford 1991, p. 155). Because emigration vents social pressure and because remittances are so vital to the economy (see Table 16.5; Shankman 1976, p. 45), every restraint by New Zealand, or by the United States or Australia, generates official concern in Apia.

The New Zealand government's efforts to restrain immigration and to send back overstayers began in 1976 and has continued intermittently (Hoadley 1989, p. 110). In 1982 the Privy Council ruled that Western Samoans born before the passage of the British Nationality and New Zealand Citizenship Act 1948 were legally entitled to New Zealand citizenship (Hoadley 1989, p. 139). New Zealand's parliament immediately overrode the court judgement, and Prime Minister Robert Muldoon urged Prime Minister Tofilau Eti to accept the status quo. In spite of public criticism at home, Eti did so. But he succeeded in negotiating a protocol to the 1962 Treaty of Friendship to the effect that Samoans resident in New Zealand would not be expelled, the Samoan immigration quota of 1100 per year would be maintained, and Western Samoa's leaders would be consulted on future changes to New Zealand immigration policy.

In 1989 it became public that Samoan immigration had exceeded 4000 the previous year through abuse of the family reunification and adoption provisions of the Immigration Act. To save the quota of 1100 per year, which political opponents and unionists in New Zealand demanded be suspended, Prime Minister Eti was obliged to announce a policy of voluntary restraint and offer to send Samoan officers to New Zealand to monitor compliance. In 1991 the newly elected National government prepared to expel an estimated 9000 Samoan overstayers.

To some Samoan critics, New Zealand, relatively large and wealthy, appeared to pressure a small poor island country for selfish reasons. However, with unemployment climbing in New Zealand, the United States and Australia, immigration quotas and policies will be under review in the 1990s, and the island country most disadvantaged in the event of impeded immigration is likely to be Western Samoa. Other irritations have arisen over import restrictions, air routes, shipping services, aid project supervision, crime control and health, safety and educational standards.

These may induce Samoan leaders to consider alternative non-traditional partners in their search for external resources. Samoa already has good relations with Japan, China, Saudi Arabia and the Organization of Petroleum Exporting Countries (OPEC), which it might cultivate. France has already extended aid and may be ready to do more either directly or through French Polynesia. South Korea, Taiwan, Indonesia and Malaysia—and maybe the Soviet Union in the long run—are countries likely to be responsive to appeals from the South Pacific. Each of these offers possibilities that an ambitious government could explore.

However, cultivating new partners will consume scarce diplomatic and administrative resources and may induce traditional benefactors to lose interest and reduce assistance. Western Samoan leaders are likely to look beyond current irritations with traditional partners to reaffirm relationships that have served them well in the past three decades.

References

Afeaki, E. 1983, 'Tonga: the last Pacific kingdom', *Politics in Polynesia*, eds R. Crocombe & A. Ali, University of the South Pacific Institute for Pacific Studies, Suva

Aiavao, U. 1991, 'Time to change tune', *Pacific Island Monthly*, vol. 61, no. 5, May, p. 30

Alatas, A. 1988, 'Indonesia and the South Pacific', Minister for Foreign Affairs, Jakarta; typescript keynote address to First Conference on the Relationship between Indonesia and the South Pacific Countries, Ujung Pandang, 5 December

Aldrich, R. 1988, *The French View of the Pacific: A Critique of Geo-political Analysis*, University of Sydney Research Institute for Asia and the Pacific, Sydney

—— 1989, 'France in the South Pacific', *No Longer an American Lake*, ed. J. Ravenhill, Allen & Unwin, North Sydney

—— 1990, *The French Presence in the South Pacific*, Macmillan, Basingstoke

Ali, A. 1982, 'Fiji: the politics of a plural society', *Politics in Melanesia*, eds R. Crocombe & A. Ali, University of the South Pacific Institute of Pacific Studies, Suva

Alley, R. ed. 1984, *New Zealand and the Pacific*, Westview Press, Boulder

'American Samoa', 1986, *Pacific Constitutions Vol. 1 Polynesia*, University of the South Pacific, Suva

Angiki, D. 1990a, 'King Solomon's mind', *Pacific Islands Monthly*, vol. 60, no. 11, November, pp. 10–11

—— 1990b, 'The time to go private', *Pacific Islands Monthly*, vol. 60, no. 11, November, pp. 12–13

Asia Pacific Research Unit, 1982a, *Cook Islands: A Trade and Investment Guide*, Wellington

227

—— 1982b, *Kiribati: A Trade and Investment Guide*, Wellington

—— 1982c, *Nauru: A Trade and Investment Guide*, Wellington

—— 1982d, *Niue: A Trade and Investment Guide*, Wellington

—— 1982e, *Tonga: A Trade and Investment Guide*, Wellington

—— 1982f, *Tuvalu: A Trade and Investment Guide*, Wellington

Australia Government, 1987a, Department of Foreign Affairs and Trade, 'Australia and Japan', *Australian Foreign Affairs Record*, vol. 58, no. 2, February, pp. 45–8

—— 1987b, Beasley, K. Hon. Minister of Defence, *The Defence of Australia*, Department of Defence, Canberra, March

—— 1987c, Department of Foreign Affairs and Trade, 'Declaration of principles guiding relations between Papua New Guinea and Australia', *Australian Foreign Affairs Record*, vol. 58, no. 10, November–December, pp. 615–16

—— 1988, Australian International Development Assistance Bureau, *Cooperation: A Review of the Australian International Aid Program 1987–88*, Australian Government Publishing Service, Canberra

—— 1988/89, *Tuvalu Country Paper*, 2nd edn, Australian International Development Assistance Bureau, Canberra

—— 1989a, *Papua New Guinea: Economic Situation and Outlook*, Australian International Development Assistance Bureau, Canberra, February

—— 1989b, Parliament Joint Committee on Foreign Affairs, Defence and Trade, *Australia's Relations with the South Pacific*, Australian Government Publishing Service, Canberra, March

—— 1989c, Parliament Joint Committee on Foreign Affairs, Defence and Trade, *Report on Visit to New Caledonia*, Australian Government Publishing Service, Canberra, May

—— 1989d, *Australia's Development Cooperation Programme with Papua New Guinea*, Australian International Development Assistance Bureau, Canberra, August

—— 1989e, Evans, G. Hon. Minister of Foreign Affairs, *Australia's Regional Security*, Department of Foreign Affairs and Trade, Canberra, December

—— 1990a, *Vanuatu Country Paper*, Australian International Development Assistance Bureau, Port Vila, February

—— 1990b, *Tuvalu Country Paper*, Australian International Development Assistance Bureau, Canberra, March

Babbage, R. 1990, *A Coast Too Long: Defending Australia Beyond the 1990s*, Allen & Unwin, North Sydney

Ball, D. ed. 1985, *The ANZAC Connection*, Allen & Unwin, North Sydney

Banks, A.S. ed. 1987, *Political Handbook of the World 1987*, CSA Publications, Birmingham, NY

Barber, D. 1991, 'Wellington notes' *Pacific Islands Monthly*, vol. 61, no. 3, March, p. 8

Bates, S. 1990, *The South Pacific Island Countries and France: A Study in Inter-state Relations*, Australian National University Department of International Relations, Canberra

Beaglehole, J.C. 1934, *The Exploration of the Pacific*, A.C. Black, London

Bedford, R. 1991, 'Migration and development in the Pacific islands', *The South Pacific*, ed. R. Thakur, Macmillan, London

Bellam, M.E.P. 1980, *The Citrus Colony: New Zealand–Cook Islands Economic Relations*, New Zealand Coalition for Trade and Development, Wellington

Biddick, T.V. 1989, 'Diplomatic rivalry in the South Pacific: the PRC and Taiwan', *Asian Survey*, vol. 29, no. 8, August, pp. 800–15.

Blaustein, A.P. and Blaustein, P.M. eds, 1985, *Constitutions of Dependencies and Special Sovereignties*, Oceana Publications, Dobbs Ferry, NY

Boss, A.H. et al. 1987, *Report of the International Observer Mission Palau Referendum December 1986*, International League for Human Rights Minority Rights Group, New York, May

Boyce, P. and Angel J. eds. 1991, *Australia in World Affairs 1981–90*, Longman Paul, Sydney, forthcoming

Boyd, M. 1969, 'The record in Western Samoa to 1945', *New Zealand's Record in the Pacific Islands in the Twentieth Century*, ed. A. Ross, Longman Paul, Auckland

—— 1987, *New Zealand and Decolonisation in the South Pacific*, New Zealand Institute of International Relations, Wellington

Britain Government, 1989, Overseas Development Administration, *Britain and the Countries of the South Pacific: Partners in Development*, London, December

Browne, C. 1989, *Economic Development in Seven Pacific Island Countries*, International Monetary Fund, Washington

Buchholz, H.J. 1987, *Law of the Sea Zones in the Pacific Ocean*, Institute of Southeast Asian Studies, Singapore

Bugota, F. 1990, 'A Review of the Achievements of the Forum Fisheries Agency in its first decade of operations' *The Forum Fisheries Agency: Achievements, Challenge and Prospects*, ed. R. Herr, University of the South Pacific Institute of Pacific Studies, Suva

Bunge, F.M. and Cooke M.W. eds, 1985, *Oceania: A Regional Study*, United States Government Printing Office and Department of the Army, Washington

Burdick, A.B. 1988, 'The Constitution of the Federated States of Micronesia', *Law, Government and Politics in the Pacific Island States*, ed. Y.H. Ghai, University of the South Pacific Institute of Pacific Studies, Suva

Campbell, I.C. 1989, *A History of the Pacific Islands*, University of Canterbury Press, Christchurch

Centre for South Pacific Studies, 1990, *Newsletter*, University of New South Wales, Kensington, NSW, various issues

Chapman, T.M. 1976, *The Decolonisation of Niue*, Victoria University Press, Wellington

Chesneaux, J. 1986, 'France in the Pacific: global approach or respect for regional agendas?', *Bulletin of Concerned Asian Scholars*, vol. 18, no. 2, April/June, pp. 73–80

Clark, R.S. and Blaustein, A.P. 1985, 'New Zealand associated states: Cook Islands', *Constitutions of Dependencies and Special Sovereignties*, eds

A.P. Blaustein & P.M. Blaustein, Oceana Publications, Dobbs Ferry, NY

Clark, R. and Roff, S.R. 1987, *Micronesia: The problem of Palau*, rev. edn, Minority Rights Groups, New York, November

Cole, R.V. 1991, 'Economic Constraints and Prospects: The Role of Regional Cooperation' *South Pacific Security: Issues and Perspectives*, eds S. Henningham and Australian National University Strategic and Defence Studies Centre, Canberra

—— and Parry, D.G. eds, 1986, *Selected Issues in Pacific Islands Development*, Pacific Policy Paper No. 2, National Centre for Development Studies, Australian National University, Canberra

Commission of the European Communities, 1989, *South Pacific and the European Community*, Brussels, June

Commission on Self-Determination, 1988, *Guam's Draft Commonwealth Act*, Guam, February

Conseil du Pacifique Sud, 1990, *Communiqué*, typescript, Papeete, 17 May

Concise World Atlas for Australia and New Zealand, 1987, George Philip & Son, London

'Cook Islands', 1986, *Pacific Constitutions Vol. 1 Polynesia*, University of the South Pacific, Suva

Cook Islands Government, 1989, Minister of Finance, 'Financial statement budget 1 April 1989–31 March 1990', typescript, n.p.

Couper, A.D. ed. 1988, *Development and Social Change in the Pacific Islands*, Routledge, London

Craig, R.D. and King, F.P. eds, 1981, *Historical Dictionary of Oceania*, Greenwood Press, London

Crocombe, R. 1980, *Cook Islands Politics: The Inside Story*, Polynesian Press, Auckland

—— 1988, 'Nauru: the politics of phosphate', *Micronesian Politics*, eds R. Crocombe & L. Mason, University of the South Pacific Institute of Pacific Studies, Suva

—— 1989a, *The South Pacific: An Introduction*, 5th edn, Longman Paul, Auckland

—— 1989b, 'Studying the Pacific', *Class and Culture in the South Pacific*, eds A. Hooper et al, University of Auckland Centre for Pacific Studies, Auckland

Crocombe, R. and Ali, A. eds, 1983a, *Politics in Polynesia*, University of the South Pacific Institute of Pacific Studies, Suva

—— 1983b, *Foreign Forces in Pacific Politics*, University of the South Pacific Institute of Pacific Studies, Suva

Daniel, P. and Sims, R. 1986, *Foreign Investment in Papua New Guinea: Policies and Practices*, Australian National University National Centre for Development Studies, Canberra

Danielsson, B. 1982, 'French Polynesia: nuclear colony', *Politics in Polynesia*, eds R. Crocombe & A. Ali, University of the South Pacific Institute of Pacific Studies, Suva

Davidson, J.W. 1967, *Samoa Mo Samoa: The Emergence of the Independent State of Western Samoa*, Oxford University Press, Melbourne

Day, A.G. 1966, *Explorers of the Pacific*, Duell, Sloan and Pearce, New York

Day, A.J. ed. 1987, *Border and Territorial Disputes*, 2nd edn, Longman, London

Delpar, H. ed. 1980, *The Discoverers: An Encyclopedia of Explorers and Exploration*, McGraw-Hill, New York

Dodge, E.S. 1976, *Islands and Empires*, University of Minnesota Press, Minneapolis

Dorrance, J.C. et al. 1990a, *The South Pacific: Emerging Security Issues and US Policy*, Institute for Foreign Policy Analysis, Washington

—— 1990b, 'The Soviet Union and the Pacific islands', *Asian Survey*, vol. 30, no. 9, September, pp. 908–25.

Douglas, N. and Douglas, N. eds. 1989, *Pacific Islands Yearbook*, 16th edn, Angus & Robertson, North Ryde, NSW

Doulman, D.J. 1986, *Licensing Distant-Water Tuna Fleets: The Experience of Papua New Guinea*, East–West Center Pacific Islands Development Program, Honolulu, May

—— 1987a, *Tuna Issues and Perspectives in the Pacific Islands Region*, East–West Center, Honolulu

—— 1987b, 'The Kiribati–Soviet Union fishing agreement', *Pacific Viewpoint*, vol. 28, no. 1, May, pp. 20–39

—— 1987c, 'Fisheries cooperation: the case of the Nauru Group', *Tuna Issues and Perspectives in the Pacific Islands Region*, ed. D.J. Doulman, East–West Center, Honolulu

—— 1991, 'Fisheries Management in the South Pacific: The Role of the Forum Fisheries Agency', *The South Pacific*, ed. R. Thakur, Macmillan, London

East–West Center, 1990, *Summit of the United States and the Pacific Island Nations October 27, 1990: Concluding Remarks and Background Papers*, Honolulu

Edo, J. 1986, *Japanese Aid to the Pacific Islands Region*, East–West Center, Honolulu

Faaniu, S. et al, 1983, *Tuvalu: A History*, University of the South Pacific Institute of Pacific Studies, Suva

Fairbairn, T.I.J. 1987, *Entrepreneurship in the Cook Islands*, East–West Center Pacific Islands Development Program, Honolulu, July

—— et al, 1991, *The Pacific Islands: Politics, Economics and International Relations*, East–West Center International Relations Program, Honolulu

Far East and Australasia 1989, 1989, Europa Publications, London

Far East and Australasia 1990, 1990, Europa Publications, London

Far East and Australasia 1991, 1991, Europa Publications, London

Federated States of Micronesia Government, 1987, 'Economic cooperation agreement signed with China', *The National Union*, vol. 2, no. 2, p. 3

—— 1989, 'FSM, Japan sign exchange of notes', *The National Union*, vol. 10, no. 12, December, p. 5

—— 1990a, 'State of the nation message', *The National Union*, vol. 11, no. 3, 30 May supplemental issue

—— 1990b, 'President took delivery of FSS Palikir from Australia', *The National union*, vol. 11, no. 3, 30 May

—— 1990c, 'FSM & Japan sign harbour agreement', *The National Union*, vol. 11, no. 4, 15 June, p. 4

—— 1990d, 'FSM, Japan sign exchange of notes', *The National Union*, vol. 10, no. 12, December, p. 5

Fiji Government, 1977, *Selected Speeches by The Right Honourable Ratu Sir Kamesese Mara, K.B.E.*, Government Printer, Suva

—— 1985, *Fiji's Ninth Development Plan 1986–1990*, Central Planning Office, Suva, November

—— 1987, Ministry of Foreign Affairs, *Foreign Policy Initiatives for the Republic of Fiji*, Suva, 19 October

—— 1989, *Fiji Trade and Investment Board Annual Report 1989*, Fiji Trade and Investment Board, Suva

—— 1990a, Ministry of Information, *Fiji Today*, Suva

—— 1990b, Bureau of Statistics, *Current Economic Statistics*, Suva, July

—— 1990c, Trade and Investment Board, *Trade and Investment News*, no. 3, March–April

—— 1991a, Bureau of Statistics, 'Provisional visitor statistics 1990', *Statistical News*, no. 3, 4 January

—— 1991b, Bureau of Statistics, 'Provisional overseas trade statistics, 1990', *Statistical News*, no. 5, 25 January

—— 1991c, Bureau of Statistics, 'Visitor statistics—December 1990', *Statistical News*, no. 15, 21 March

Fiji Focus, 1982, vol. 1, no. 4, p. 16

Fiji Times, 1990a, 'Deregulation a mistake: Punja', 29 September

—— 1990b, 'Lee praises deregulation', 2 October

—— 1990c, 'Deregulation would increase business efficiency, says Lee', 8 October

—— 1990d, 'Need to lift protection—Naisoro', 8 October

Fisk, E.K. and Mellor, C.S. 1986, *Tuvalu Trust Fund Appraisal Study*, Report No. 16, Australian Development Assistance Bureau, Canberra, July

Forum Fisheries Agency 1990, *Approved Work Programme 1990/91, Approved Budget 1990/91*, Honiara, May

France Government, 1988, Annual Meeting of French Civil and Military Authorities of the South Pacific 19–21 February 1988, Noumea; typescript provided by French Embassy, Port Vila

Fraser, H. 1987, *New Caledonia: Anti-Colonialism in a Pacific Territory*, Discussion Paper 2 1987–88, Parliament of the Commonwealth of Australia Legislative Research Service, Canberra

—— 1990, 'Tonga special report', *Pacific Report*, vol. 3, no. 23, 6 December, pp 3–5

'French Polynesia' 1986, *Constitutions of Dependencies and Special Sovereignties*, eds A.P. Blaustein and P.M. Blaustein, Ocean Publications, Dobbs Ferry, New York

French Polynesia Territorial Government 1990, *Report of Visit of President François Mitterrand*, typescript, Papeete

—— 1991a, *La polynésie en bref*, Institut Territorial de la Statistque, Papeete

—— 1991b, *Allocution de M. Gaston Flosse, Président du Gouvernement*, typescript, Papeete, 9 April

Friis, H.R. ed. 1967, *The Pacific Basin: A History of Its Geographical Exploration*, American Geographical Society, New York

Fry, G.E. 1981, 'Regionalism and international politics of the South Pacific', *Pacific Affairs*, vol. 54, no. 4, Fall, pp. 455–84

—— 1989a, 'Special report: the 29th South Pacific Conference, Agana, Guam, 9–11 October 1989', *Pacific Research*, vol. 2, no. 4, November, p. 28

—— 1989b, 'Report on the Tenth Meeting of the Committee of Representatives of Governments and Administrations, South Pacific Commission, Noumea, 22–27 May 1989', Canberra, draft

—— 1990, *Peacekeeping in the South Pacific: Some Questions for Prior Consideration*, Working Paper 1990/7, Department of International Relations, Canberra, September

—— 1991a, 'The politics of South Pacific regional co-operation', *The South Pacific: Problems and Prospects*, ed. R. Thakur, Macmillan, London

—— 1991b, 'Australia and the South Pacific', *Australia in World Affairs 1981–90*, eds P. Boyce and J. Angel, Longman Paul, forthcoming

—— 1991c, "Constructive commitment" with the South Pacific: Monroe Doctrine or new "partnership"?' *Australia's Regional Security*, ed. G. Fry, Allen & Unwin, North Sydney, NSW

Gerston, L. 1991, 'Political stagnation in Palau', *New Zealand International Review*, vol. 16, no. 2, March/April, pp. 24–7

Ghai, Y.H. 1988, 'Constitution making and decolonisation', *Law, Politics and Government in the Pacific Island States*, ed. Y.H. Ghai, University of the South Pacific Institute of Pacific Studies, Suva

Gill, G. 1989, 'Soviet interests in the Pacific', *No Longer an American Lake?*, ed. J. Ravenhill, Allen & Unwin, North Sydney

Gittings, D. 1991, 'Tonga's missing millions', *Pacific Islands Monthly*, vol. 61, no. 5, May, pp. 10–17

Griffin, J. ed. 1974, *A Foreign Policy for an Independent Papua New Guinea*, Angus & Robertson, Sydney

Gubon, F. 1987, 'History and role of the Forum Fisheries Agency', *Tuna Issues and Perspectives in the Pacific Islands Region*, ed. D.J. Doulman, East–West Center, Honolulu

Guest, S. 1990a, 'Questions for Niue', *Islands Business*, vol. 16, no. 9, p. 59

—— 1990b, 'Rex, 82, shows his experience again', *Islands Business*, vol. 16, no. 11, November, p. 29

Haas, M. 1989, *The Pacific Way: Regional Cooperation in the South Pacific*, Praeger, New York

Hamnett, M.P. and Kiste, R.C. 1988, 'Issues and interest groups in the Pacific Islands', unpublished report, United States Information Service Research Office, Washington, December

Hayes, P. et al. 1986, *American Lake: Nuclear Peril in the Pacific*, Penguin, Ringwood, Vic.

Hegarty, D. 1983, 'The change of government, 1981', *Solomon Islands Politics*, ed. P. Larmour, University of the South Pacific Institute of Pacific Studies, Suva

—— 1987, *Libya and the South Pacific*, Australian National University Strategic and Defence Studies Centre, Canberra

—— 1989a, 'The Soviet Union in the South Pacific in the 1990s', *The Soviets in the Pacific in the 1990s*, ed. R. Babbage, Pergamon Press, Rushcutters Bay, NSW

—— 1989b, 'Papua New Guinea in 1988: political crossroads?' *Asian Survey*, vol. 39, no. 2, February, pp. 181–8

—— and Polomka, P. eds 1989, *The Security of Oceania in the 1990s. Vol. 1: Views from the Region*, Australian National University Strategic and Defence Studies Centre, Canberra

Henningham, S. 1989, *France and the South Pacific: Problems and Prospects*, Australian National University Peace Research Centre, Canberra, February

—— 1990, 'Keep the tricolour flying: the French Pacific into the 1990s', *Sydney Talk: Australia in the South Pacific*, ed. G. McCall, University of New South Wales Centre for South Pacific Studies, Kensington; also in *The Contemporary Pacific*, vol. 1. nos 1 & 2, Spring & Fall 1989, pp. 97–132

—— and Ball, D. eds 1991, *South Pacific Security: Issues and Perspectives*, Australian National University Strategic and Defence Studies Centre, Canberra

Herr, R. ed. 1990, *The Forum Fisheries Agency: Achievements, Challenges and Prospects*, University of the South Pacific Institute of Pacific Studies, Suva

—— 1991a, 'Soviet and Chinese interests in the South Pacific', *Strategic Cooperation and Competition in the Pacific Islands*, ed. F. Mediansky, National Defense University Press, Washington, forthcoming

—— 1991b, 'Future roles of regional organizations—regionalism and subregional groupings', *Strategic Cooperation and Competition in the Pacific Islands*, ed. F. Mediansky, National Defense University Press, Washington, forthcoming

Hoadley, S. 1989, *The New Zealand Foreign Affairs Handbook*, Oxford University Press, Auckland

—— 1991a 'New Zealand's South Pacific strategy', *Strategic Cooperation and Competition in the Pacific Islands*, ed. F. Mediansky, National Defense University, Washington, forthcoming

—— 1991b, 'New Zealand's international aid', *Beyond New Zealand II: Foreign Policy into the 1990s,* eds R. Kennaway, J. Henderson, Longman Paul, Auckland

—— 1991c, 'Japan's policies in the South Pacific', *New Zealand International Review*, vol. 16, no. 3, May/June

Hooper, A. et al. eds, 1987, *Class and Culture in the South Pacific*, Centre for Pacific Studies, Auckland

Horiguchi, R.Y. 1987, 'New aid programs reflect Japan's strategic concern for sea lines', *Pacific Defence Reporter*, vol. 13, no. 4, April, p. 43

Howorth, R. 1990, 'Mineral resources potential of Southwest Pacific island nations', *Sydney Talk: Australia in the South Pacific*, ed. G. McCall, University of New South Wales Centre for South Pacific Studies, Kensington

Hoyle, J.H.A. 1985, 'The security of small island states', *The ANZAC Connection*, ed. D. Ball, Allen & Unwin, North Sydney, pp. 68–81

Hughes, A.V. 1987, 'High speed on an unmade road: Solomon Islands' joint-venture route to a tuna fishery', *Tuna Issues and Perspectives in the Pacific Islands Region*, ed. D.J. Doulman, East–West Center, Honolulu

Institute Territoriale de la Statistique et des Études Économiques, 1990, *Information Statistique Rapid Nouvelle-Caledonia*, Noumea, vol. 197, no. 97, August

Isala, T. 1983, 'Tuvalu—atoll nation' *Politics in Polynesia*, eds R. Crocombe and A. Ali, University of the South Pacific Institute of Pacific Studies, Suva

Islands Business, 1990, 'Inside oil on Naisoro', vol. 16, no. 12, December, p. 8

Islands Business Pacific 1991a, 'Samoa's dollars come home', vol. 17, no. 2, February, p. 38

—— 1991b, 'The kingdom strikes back', vol. 17, no. 4, April, pp. 24–5

—— 1991c, 'Saying no to the waste trade', vol. 17, no. 4, April, p. 40

Iuta, T. et al. 1980, *Politics in Kiribati*, University of the South Pacific Institute of Pacific Studies, Suva

Jackson, R.H. 1990, *Quasi-states: sovereignty, international relations and the Third World*, Cambridge University Press, Cambridge

Jennings, P. 1990, 'South Pacific islands', *Yearbook on International Communist Affairs*, ed. R. Starr, Hoover Institution Press, Stanford, pp. 267–80

Johnson, G. 1986, 'Collision course at Kwajalein', *Bulletin of Concerned Asian Scholars*, vol. 18, no. 2, April–June, pp. 28–39

—— 1988, 'Politics in the Marshall Islands', *Micronesian Politics*, eds R. Crocombe & A. Ali, University of the South Pacific Institute of Pacific Studies, Suva

Kanasugi, K. 1988, 'Japanese aid policy in the South Pacific region', *Pacific Economic Bulletin*, vol. 3, no. 1, June

Kaspar, W., Bennett, J. and Blandy, R. 1988, *Fiji: Opportunity from Adversity?*, Centre for Independent Studies, St Leonards, NSW

Kay, R. Ed. 1972, *The Australian–New Zealand Agreement 1944*, Government Printer, Wellington

Keith-Reid, R. 1990a, 'Solomon Mamaloni defends his wicket', *Islands Business*, vol. 16, no. 11, November, pp. 18–23

—— 1990b, 'Men of the year: brave challenge by reformers', *Islands Business*, vol. 16, no. 12, pp. 16–21

—— 1991, 'Problems cooking', *Islands Business Pacific*, vol. 17, no. 8, August, pp. 16–18

Kengalu, A.M. 1988, *Embargo: The Jeanette Diana Affair*, Robert Brown & Associates, Bathurst

King, D.M. 1987, 'Global tuna markets: a Pacific island perspective', *Tuna Issues and Perspectives in the Pacific Islands Region*, ed. D.J. Doulman, East–West Center, Honolulu

Kiribati Government, 1989, Statistics Office, *Kiribati Statistics Yearbook 1988*, Bairiki, Tarawa, June

Kiste, R.C. 1990, 'The United States and the Pacific islands', Honolulu; typescript prepared for Workshop on Australia, New Zealand and the United States: National Evolution and Alliance Relations, Canberra, December

Kite, S. 1977, 'The Pacific nations and international organizations', *Pacific Perspectives*, vol. 6, no. 1, pp. 6–32

Kubuabola, J.Y. 1990, 'Seminar on Reserve Bank of Fiji Policies Pertaining to Foreign Trade and Investments in Fiji', Reserve Bank of Fiji, Suva, 14 September; photocopied seminar notes

Larmour, P. 1983a, 'The Mamaloni government 1981–1993', *Solomon Islands Politics*, ed. P. Larmour, University of the South Pacific Institute of Pacific Studies, Suva

—— 1983b, *Solomon Islands Politics*, University of the South Pacific Institute of Pacific Studies, Suva

Les Nouvelles calédoniennes, 1990a, 'L'École d'état-major neo zelandaise en Caledonie', 14 September, p. 7

—— 1990b, 'Cooperation scientifique: la Nouvelle-Caledonie veut joues un role accru', 11 November

Lini, H. 1982, 'Vanuatu: overcoming pandemonium', *Politics in Melanesia*, eds R. Crocombe & A. Ali, University of the South Pacific Institute of Pacific Studies, Suva

—— 1990, 'Immigration: deportation orders issued', *Pacific Islands Profile: Vanuatu's News Magazine*, no. 3, September, p. 17

Lini, W. 1983, *Statement to the 38th Session of the United Nations General Assembly*, United Nations, New York

Loomis, T. 1990, *Pacific Migrant Labour, Class and Racism in New Zealand*, Avebury, Aldershot

Low-O'Sullivan, M. 1989, 'Fiji's foreign policy: a change in direction?', *Review 17*, University of the South Pacific, vol. 10, no. 17, pp. 32–40

Luard, E. 1974, *The Control of the Sea-bed*, Heinemann, London

Macdonald, B. 1982, *Cinderellas of the Empire: Towards a History of Kiribati and Tuvalu*, Australian National University Press, Canberra

—— 1988, *In Pursuit of the Sacred Trust: Trusteeship and Independence in Nauru*, New Zealand Institute of International Affairs, Wellington

MacKinnon, M. 1990, 'At Vava'u, an exercise in keeping in step', *Islands Business*, vol. 16, no. 12, December, pp. 59–60

MacQueen, N. 1990, *The South Pacific: Regional Subsystem or Geographical Expression?*, Australian National University Strategic and Defence Studies Centre, Canberra

McCall, G. ed. 1990, *Sydney Talk: Australia in the South Pacific*, University of New South Wales Centre for South Pacific Studies, Kensington

McHenry, D.F. 1975, *Micronesia: Trust Betrayed: Altruism vs Self-Interest*

in American Foreign Policy, Carnegie Endowment for International
    Peace, New York
McPhetres, A. 1988, 'The Northern Mariana Islands: US commonwealth',
    Micronesian Politics, eds R. Crocombe & L. Mason, University of the
    South Pacific Institute of Pacific Studies, Suva
Maiava, I. 1988, '*Western Samoa*', commissioned study, US Information
    Agency Office of Research, Washington, November; typescript
Maketu, B.T. 1988, *Defence in Papua New Guinea: Introductory Issues*,
    Australian National University Strategic and Defence Studies Centre,
    Canberra, August
Mangnall, K. 1990a, 'A tale of two hotels', *Pacific Islands Monthly*,
    vol. 60, no. 9, September, pp. 10–14
—— 1990b, 'Vanuatu's economy spins on a high', *Pacific Islands Monthly*,
    vol. 60, no. 9, September, pp. 26–7
Martin, G. 1991, 'France as a South Pacific Actor', *The South Pacific*, ed.
    R. Thakur, Macmillan, London
Mediansky, F.A. 1988, 'Australia and the Southwest Pacific', *In Pursuit
    of National Interests: Australian Foreign Policy in the 1990s*, eds F.A.
    Mediansky and A.C. Palfreeman, Pergamon Press, Sydney
—— ed. 1991, *Strategic Cooperation and Competition in the Pacific
    Islands*, National Defense University Press, Washington, forthcoming
Mediansky, F.A. and Palfreeman, A.C. eds 1988, *In Pursuit of National
    Interests: Australian Foreign Policy in the 1990s*, Pergamon Press,
    Sydney
Meleisea, M. 1987, *Lagaga: A Short History of Western Samoa*, University
    of South Pacific, Suva
Meleisea, M. and Schoeffel, P. 1983, 'Western Samoa', *Politics in Poly-
    nesia*, eds R. Crocombe and A. Ali, University of the South Pacific,
    Suva
Mero, J.L. 1959, *The Finding and Processing of Deep-sea Manganese
    Nodules*, University of California Press, Berkeley
Micronesian Investment Quarterly, 1990a, 'Registry business surging',
    vol. 1, no. 2, 2nd quarter
—— 1990b, '$150 million tourism project proposed', vol. 1, no.4, 3rd
    quarter
—— 1990c, 'Japanese firm to make Palauan coins', vol. 2, no. 1, 4th
    quarter
—— 1990d, 'Palau economy expanding', vol. 2, no. 1, 4th quarter
Milne, S. 1987, 'The Cook Islands tourist industry: ownership and plan-
    ning', *Pacific Viewpoint*, vol. 28, no. 2, October, pp. 119-38
—— 1990, 'The economic impact of tourism in Tonga', *Pacific Viewpoint*,
    vol. 31, no. 1, May, pp. 24–43
Mullin, C.J. 1990, 'US goals in South Pacific: democracy, growth, stabil-
    ity', USIS press release, Washington, 3 May; typescript
'Naura', 1986a, *Constitutions of the Countries of the World*, eds A.P.
    Blaustein and G.H. Flanz, Oceana Publications, Dobbs Ferry, NY
—— 1986b, *Pacific Constitutions Vol. 2 Independent states of Melanesia
    and Micronesia*, University of the South Pacific, Suva
Neemia, U.F. 1986, *Cooperation and Conflict: Costs, Benefits and*

National Interests in Pacific Regional Cooperation, University of the South Pacific Institute of Pacific Studies, Suva

New Caledonia Territorial Government, 1988, 'Loi no 88–1028 du 9 novembre 1988 portant dispositions statutaires et preparatoires a l'autodetermination de la Nouvelle-Caledonia en 1998', *Journal officiel de la Nouvelle-Caledonie*, vol. 133, no. 6592, 17 November

—— 1990a, 'Le partage des credits de developpement', *Lettre du Delegue*, no. 7, March, p. 3

—— 1990b, 'Les mission du Prefet Delegue: developpement économique et cooperation regionale', *Lettre du Delegue*, no. 9, May, pp. 3–4

—— 1990c, 'L'économie caledonienne sur la bonne voie', *Lettre du Delegue*, no. 9, May, pp. 5–6

—— 1990d, 'La France au sein de la CPS', *Lettre du Delegue*, no. 10, June–July, pp. 10–11

—— 1990e, 'Bilan de deux ans des accords de Matignon', *Lettre du Delegue*, no. 11, August–September, pp. 3–9

—— 1990f, 'New Caledonia', Noumea; typed information sheet distributed to visitors

New Zealand Herald, 15 December 1987, 'French phones call up Niuean protest'

—— 13 April 1989

—— 24 June 1989

—— 24 July 1989

—— 30 January 1990

—— 10 March 1990

—— 14 April 1990

—— 9 May 1990

—— 10 May 1990, 'Polynesian protest against atoll sale'

—— 25 May 1990

—— 24 August 1990, 'Vila: safe haven for worried shipowners'

—— 22 November 1990

—— 25 January 1991, 'N-protests weakening'

—— 6 February 1991

—— 19 March 1991, 'Fiji backing down on incentives say firms'

—— 27 March 1991

New Zealand Government 1974, Ministry of Foreign Affairs, *Report for the Year ended 31 March 1974* Government Printers, Wellington

—— 1987a, Ministry of Foreign Affairs, 'Brief visit by Japanese ministers', *New Zealand Foreign Affairs Review*, vol. 37, no. 2, January, p. 22

—— 1987b, Ministry of Defence, *Defence of New Zealand: Review of Defence Policy 1987*, Government Printer, Wellington

—— 1987c, Ministry of Foreign Affairs, *United Nations Handbook 1987*, Wellington

—— 1988, Department of Trade and Industry and Ministry of Foreign Affairs, *Investment Opportunities in the Republic of Kiribati*, Wellington, March

—— 1989, Ministry of External Relations and Trade, 'Jobs for the boys',

Development: New Zealand's Cooperation with Developing Countries, vol. 12, no. 2, September, p. 7

—— 1990a, South Pacific Policy Review Group, *Towards a Pacific Islands Community*, Wellington, May

—— 1990b, Ministry of External Relations and Trade, *The South Pacific Forum*, Information Bulletin No. 32, Wellington, November

—— 1991, *The Defence of New Zealand: A Policy Paper*, Government Printer, Wellington

'Niue', 1986, *Pacific Constitutions Vol. 1 Polynesia*, University of the South Pacific, Suva

Noguchi, Y. 1990, 'Statement at the Thirtieth South Pacific Conference on October 31, 1990'; typescript provided by the Japanese Consulate General, Auckland

North, D. 1990, 'Drawing water lines for the islands', *Pacific Islands Monthly*, vol. 60, no. 10, October, pp. 24–5

—— 1991, 'Taxes and tourism on top', *Pacific Islands Monthly*, vol. 61, no. 2, February, pp. 12–18

Numata, S. 1990, 'Japan's cooperation with the South Pacific region', *Pacific Economics Bulletin*, vol. 5, no. 2, December, pp. 8–14

Olewale, E. 1974, 'Discussion topic: that PNG must have a truly independent foreign policy', *A Foreign Policy for an Independent Papua New Guinea*, ed. J. Griffin, Angus & Robertson, Sydney, pp. 67–71

Oliver, D.L. 1951, *The Pacific Islands*, rev. edn, Doubleday, Garden City, NY

Pacific Constitutions Vol. 1 Polynesia, 1986, University of the South Pacific, Suva

Pacific Constitutions Vol. 2 The Independent States of Melanesia and Micronesia, 1986, University of the South Pacific, Suva

Pacific Economic Bulletin, 1990a, 'Country data: Kiribati', vol. 5, no. 2, December, pp. 56–8

—— 1990b, 'Country data: Papua New Guinea', vol. 5, no. 2, December, pp. 59–61

—— 1990c, 'Country data: Solomon Islands', vol. 5, no. 2, December, pp.62–4

Pacific Islands Monthly, 1990a, 'Building a tax haven', vol. 60, no. 12, December, pp. 35–6

—— 1990b, 'Monarch sees power in burning tyres', vol. 60, no. 12, December, p. 38

—— 1991a, 'New signs of promise on Niue', vol. 61, no. 3, March, p. 35

—— 1991b, 'Working on the differences', vol. 61, no. 3, March, pp. 52–3

—— 1991c, 'Quota cut shocks garment industry', vol. 61, no. 3, April, p. 32

—— 1991d, 'New Korean fish treaty', vol. 61, no. 3, April, p. 35

—— 1991e, 'Fishing stalemate', vol. 61, no. 3, April, p. 33

Pacific Islands Profile: Vanuatu's News Magazine, 1990, 'Constitutional review', vol. 3, September, p. 19

'Papua New Guinea', 1985, *Constitutions of the Countries of the World*, eds A.P. Blaustein & G.H. Flanz, Oceana Publications, Dobbs Ferry, NY

—— 1986, *Pacific Constitutions Vol 2 The Independent States of Melanesia and Micronesia*, University of the South Pacific, Suva

Papua New Guinea Government, 1974, Central Planning Office, 'Papua New Guinea's Eight Aims', *Strategies for Nationhood: Programmes and Performance*, Government Printer, Port Moresby, September

—— 1975, Central Planning Office, 'Foreign relations and trade: policy and the Eight Aims', *Programmes and Performance 1975–76*, Government Printer, Port Moresby, October

—— 1980, Ministry of Foreign Affairs, 'Diplomatic directory', *Papua New Guinea Foreign Affairs Review*, vol. 1, no. 1, September–December, pp. 55-6

—— 1986, Ministry of Foreign Affairs, 'Diplomatic directory' and 'Diplomatic relations', *Papua New Guinea Foreign Affairs Review*, vol. 6, no. 1, January–March, pp. 48–9

—— 1990a, National Statistical Office, *Abstract of Statistics*, Port Moresby, June quarter

—— 1990b, Bank of Papua New Guinea, *Quarterly Economic Bulletin*, vol. 18, no. 2, June

Pearsal, S. 1990, 'Emergence of the South Pacific Regional Environment Programme: a case study in Pacific regionalism', *Pacific Viewpoint*, vol. 31, no. 1, May, pp. 1–23

Peattie, M.R. 1988, *Nan'yo: The Rise and Fall of the Japanese in Micronesia 1885–1945*, University of Hawaii Press, Honolulu

Plant, C. ed. 1977, *New Hebrides: The Road to Independence*, University of the South Pacific Institute of Pacific Studies, Suva

Pokawin, S.P. 1982, 'Papua New Guinea: aftermath of colonialism', *Politics in Melanesia*, eds R. Crocombe & A. Ali, University of the South Pacific Institute of Pacific Studies, Suva

Polomka, P. 1990, *Bougainville: Perspectives on a Crisis*, Australian National University Strategic and Defence Studies Centre, Canberra

Premdas, R.R. 1975, 'Papua New Guinea: internal problems of rapid political change', *Asian Survey*, vol. 15, no. 12, December, pp. 1054–76

—— 1977, *Toward a Papua New Guinea Foreign Policy: Constraints and Choice*, University of California Center for South Pacific Studies, Santa Cruz, January

Premdas, R.R. and Howard, M.C. 1989, 'Vanuatu's foreign policy: contradictions and constraints', *Politics and Government in Vanuatu: From Colonial Unity to Post-Colonial Disunity*, eds R.R. Premdas & J.S. Steeves, James Cook University Centre for Southeast Asian Studies, Townsville

Premdas, R.R. and Steeves, J.S. eds, 1989, *Politics and Government in Vanuatu: From Colonial Unity to Post-Colonial Disunity*, James Cook University Centre for Southeast Asian Studies, Townsville

Prescott, V. 1988, 'Maritime boundaries in the Southwest Pacific region', *Development and Social Change in the Pacific Islands*, ed. A.D. Couper, Routledge, London

Pryor, P.T.I. 1988, 'The Pacific islands and ASEAN: prospects for inter-regional co-operation', *The Indonesia Quarterly*, vol. 16, no. 1, January, pp. 48–71

Quimby, F. 1988, 'The yin and yang of Belau: a nuclear free movement struggles with the quest for economic development', *Micronesian Politics*, eds R. Crocombe & L. Mason, University of the South Pacific Institute of Pacific Studies, Suva

Rampell, E. 1990, 'Geoffrey Henry: Prime Minister, Cook Islands', *Pacific Islands Monthly*, vol. 60, no. 7, pp. 51–3

Ranney, A. and Penniman, H.R. 1985, *Democracy in the Islands: The Micronesian Plebiscites of 1983*, American Enterprise Institute for Public Policy Research, Washington

Revenhill, J. ed. 1989, *No Longer an American Lake*, Allen & Unwin, North Sydney

Rensch, K.H. 1982, 'Wallis and Futuna: total dependency', *Politics in Polynesia*, eds R. Crocombe & A. Ali, University of the South Pacific Institute of Pacific Studies, Suva

Ritova, S. 1991, 'Coleman's move', *Islands Business Pacific*, vol. 17, no. 2, February, pp. 31–3

Ritterbush, D. and Patolo, T.F.K. 1988, 'Kingdom of Tonga', research report, US Information Service Office of Research, Washington, November; typescript

Rix, A. 1990, *Japan's Aid Program: A New Global Approach*, Australian International Development Assistance Bureau, Canberra, April

Robertson, M. 1986, 'The South Pacific Regional Trade and Economic Cooperation Agreement: a critique', *Selected Issues in Pacific Islands Development*, Pacific Policy Paper No. 2, eds R.V. Cole & D.G. Parry, National Centre for Development Studies, Australian National University, Canberra

Robie, D. 1989, *Blood on their Banner: Nationalist Struggles in the South Pacific*, Zed Books, London

—— 1991, 'Stormin' Pohiva fights on', *Pacific Islands Monthly*, vol. 61, no. 4, April, pp. 12–15

Rose, B. 1989, 'Nauru: the fall of de Roburt', *Pacific Islands Monthly*, vol. 59, no. 21, October, p. 7

Ross, K. 1990, *Prospects for Crisis Prediction: A South Pacific Case Study*, Australian National University Strategic and Defence Studies Centre, Canberra

Roughan, J. 1988, 'The Solomon Islands', commissioned study, US Information Agency Office of Research, Washington, November; typescript

Rubinstein, D.H. 1988, 'The Federated States of Micronesia', commissioned study, US Information Agency Office of Research, Washington, November; typescript

Saemala, F. 1982, 'Solomon Islands: uniting the diversity', *Politics in Melanesia*, eds R. Crocombe & A. Ali, University of the South Pacific Institute of Pacific Studies, Suva

—— 1989, 'Security goals and strategies in the Solomon Islands', *The Security of Oceania in the 1990s. Vol 1: Views from the region*, eds D. Hegarty and P. Polomka, Australian National University Strategic and Defence Studies Centre, Canberra

Saffu, Y. 1988, 'Papua New Guinea in 1987: Wingti's coalition in a disabled system', *Asian Survey*, vol. 28, no. 2, February, pp. 242–51

Schug, D.M. and Galea'i, A.P. 1987, 'American Samoa: the tuna industry and the economy', *Tuna Issues and Perspectives in the Pacific Islands Region*, ed. D.J. Doulman, East–West Center, Honolulu

Shankman, P. 1976, *Migration and Underdevelopment: The Case of Western Samoa*, Westview Press, Boulder

Sharma, D. 1991, 'To free or not to free', *Islands Business Pacific*, vol. 17, no. 3, March, pp. 16–18

Short, I. 1983, 'The Cook Islands: politics as a way of life. Part 2, The new era', *Politics in Polynesia*, eds R. Crocombe & A. Ali, University of the South Pacific Institute of Pacific Studies, Suva

Sitai, D. 1983, 'Low-cost diplomacy', *Solomon Islands Politics*, ed. P. Larmour, University of the South Pacific Institute of Pacific Studies, Suva

Slatyer, A.J. 1987, 'Tuna and the impact of the Law of the Sea', *Tuna Issues and Perspectives in the Pacific Islands Region*, ed. D.J. Doulman, East–West Centre, Honolulu

Smith, R.H. and Pugh, M.C. 1991, 'Micronesian trust territories—imperialism continues?', *The Pacific Review*, vol. 4, no. 1, pp. 36–44

Smith, T.R. 1972, *South Pacific Commission: An Analysis after Twenty-five Years*, Price Milburn for the New Zealand Institute of International Affairs, Wellington

Solomon Islands Government, 1983, Ministry of Foreign Affairs and International Trade, *Solomon Islands Foreign Affairs and Trade Relations*, Honiara, March

—— 1985, Ministry of Economic Planning, *Solomon Islands National Development Plan 1985–1989*, Honiara, August

—— 1987, Office of the Prime Minister, *Programme of Action 1987–1989 of the National Development Plan 1985–1989*, Honiara, June

—— 1988a, *Socio-economic Development Strategies and External Assistance Priorities*, Honiara; prepared for the Round Table Meeting at Geneva, October, vol. 1

—— 1988b, *Development Co-operation and Aid Co-ordination*, Honiara; prepared for the Round Table Meeting at Geneva, October, vol. 2

—— 1988c, *Sectoral Strategies and Priority Development Projects*, Honiara; prepared for the Round Table Meeting at Geneva, October, vol. 3

—— 1989, Ministry of Foreign Affairs and Trade Relations, *Solomon Islands Foreign Affairs and Trade Relations,* Honiara

—— 1990, *Central Bank of Solomon Islands Quarterly Review*, vol. 4, no. 4, Honiara

—— 1991, *Central Bank of Solomon Islands Annual Report*, Honiara, April

Somare, M. 1974, *The Emerging Role of Papua New Guinea in World Affairs*, Australian Institute of International Affairs, Melbourne, 14 June

South Pacific Commission, 1989a, *South Pacific Economies: Statistical Summary No. 11: 1987*, Noumea

—— 1989b, *South Pacific Commission Budget*, Working Paper 2, presented to the Tenth Committee of Regional Governments and Administrations, Noumea, 22–27 May

—— 1990, *South Pacific Commission: History, Aims and Activities*, Noumea

South Pacific Forum, 1987, *Business and Investment Environment in South Pacific (Fiji, Papua New Guinea, Solomon Islands, Tonga, Vanuatu)*, South Pacific Bureau for Economic Cooperation, Suva, and Asian and Pacific Development Centre, Kuala Lumpur

—— 1989, *Forum Secretariat Annual Report 1988/1989*, South Pacific Forum Secretariat, Suva

—— 1991, *Forum Secretariat Annual Report 1990/91*, Suva

Starr, R. ed. 1990, *Yearbook on International Communist Affairs*, Hoover Institution Press, Stanford

Steeves, J.S. 1989, 'Political and constitutional crisis in Vanuatu', *Politics and Government in Vanuatu: From Colonial Unity to Post-Colonial Disunity*, eds R.R. Premdas & J.S. Steeves, James Cook University Centre for Southeast Asian Studies, Townsville

Taitanto, C. 1988, 'Guam: the struggle for civil and political rights', *Micronesian Politics*, eds R. Crocombe & L. Mason, University of the South Pacific Institute of Pacific Studies, Suva

Talu, A. et al. 1979, *Kiribati: Aspects of History*, Ministry of Education, Training and Culture, Tarawa

Tanham, G.K. 1990, *New Caledonia: The Fragile Peace*, Rand Corporation, Santa Monica, June

Tanham, G.K. and Wainstein, E.S. 1990, *Papua New Guinea Today*, Rand Corporation, Santo Monica, June

Teiwaki, R. 1988a, 'Kiribati: nation of water' *Micronesian Politics*, eds R. Crocombe & L. Mason, University of the South Pacific Institute of Pacific Studies, Suva

—— 1988b, *Management of Marine Resources in Kiribati*, University of the South Pacific Institute of Pacific Studies, Suva

Thambipillai, P. 1988, 'Asian and the Pacific islands: bilateral and multilateral relations', *The Indonesia Quarterly*, vol. 16, no. 1, January, pp. 72–83

Thakur, R. ed. 1991, *The South Pacific*, Macmillan, London

Timiti, U. and Tewai, T. 1979, 'Gestation: towards independence', *Kiribati: Aspects of History*, A. Talu et al., Ministry of Education, Training and Culture, Tarawa

Togo, T. 1990, 'Address at the Japan–SPF Dialogue August 4, 1990'; typescript provided by the Japanese Consulate General, Auckland

Tonga Government, 1987a, *Estimates of Revenue and Expenditure and the Development Estimates for the Year 1987–88*, Government Printer, Nuku'alofa

—— 1987b, Central Planning Department, *Fifth Five-Year Development Plan 1986–1990*, Nuku'alofa, December

—— 1987c, *Report of the Minister of Foreign Affairs for the Year 1986*, Government Printer, Nuku'alofa

—— 1988, Statistics Department, *Statistical Abstract 1987*, Nuku'alofa, December

—— 1989, *Investing in Tonga*, Bank of Tonga, Nuku'alofa

—— 1990, National Reserve Bank of Tonga, *Quarterly Bulletin*, vol. 1, no. 2

Trade News of the South Pacific, 1990a, 'New push for Solomons tourism', no. 20, September/October, p. 11

—— 1990b, 'Waste dumping plan for Kiribati', no. 20, September/October, p. 35

—— 1990c, 'Fiji's export drive into the Pacific', no. 20, September/ October, pp. 13–26

—— 1991, 'Fiji to control own oil supplies', no. 23, January/February, pp. 1–3

Tuvalu Government, 1990, 'Tuvalu Trust Fund', Funafuti; photocopied typescript

Union of International Associations, 1988, *Yearbook of International Organisations 1988/89*, 6th edn, K.G. Saur, Munich

United Nations, 1964, *Everyman's United Nations*, 7th edn, United Nations Office of Public Information, New York

—— 1983, *The Law of the Sea: United Nations Convention on the Law of the Sea*, United Nations Office of Public Information, New York

—— 1986, United Nations Industrial Development Organisation, *Pacific Islands States: Papua New Guinea, Fiji, Solomon Islands, Western Samoa, Vanuatu, Tonga, Kiribati, FSM and Micro States*, Vienna, 21 July

—— 1988, *United Nations International Trade Statistics Yearbook 1987*, New York

Uregei, Y.C. 1982, 'New Caledonia: confrontation to colonial rule', *Politics in Melanesia*, eds R. Crocombe & A. Ali, University of the South Pacific Institute of Pacific Studies, Suva

Vanuatu Government, 1988, *Socio-economic Development Strategies and External Assistance Priorities*, Port Vila, prepared for the Round Table Meeting at Geneva, October

—— 1989a, *Second National Development Plan 1987–1991*, Port Vila

—— 1989b, Reserve Bank of Vanuatu, *Quarterly Economic Review*, vol. 4, no. 4, December

—— 1990, Statistics Office, *Vanuatu Statistical Bulletin: Statistical Indicators 1990: 1st Quarter*, Port Vila

Victor, J.C. 1990, 'France in the Pacific', *Pacific Review*, vol. 3, no. 4, pp. 343–8

Viviani, N. 1970, *Nauru: Phosphate and Political Progress*, Australian National University Press, Canberra

Vurobaravu, N. 1989, 'The Vanuatu Foreign Service: an overview', Port Vila; Ministry of Foreign Affairs typescript, approved by Cabinet and released November 1989

Walker R. and Sutherland, W. eds, 1988, *The Pacific: Peace, Security, and the Nuclear Issue*, United Nations University, Tokyo

Watanabe, A. 1991, 'The Pacific islands and Japan', *Strategic Cooperation and Competition in the Pacific Islands*, ed. F. Mediansky, National Defense University Press, Washington, forthcoming

Watters, R. 1987, 'Mirab societies and bureaucratic elites', *Class and Culture in the South Pacific*, eds A. Hooper et al., Centre for Pacific Studies, Auckland

Weisgall, J.M. 1985, 'Micronesia and the nuclear Pacific since Hiroshima', *SAIS Review*, John Hopkins University, vol. 5, no. 2, Fall, pp. 41–55

Western Samoa Government, 1987, Department of Economic Development, *Western Samoa's Sixth Development Plan 1988–1990*, Apia, December

—— 1988, *Western Samoa: Socio-economic Situation, Development Strategy, and Assistance Needs*, Apia, October

—— 1989, *Central Bank of Samoa Bulletin*, vol. 4, no. 1

—— n.d., *Investing in Western Samoa: A Brief Guide to Entrepreneurs*, Apia

Williams, I. 1991a, 'Freedom at last!', *Pacific Islands Monthly*, vol. 61, no. 2, February, pp. 10–12

—— 1991b, 'Where the phosphate and time are running out', *Pacific Islands Monthly*, vol. 61, no. 3, March, pp. 19–22

Wolfers, E.P. 1981, 'Papua New Guinea in 1980: a change in government, aid, and foreign relations', *Asian Survey*, vol. 21, no. 2, February, pp. 274–84

World Bank, 1987, *Fiji: A Transition to Manufacturing*, Washington

—— 1988, *Papua New Guinea: Policies and Prospects for Sustained and Broad-Based Growth*, Washington, vol. 1

—— 1991a, *Papua New Guinea—Structural Adjustment, Growth and Human Resource Development*, Washington, May 1

—— 1991b, *Toward Higher Growth in Pacific Island Economies*, Washington, January 18

Yasutomo, D.T. 1986, *The Manner of Giving: Strategic Aid and Japanese Foreign Policy*, Lexington Books, Lexington

Yusuf, S. and Peters, R.K. 1985, *Western Samoa: The Experience of Slow Growth and Resource Imbalance*, Staff Working Paper, World Bank, Washington

Index

983 371SC1 FM 6098
11/93 32550 m